世界大师原典文库
(中文导读插图版)

总主编 杨慧林 金莉

# The Second Treatise of Government

# 政府论（下篇）

［英］约翰·洛克（John Locke） 著
王 涛 导读

中国人民大学出版社
·北京·

## 世界大师原典文库（中文导读插图版）
## 编委会

### 总主编

杨慧林　中国人民大学　　　　金　莉　北京外国语大学

### 编　委

| | | | |
|---|---|---|---|
| 常　乐 | 沈阳建筑大学外语学院 | 刘小枫 | 中国人民大学文学院 |
| 陈世丹 | 中国人民大学外语学院 | 栾述文 | 中国石油大学文学院 |
| 陈万会 | 聊城大学外语学院 | 彭　工 | 中国科学院大学外语学院 |
| 程朝翔 | 北京大学外语学院 | 史宝辉 | 北京林业大学外语学院 |
| 方开瑞 | 广东外语外贸大学英语语言文化学院 | 史彤彪 | 中国人民大学法学院 |
| | | 石运章 | 山东农业大学外语学院 |
| 高宏存 | 国家行政学院社会和文化部 | 谭少兵 | 北京青年政治学院图书馆 |
| | | 唐蔚明 | 三亚学院外语学院 |
| 郭　涛 | 北方工业大学文法学院 | 王健芳 | 贵州大学外国语学院 |
| 郭英剑 | 中央民族大学外语学院 | 王立非 | 对外经济贸易大学英语学院 |
| 韩东晖 | 中国人民大学哲学院 | | |
| 鞠玉梅 | 曲阜师范大学外语学院 | 王守仁 | 南京大学外语学院 |
| 孔令翠 | 四川师范大学外语学院 | 文　旭 | 西南大学外语学院 |
| 兰　萍 | 西南交通大学外语学院 | 吴亚欣 | 山西大学外语学院 |
| 李常磊 | 济南大学外语学院 | 修旭东 | 鲁东大学外语学院 |
| 李　红 | 重庆大学外语学院 | 杨蕾达 | 海南师范大学外语学院 |
| 李京廉 | 北京理工大学外语学院 | 杨连瑞 | 中国海洋大学外语学院 |
| 李丽生 | 云南师范大学外语学院 | 杨仁敬 | 厦门大学外语学院 |
| 李　毅 | 山东财经大学外语学院 | 杨瑞龙 | 中国人民大学经济学院 |
| 李正栓 | 河北师范大学外语学院 | 杨若东 | 北京交通大学语言学院 |
| 李佐文 | 中国传媒大学外语学院 | 张　潮 | 琼州学院外国语学院 |
| 刘白玉 | 山东工商学院外语学院 | 赵　雯 | 东北大学外语学院 |
| 刘世生 | 清华大学外语学院 | 资谷生 | 云南农业大学外语学院 |

### 统　筹

鞠方安　中国人民大学出版社外语分社

## 出版说明

对于古今学问、中西思想的会通之难，王国维先生的感悟最为深切："如执近世之哲学，以述古人之说，谓之弥缝古人之说则可，谓之忠于古人则恐未也……欲求其贯串统一，势不能不用语意更广之语；然语意愈广者，其语愈虚，于是古人之说之特质渐不可见，所存者其肤廓耳。译古书之难，全在于是。"今人之于古人的"以意逆志"尚且如此，又遑论国人之于西人？于是王国维先生认为"外国语中之无我国'天'字之相当字，与我国语中之无 God 之相当字无以异"；经典之妙，"无论何人，不能精密译之"。[1]

译事之难如是，中国人研读西学经典却不能不借助译本。译本或如业师，指点迷津、功不可没，然入门之后能否一窥堂奥，阡陌纵横如何辨知虚实，则不能不溯本求源。因而阅读原典、溯本求源、汲取学养为会通中西之要素之一。

在本文库编委会专家、学者们的指导下，我们精选了西方历代名家经典著作的权威版本，辅之以中文导读，配以精美插图，分批推出"世界大师原典文库（中文导读插图版）"，供读者对比、品味、研读。

本文库内容涵盖哲学、文学、历史学、法学、政治学、经济学、社会学、心理学、人类学等，力求满足相关领域专家、学者的学术需求，力求帮助学生开阔视野、涵养通识，同时也特别为外语教师、外语类大学生、外语学习者和外语爱好者提供便捷实用的参考资料。

世界之大，在于和而不同；学问之大，在于海纳百川；心灵之大，在于兼容并蓄。我们相信，"世界大师原典文库（中文导读插图版）"会成为各界读者阅读、研究和收藏的精神大餐。

杨慧林　教授（中国人民大学副校长、博士生导师）
金　莉　教授（北京外国语大学副校长、博士生导师）
2012 年 9 月

---

[1] 王国维：《书辜氏汤生英译〈中庸〉后》，见傅杰编校：《王国维论学集》，473—474 页，昆明，云南人民出版社，2008。

# 导 读

王 涛

## 一、洛克的生平

1632年，约翰·洛克出生于一个名叫Wrington的村庄。这个村庄位于英格兰西部的萨默塞特郡（Somerset）。洛克的家庭最多只能称得上是一个下层的清教绅士家庭。父亲家一方原是裁缝，母亲家一方则为制革匠。洛克的父亲在英国内战中加入了议会军，战后做了一名不算成功的律师。可以说，洛克的家庭并没有为他的成长提供不同寻常的知识背景与社会地位。

在父亲从军时的军团首长亚历山大·波帕姆（Alexander Popham）的帮助下，洛克的人生才算有了一个转机。1647年，洛克在波帕姆的帮助下进入伦敦的威斯敏斯特学堂就读。1652年，时年20岁的洛克进入牛津大学最好的学院——基督教会学院（Christ Church）——就读。在牛津大学，洛克接受的仍然是中世纪式的教育。虽然洛克日益对这种陈旧的知识丧失了兴趣，但他还是于1656年2月顺利地获得了文科学士学位，并接着攻读硕士学位。1658年6月，洛克获得了文科硕士学位，并被选为基督教会学院的高级学生。作为高级学生，洛克已经是学院的职员了，但是这个职位并不是永久性的。洛克在1660年被选为希腊语的讲师，1663年被选为修辞学的讲师。在此期间，洛克写了两篇关于宗教宽容的政治短论。这两篇短论并没有公开发表。1967年，菲利普·艾布拉姆斯将其从洛克的手稿中整理出来，以《约翰·洛克：政府短论两篇》为题出版。[1]这本书成为学者们研究洛克早期政治思想与宗教思想的重要文本。

1663年，洛克面临着一个重大的人生选择。按照基督教会学院的规定，学院的55名学者必须成为神职人员，只有5个名额可被分配到医学（2个）、法学（2个）与道德哲学（1个）中。对于洛克来说，成为一名教士显然是最稳妥的做法，但是他还是放弃了。1663年的平安夜，洛克被选为道德哲学学监，为期一年。在此期间，洛克写了一篇关于自然法的讲稿。1954年，凡·列登将其从洛克的手稿中整理出来，以《自然法辩难》为题出版。[2]这本书成为学者们研究洛克自然法思想的最重要文本。

1665年，洛克离开牛津大学，作为外交人员出访了勃兰登堡（Brandenburg）。之后，洛克又被邀请出访西班牙、瑞典，但是他都拒绝了。1666年，洛克回到了牛津，和几位朋友进行医学研究。其实之前在牛津的时候，洛克就已经对化学、医学等自然科学产生了巨大的兴趣，与许多这方面的学者相互学习。其中最为著名的就是"现代化学之父"罗伯特·波义耳（Robert Boyle）。最终，洛克通过各种渠道使得自己在基督教会学院获得了一个非教士的职位。

洛克人生的第二个转折点是1666年夏天与上议院议员安东尼·阿什利·库珀（Anthony Ashley Cooper, 1621—1683）的相遇。后者又被称为Lord Ashley，即后来的沙夫茨伯里第一伯爵（First Earl of Shaftesbury）。两人相互颇为赏识，而且由于洛克在牛津的职位并不要求上课，所以当阿什利于1667年邀请他做自己的私人医生去伦敦生活时，洛克便离开了牛津。

在牛津大学的近15年间，洛克虽然写了一些政治作品，但是就他个人在牛津大学所获得的学术发展而言，化学与医学方面的研究才是最重要的。跟随阿什利来到伦敦后，洛克渐渐进入到了英国政治活动的中心地带，从而对政治开始了更深入的

---

[1] John Locke: *Two Tracts on Government* / Edited with an Introduction, Notes and Translation by Philip Abrams, Cambridge University Press, 1967.

[2] John Locke: *Essays on the Law of Nature* / the Latin text, with a translation, introduction and notes, together with transcripts of Locke's shorthand in his journal for 1676, edited by W. von Leyden, Clarendon Press, 1954.

思考。从1667年到1683年,沙夫茨伯里可以说是查理二世宫廷中最富权势的政治人物,并且是议会中辉格党派的领袖。从1673年开始,沙夫茨伯里极为关注查理二世宫廷中的天主教倾向于法国式的绝对主义国家走向。其中最令他担忧的是,查理二世的弟弟,信仰罗马天主教的约克公爵(Duke of York)很有可能继承王位。1675年,由于身体健康问题,洛克离开英国,在法国待了三年半。洛克1679年回到英国时,沙夫茨伯里与国王之间的政治斗争已经进入白热化阶段。1679年5月,沙夫茨伯里的支持者们在下议院提出了《排除法案》(Exclusion Bill),试图将约克公爵从王位继承席中排除出去(1678年至1681年这段时间被称为"排除危机")。这一政治努力失败了,查理二世解散了议会,而沙夫茨伯里也于1681年以"谋反罪"被捕。沙夫茨伯里于1682年逃离英国,来到荷兰,次年患病身亡。

作为沙夫茨伯里的助手与密友,洛克在此期间也随时可能遭到政治迫害,所以他于1683年离开英国来到荷兰。此时洛克已年过五十,没有任何著作发表。如果洛克在当时遭遇不幸,也许我们现在都不会记得洛克这个人了。洛克在荷兰待了7年,直到光荣革命之后,才于1689年2月12日回到英国。接着,洛克连续发表了三部作品:《论宗教宽容》(匿名)[1]、《政府论两篇》(匿名)与《人类理解论》。

洛克以身体欠佳为由,拒绝了威廉三世提供的许多官职。之后,洛克受他的好友马莎姆夫人(Damaris Cudworth Masham)的邀请,住在她与丈夫在伦敦北部艾塞克斯郡(Essex)的宅邸中。在人生的最后十几年中,洛克并没有隐居于世外。他担任贸易局与下议院的顾问,积极参与政治活动。1700年,由于健康状况日益恶化,洛克辞去了公职。1704年,洛克与世长辞。洛克晚年的著作还包括:1690年出版的《理解能力指导散论》[2]、

---

[1] 中译本参见:[英]洛克:《论宗教宽容:致友人的一封信》,吴云贵译,北京,商务印书馆,2009。
[2] 中译本参见:[英]洛克:《理解能力指导散论》,吴棠译,北京,人民教育出版社,2005。

1691年出版的《论降低利息和提高货币价值的后果》[1]、1693年出版的《教育片论》[2]以及1695年出版的《基督教的合理性》[3]等。

## 二、《政府论（下篇）》的语境

要想理解一部经典作品，我们首先必须了解思想家为什么要写这部作品。要回答这一问题就必须知道思想家的写作背景，即这部作品的语境。我将结合洛克创作《政府论（下篇）》的政治背景与思想史背景来介绍一下这本书的语境。

首先我们需要说明一下《政府论两篇》的创作过程与创作目的。《政府论两篇》发表于光荣革命之后的1689年，但是洛克其实早已开始写作这两篇政治短论。根据拉斯莱特的细致考据，《政府论（下篇）》其实早于《政府论（上篇）》成型。[4] 1675年在法国的时候，洛克已经开始集中精力思考政府的性质与来源问题。1679年，洛克已经开始写《政府论（下篇）》了，而且很有可能已几近完成。1680年初，罗伯特·费尔默（Robert Filmer, 1588—1653）的《父权制》（*Patriarcha*, 1680）被再次出版。托利党人出版这本写于1631年左右的书是想为绝对君主制辩护。一时间，相关思想甚嚣尘上。基于这一事态，洛克并没有继续完善《政府论（下篇）》，而是开始写《政府论（上篇）》以驳斥费尔默的观点。拉斯莱特的这一考证的重大结论是：《政府论（下篇）》早于光荣革命写成。因此，它并不是对革命的辩护（传统的观点），而是对革命的呼唤。

《政府论两篇》一方面想要反驳费尔默父权制思想，以及流行于欧洲的绝对主权学说，另一方面则是为英国的宪政危机开

---

[1] 中译本参见：[英]洛克：《论降低利息和提高货币价值的后果》，徐式谷译，北京，商务印书馆，1997。
[2] 中译本参见：[英]洛克：《教育片论》，熊春文译，上海，上海人民出版社，2006。
[3] 中译本参见：[英]洛克：《基督教的合理性》，王爱菊译，武汉，武汉大学出版社，2006。
[4] [英]彼得·拉斯莱特：《洛克〈政府论〉导论》，冯克利译，北京，生活·读书·新知三联书店，2007。

出理论药方,为政治新道路指出方向。这里我们需要结合欧洲当时的思想史背景与英国的宪政危机来做进一步的考察。

17世纪是现代民族国家的创生时期。如何阐述一种不同于中世纪的国家学说成为所有政治学说的首要任务。最早对这一时代命题做出回应的是国家理性学说。这一学说诞生于意大利,在16世纪中晚期获得了主导地位。国家理性学说强调,为了应对多变的国家政局与险恶的国际环境,统治者应当享有超脱宗教与道德束缚的最高权力。与此同时,现代主权思想之父,法国思想家让·博丹(Jean Bodin, 1530—1596)于1576年出版了《共和国六书》。博丹在此书中提出了一种更具科学性的绝对主权概念,对欧洲知识界与政治界产生了巨大的影响。近代自然法之父,荷兰思想家胡果·格劳秀斯(Hugo Grotius, 1583—1645)虽然在《战争与和平法权》一书中批判了博丹的主权学说,为其设定了一些实质性限制,但是仍然无法彻底摆脱绝对主权的必要性。17世纪可以说是法国的世纪,而"太阳王"路易十四统治下的法国则是这种绝对主权国家的代表。

欧洲大陆的绝对主义新思潮迅速进入到了英国。虽然英国有着悠久的普通法传统与古老宪章传统,这种极富魅力的主权学说还是受到了不少人的吹捧。都铎王朝崩溃后,整个17世纪英国处于不断的宪政危机中。绝对主权学说是重塑英国国家秩序的一个重要思潮。1603年至1625年间在位的英国国王詹姆斯一世通过吸收博丹的主权学说来改造英国的传统政治学说。这位颇具理论家水平的国王在一系列的演讲与论文中将国王阐述为上帝的直接代言人、所有世俗法律的直接来源地、对整个王国所有领域拥有绝对权力的统治者。费尔默在《父权制》等作品中,同样反驳了英国传统的普通法传统与人民同意理论,批判了混合君主制与有限君主制,只不过费尔默是通过圣经解释学重塑一种更为抽象、更为极端的父权制思想来为此张目的。如果说詹姆斯一世与费尔默的学说仍然是在法国主权学说的启发下对传统学说的偷梁换柱,那么霍布斯(Thomas Hobbes, 1588—1679)的主权学说则完全呈现出一种全新的理论深度。霍布斯采用了自然权利、同意、社会契约等新式话语,利用精密

的逻辑推理论证了绝对主权的必要性与正当性。

虽然绝对君主制思想来势汹汹，但是英国的宪政主义传统以及议会对绝对王权的抵制亦不曾间断。1649年，查理一世成为第一位被公开处决的国王。随后，世界上第一个共和政体在英国诞生。在17世纪的后半期，查理二世复辟。虽然秩序复原，但人心晃荡，危机四伏，前途不明。国王与议会之间的政治角力日趋激烈，思想界同样针锋相对。扎根于古老传统的学说落后于时代，已无法对抗绝对主权浪潮。洛克试图用新式的自然法学说来为英国的宪政分权政体注入新的生命。若要防止专制政府的出现，就必须防止任何主体（无论是人民、议会还是国王）握有绝对权力，因此洛克精心构建了不同权力的动态宪法关系，同时将一种自然权利理论作为其基础。这种学说彻底转化了传统宪政思想的内涵与逻辑，成为现代宪制民主思想的起点。

### 三、《政府论（下篇）》与洛克的其他作品

洛克并不是现代学科划分基础上的政治学者，他在哲学、神学、经济学、教育学等各个领域都颇有建树。洛克是英国经验主义哲学传统的开创者，他的《人类理解论》深深地影响了后来的贝克莱（George Berkeley）、休谟（David Hume）、密尔（J. S. Mill）等英国哲学家。洛克的《论宗教宽容》与《基督教的合理性》是近代自然神学思想的代表作。《教育片论》的英文版在18世纪共出了21版，并被翻译成荷兰语、法语、瑞典语、德语和意大利语，成为现代教育思想的经典著作。一位经典思想家并不是在某一特定范围内进行理论思考的人。他不仅需要思考人类的政治制度设计问题，更重要的是，他还需要思考人类的知识来源，关照人类的灵魂与信仰，反思人类的社会生活。也就是说，他必须在一个整全的视野中考察人与自己、人与他人、人与世界的关系。

当我们试图去理解洛克的政治学说时，我们必须将其作为洛克整个思想的一部分来加以研究，而不可孤立地对其加以简单的评判。当然，这里还有另一个更为直接的原因。作为一部

政治学作品，《政府论（下篇）》没有严谨的定义与推理，没有一个清晰完整的理论体系。它以极为通俗易懂的语言来阐述极为简明有力的政治论断，而没有形而上学、道德哲学、神学层面上的深入分析。当我们回过头去看这一自由主义的奠基之作时，很多人都会不满意这种略显粗糙的理论论证。因此，我们可以通过结合洛克的其他作品来加深对《政府论（下篇）》的理解。

我们可以去思考，洛克的《自然法辩难》与《人类理解论》是否可以为《政府论（下篇）》提供一个道德哲学基础（特别是其中的自然法学说）？洛克的《政府短论两篇》、《论宗教宽容》与《基督教的合理性》是否可以调和宗教与政治、信仰与理性之间的张力？《教育片论》是否可以为如何培养新政治所需要的新公民提供充分的说明？在整体上，这些写于不同时期、针对不同议题的著作是否存在一个融贯的逻辑，是否可以为人类提供一幅整全的图景？对这些问题的回答，将决定我们如何看待《政府论（下篇）》的价值与意义。

### 四、《政府论（下篇）》的影响

洛克的《政府论（下篇）》已经成为西方政治学的不朽名著。对洛克的学术研究从未间断，甚至达到了学派分立的程度。洛克与当今政治学理论之间的关联也是千丝万缕。由于篇幅有限，这篇导读将不介绍对洛克的研究学说史。我将介绍的是《政府论（下篇）》在18世纪的直接影响，主要包括在英国本土的影响与在美洲的影响。

之前我们已经提到，《政府论（下篇）》并不是对光荣革命的事后辩护。更值得我们注意的一点是，人们事后也并不是从《政府论（下篇）》的角度来理解整个事件的。光荣革命之后，英国议会颁布的《权利法案》并没有赋予人民以主权与革命权，并没有将政府的合法性奠定在人民的同意之上。《权利法案》并没有将光荣革命描述为"革命"，而是将其描述为：奥兰治的威廉（William of Orange）在詹姆斯二世放弃王位出逃法国后（而非被废除），凭借与玛丽（詹姆斯二世的女儿）的婚姻关系对英

国王位的继承。这也是当时大部分人（包括辉格党人）的观点。洛克对这种保守的做法极为不满，因为这否认了1688年这一政治事件所蕴含的革命内涵，重又回到世袭君主制的老路上。考虑到洛克的这种反潮流的激进立场，我们就不难理解他为何要匿名出版《政府论两篇》了。这还有利于我们理解《政府论（下篇）》在18世纪英国的遭遇。

早期的一些政治思想史著作将洛克描述为光荣革命的代言人，似乎洛克的学说带来了英国甚至整个西方政治思想界的转向，引领着后来者一步步建立了现代自由世界。这种对思想家的标签化、对思想史的意识形态化被证明是与历史不符的。历史学家们发现，由于《政府论两篇》的激进性，在光荣革命之后的政治讨论中，《政府论两篇》很少被人提及。辉格党人谨小慎微，将人民革命学说拒之门外。托利党人即使提及洛克，也是对其加以抨击。还有学者指出，18世纪时常出现的现实政治话语是人的自然社会性、公民人文主义、帝国、古老宪章、政治经济学等，而不是洛克的个人权利、社会契约、人民革命等。而且，18世纪后半期，思想史上占据主导的是功利主义思潮。洛克的自然法学说、社会契约论都遭到了休谟、边沁（Jeremy Bentham）等人的评判。

对洛克神话的这一颠覆略有些矫枉过正。在18世纪的上半期，虽然洛克的政治学说作为一个整体并没有获得普遍的接受与发展，但是洛克学说通过一定的转化被应用到了政治领域中。例如，某些辉格党人对议会的专断行为提出抗议时，会以相对温和的方式引用洛克的学说。某些对父权制思想死灰复燃保持警惕的人，通过洛克的学说对这种思想毒草加以批判。1760年乔治三世上台，这位具有绝对王权野心的国王试图恢复王权的往昔荣耀。此时，洛克的《政府论两篇》重又被许多人直接谈论。洛克的学说成为主张参政权、地方自治权的自由派人士（甚至一些"社会主义"倾向的人）的理论武器。就学术界而言，洛克的《政府论（下篇）》在苏格兰与欧洲大陆被一些思想家认真对待，例如格肖姆·卡迈克尔（Gershom Carmichael）、让·巴贝拉克（Jean Barbeyrac）。那些继承自然法传统的思想家特别重视

洛克所做出的理论贡献。即使是现代学者提出的那些18世纪英国主流思潮其实也并非与洛克的学说截然不同。后革命时代的诸多政治作品具有鲜明的折中色彩，许多学说将洛克的政治学进行了改造性的解释与吸收。

大部分西方学者都会同意，洛克的学说对18世纪的英国并无巨大的影响，但是究竟是否全无影响则并无定论。相比较而言，关于洛克对18世纪的美国的影响，学者们则更是众说纷纭。其中一个重要因素是，如何理解美国革命与建国时期的思想根源，决定了我们如何理解美国的立国之本，而这对美国当代的政治学会产生直接的影响。

在20世纪60年代之前，人们都认为洛克是美国国父的精神导师，是美国自由主义传统与个人主义精神的缔造者。这一传统生生不息，直到今天仍然是美国人的精神财富。1773年《波士顿公报》发布《政府论（下篇）》的出版公告时写道，这是"对人的权利与英国人的权利的最好阐述……胜过所有其他用我们的语言写就的政府评述"。在对1765年的《印花税法》和1766年的《宣示法案》的抵抗活动中，《政府论（下篇）》是被引用最多的文献。"无代表不纳税"的口号显然来自洛克。而且，英国议会中对殖民地的同情者与强硬派也都在洛克的学说上做文章。

20世纪60年代后，史学界有了新的发现。学者们指出，洛克的学说其实并没有在独立战争之前占据主导地位。当时美洲殖民地的人民主要是借助于共和主义的思想来认识自身的地位，评价英国的殖民地政策。人们认为，重商主义政策与帝国控制带来了统治者的腐败与人民的奴役，导致地方自治、公民政治参与、共同善的谋求无从谈起。《政府论（下篇）》中的自然状态、个人私利、社会契约等学说并无法为这种看法提供理论支持。以波考克（J. G. A. Pocock）为代表的一些学者认为，以古罗马共和精神、马基雅维利、哈林顿等人构成的共和主义思潮，而非洛克的那种自由主义思潮才是当时美洲的意识形态。此外，还有学者发现，苏格兰启蒙运动、普通法传统对美洲的影响也非常大。这一思想史研究的目的是，为在当代复兴共和主义（以

取代自由主义）寻找历史基础。针对这种重大修正，20世纪80年代末到90年代，不少学者又对其提出了质疑。

就学界对于洛克对美国的影响的研究而言，一个重要的特征是，将洛克的学说作为资本主义、个人主义、自由主义等现代思潮的代言人来加以使用。新近的研究已经开始全面反思这种理解的准确性。显然，若想准确定位洛克的影响首先必须准确理解洛克的学说。

## 五、几点说明

1. 洛克的《政府论（上篇）》与《政府论（下篇）》在出版时是一本书的两个部分。本书将洛克的《政府论（下篇）》单独出版是基于以下几点考虑：首先，《政府论（上篇）》是洛克对费尔默的学说的批判，《政府论（下篇）》才是洛克的立论所在。其次，虽然《政府论（上篇）》有助于我们理解《政府论（下篇）》，但直接阅读《政府论（下篇）》并不影响现代读者对《政府论（下篇）》基本观点的了解（虽然不够深入和全面）。再次，西方的教学活动与学术研究也集中于《政府论（下篇）》（中国的情况也是如此），因此对于大部分读者来说，阅读《政府论（下篇）》应当能够满足他们的基本需求。最后，在西方出版史上，将《政府论（下篇）》单独出版的做法也是较为普遍的。商务印书馆的"汉译名著丛书"也是将《政府论（上篇）》与《政府论（下篇）》分开出版。所以，我们也借鉴了这一做法，以降低书价与书的重量，方便读者。尽管如此，我们并不能否认《政府论（上篇）》与《政府论（下篇）》之间的关系。因此,在涉及《政府论（上篇）》的地方，我会在导读与脚注中给出一个基本的说明。

2. 本书中的导读试图为一般读者提供一个进入文本的背景性介绍。这个介绍首先包括历史的介绍，即为什么某个问题会在洛克的那个时代成为一个重要的问题。这个问题产生的时代背景是什么。其次，它还包括理论的介绍，即这个问题为什么会成为一个重要的理论问题，它在思想史上的起源以及它在洛克的理论中的位置是什么。此外，它还包括洛克的基本论点与论证逻辑，我们可以对洛克的论点提出哪些疑问，我们应当去追问哪些问题。我并没有对洛克的思想做深入全面的分析，毕竟这是"导读"而不是"研究"。对于在政治学、法学、社会学方面有一定积累的读者来说，这些介绍可能略显简单，但其中可能也会有一些小小的启发。在每篇导读后面，我列出了"延伸阅读材料"。这些材料来自本人多年研究的积累，对于想要深入研究《政府论（下篇）》与洛克思想的读者来说，应该会有所帮助。

3. 本书的脚注参考了皮特·拉斯莱特在权威英文版的《政府论两篇》中所做的脚注。在此感谢这位前辈的卓越贡献。

2013 年 3 月

王涛，华东政法大学科学研究院助理研究员。中国人民大学法学博士，牛津大学哲学院访问学者。研究方向为西方法哲学、西方法律思想史。

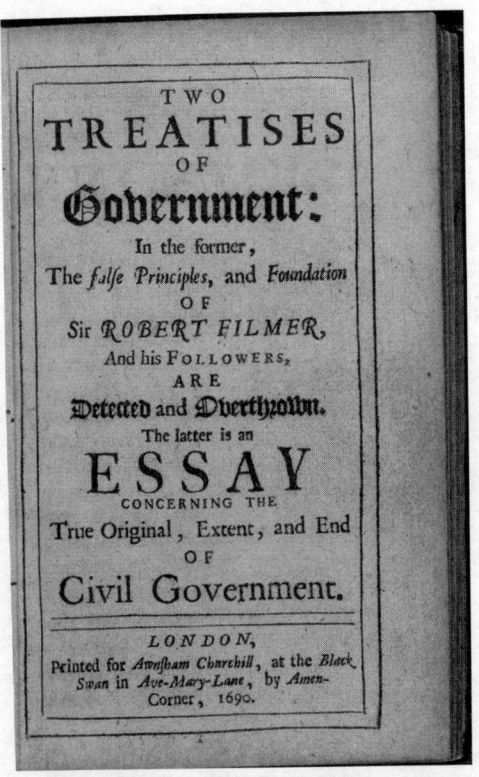

《政府论两篇》于1690年在伦敦首次出版时的封面

# CONTENTS

The Preface ································································· 1
Chapter I　　The Introduction ········································· 4
Chapter II　　Of the State of Nature ································ 12
Chapter III　　Of the State of War ··································· 25
Chapter IV　　Of Slavery ·················································· 36
Chapter V　　Of Property ················································· 45
Chapter VI　　Of Paternal Power ····································· 67
Chapter VII　　Of Political or Civil Society ························ 90
Chapter VIII　　Of the Beginning of Political Societies ·········· 106
Chapter IX　　Of the Ends of Political Society and Government ···· 133
Chapter X　　Of the Forms of a Commonwealth ··············· 140
Chapter XI　　Of the Extent of the Legislative Power ·········· 149
Chapter XII　　Of the Legislative, Executive, and Federative Power of the Commonwealth ··················· 162
Chapter XIII　　Of the Subordination of the Powers of the Commonwealth ···························· 172
Chapter XIV　　Of Prerogative ············································· 185
Chapter XV　　Of Paternal, Political, and Despotical Power, Considered Together ·································· 198

| Chapter XVI | Of Conquest | 207 |
| Chapter XVII | Of Usurpation | 227 |
| Chapter XVIII | Of Tyranny | 234 |
| Chapter XIX | Of the Dissolution of Government | 245 |

# The Preface

Reader,

Thou hast here the beginning and end of a discourse concerning government; what fate has otherwise disposed of the papers that should have filled up the middle, and were more than all the rest, it is not worth while to tell thee. These, which remain, I hope are sufficient to establish the throne of our great restorer, our present king William; to make good his title in the consent of the people; which being our only one of all lawful governments, he has more fully and clearly than any prince in Christendom; and to justify to the world the people of England, whose love of their just and natural rights, with their resolution to preserve them, saved the nation when it was on the very brink of slavery and ruin. If these papers have that evidence, I flatter myself is to be found in them, there will be no great miss of those which are lost, and my reader may be satisfied without them. For I imagine, I shall have neither the time nor inclination to repeat my pains, and fill up the wanting part of my answer, by tracing Sir Robert again through all the windings and obscurities which are to be met with in the several branches of his wonderful system. The king, and body of the nation, have since so thoroughly confuted his hypothesis, that I suppose nobody hereafter will have either the confidence to appear against our common safety, and be again an advocate for slavery; or the weakness to be deceived with contradictions dressed up in a popular style and well turned periods. For if any one will be at the pains himself, in those parts which are here untouched, to strip Sir Robert's discourses of the flourish of doubtful expressions, and endeavour to reduce his words to direct, positive, intelligible propositions, and then compare them one with another, he will quickly be satisfied there was never so much glib nonsense put together in well sounding English. If he think it not worth while to examine his works all through, let him make an experiment in that part where he treats of usurpation; and let him try whether he can, with all his skill, make Sir Robert intelligible, and consistent with himself, or common sense. I should not speak so plainly of a gentleman, long since past answering, had not the pulpit, of late years, publicly owned his doctrine, and made it the current divinity of the times. It is necessary those men, who, taking on them to be teachers, have so dangerously misled others, should be openly showed of what authority this their patriarch is, whom they have so blindly followed; that so they may either retract what upon so ill grounds they have vented, and cannot be maintained; or else justify those principles which they have preached up for gospel, though they had no better an author than an English courtier. For I should not have writ against Sir Robert, or taken the pains to show his mistakes, inconsistencies, and want of (what he so much boasts of, and pretends wholly to build on) scripture-proofs, were there not men amongst us, who, by crying up his books, and espousing his doctrine, save me from the reproach of writing against a dead adversary. They have been so zealous in this point, that, if I have done him any wrong, I cannot hope they should spare me. I wish, where they have done the truth and the public wrong, they would be as ready to redress it, and allow its just weight to this reflection, viz. that there cannot be done a greater mischief to prince and people, than the propagating wrong notions concerning government; that so at last all times might not have reason to complain of the "drum ecclesiastic." If any one, really concerned for truth, undertake the confutation of my hypothesis, I promise him

either to recant my mistake, upon fair conviction; or to answer his difficulties. But he must remember two things,

First, That cavilling here and there, at some expression, or little incident of my discourse, is not an answer to my book.

Secondly, That I shall not take railing for arguments, nor think either of these worth my notice: though I shall always look on myself as bound to give satisfaction to any one, who shall appear to be conscientiously scrupulous in the point, and shall show any just grounds for his scruples.

I have nothing more, but to advertise the reader that A stands for our author, and O for his Observations on Hobbes, Milton, &c. And that a bare quotation of pages always means pages of his *Patriarcha*, edit. 1680.

# Chapter *I*
## The Introduction

### 导 读

当代的读者（特别是中国的读者）翻开《政府论（下篇）》第一章，也许马上就会皱起眉头，因为在第一章的第二行就出现了"亚当"、"上帝"这样的字眼，而这些字眼在接下来的几行中不断映入眼帘。这种神学词汇通常不会出现在当代政法著作中，更不要说出现在首页中。但是在洛克写作的年代，这些词汇充斥于通常的日常用语、道德话语与政治讨论中。上帝创造了世界，《圣经》解释了人类的起源与发展历程，这是那个时代的常识。如何用上帝之眼来考察世间的万事万物是那个时代几乎所有思想家无法回避的一个问题。即使是少数的无神论思想家也不得不花很大的篇幅来解释"无神"意味着什么。

洛克同时代的大部分政治著作都可以被归为宽泛意义上的政治神学著作，《政府论两篇》也是如此。虽然"上帝"与圣经故事不时地出现在《政府论（下篇）》中，但是《政府论（下篇）》的主体部分几乎不包含神学内容。当代的读者也能相对比较容易地领会其中的论点与论证思路。这第一章之所以具有浓厚的神学色彩，是因为它是对《政府论（上篇）》的总结，而《政府论（上篇）》则是对一部政治神学作品（费尔默的《父权制》）的批判。

《政府论（下篇）》仅仅是《政府论两篇》的下半部分，其上半部分是《政府论（上篇）》。上下两篇在发表时候是合在一起的，但由于人们更为重视《政府论（下篇）》，所以就出现了许多下篇的单行本。在我们熟知的商务印书馆的汉译名著中，上篇与下篇也被分开来出版。从历史上看，《政府论（上篇）》一直受到冷遇。《政府论（上篇）》的美国版与法文版分别到1947年与1963年才出现。学界对洛克政治思想的研究也集中于《政府论（下篇）》，对《政府论（上篇）》的研究论文与著作可谓寥若辰星。《政府论（上篇）》之所以无人问津，正是因为人们认为它是对一部过时了的政治神学著作的反驳，所以它本身也是一部过时的作品。

　　这部所谓过时了的政治神学著作是费尔默的《父权制》。洛克在《政府论（下篇）》还没有写完的情况下停笔去反驳费尔默，并在《政府论（下篇）》的开篇专设一章来总结他的反驳观点。这一方面说明，费尔默的学说在当时产生的影响很大，而且它对洛克的学说构成了严重的挑战；另一方面还说明，洛克认为只有反驳了费尔默的学说，才能为他在《政府论（下篇）》中将要进行的立论扫清障碍。因此，如果想要全面地了解洛克的学说，必须要将《政府论（上篇）》与《政府论（下篇）》结合起来。

　　在之前的"导读"中，我们曾提到过费尔默的《父权制》。这里我们再来简单说明一下《父权制》的观点以及洛克对它的批判。《父权制》总的观点可以概括为：上帝在创世的时候，将对世界的统治权交给了人类的第一位父亲：亚当。亚当的统治权被他的子孙所继承，这些子孙就是各个君主。由于君权来自神授，所以这些君主对其臣民享有天然的、正当的统治权。由于君主的王权是通过继承亚当对全人类的父权而获得的，因此王权就是一种父权性质的统治权。所有的臣民都是君主的"子女"，他们天生就应当服从君主的统治。很显然这种君权神授的父权理论与洛克将要论证的人的自由平等、国家来自人民的同意、法治政府以及人民的革命权等论点针锋相对。

　　洛克在《政府论（上篇）》中一方面通过复杂的圣经解释学来说明费尔默对《圣经》的理解是错误的，另一方面则对这种政治神学提出了根本的质疑。洛克不仅驳斥了费尔默的学说，而且还在暗中驳斥了其背后的政治学研究方法：即《圣经》与基督教教义的解释学。洛克将一种神学论证方法转移到理性论证方式。就此而言，《政府论（上篇）》意义重大，因为它转化了政治学的研究方法。只有基于这个转化，《政府论（下篇）》的理性论证才能顺利展开，才能产生划时代的启蒙作用。

如今，《政府论（下篇）》中的许多观点都已成为我们这个时代的常识。当我们回过头去探索这些常识的来源时，我们会发现它们并不是横空出世的。《政府论（下篇）》与《政府论（上篇）》都是对既有思想的深刻反思，对人类根本问题的深入探索。我们既生活在当下，也生活在历史中，还生活在不确定的未来中，轻易地将伟大作品的某一部分定义为"过时"是对人类根本处境的严重误解。

**延伸阅读材料：**

1. [英]洛克：《政府论（上篇）》，叶启芳、瞿菊农译，北京，商务印书馆，2005。

2. [英]菲尔默：《"父权制"及其他著作》，北京，中国政法大学出版社，2003。

3. Robert Faulkner, Preface to Liberalism: Locke's First Treatise and the Bible, *The Review of Politics*, Vol. 67, No. 3 (Summer, 2005), pp.451–472.

4. Michael P. Zuckert, An Introduction to Locke's First Treatise: Locke and the Old Testament. In *Launching Liberalism: On Lockean Political Philosophy*, University of Kansas Press, 2002, pp.129–146.

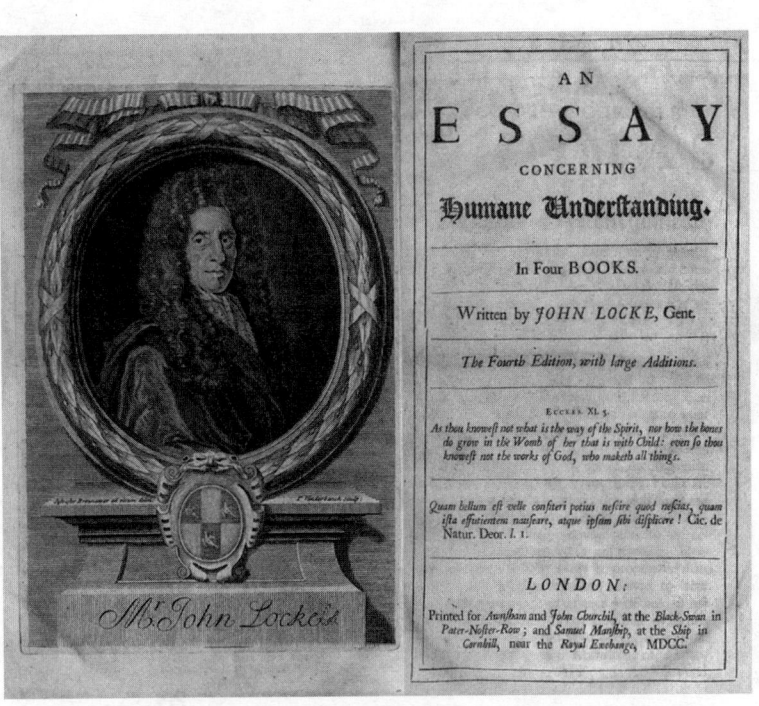

洛克的另一部伟大著作《人类理解论》一书的封面

## § 1.

It having been shown in the foregoing discourse[1],

1. That Adam had not, either by natural right of fatherhood, or by positive donation from God, any such authority over his children, or dominion over the world as is pretended.

2. That if he had, his heirs yet had no right to it.

3. That if his heirs had, there being no law of nature, nor positive law of God, that determines which is the right heir in all cases that may arise, the right of succession, and consequently of bearing rule, could not have been certainly determined.

4. That if even that had been determined, yet the knowledge of which is the eldest line of Adam's posterity, being so long since utterly lost, that in the races of mankind and families of the world, there remains not to one above another the least pretence to be the eldest house, and to have the right of inheritance.

All these premises having, as I think, been clearly made out, it is impossible that the rulers now on earth should make any benefit, or derive any the least shadow of authority from that, which is held to be the fountain of all power, "Adam's private dominion and paternal jurisdiction;" so that he that will not give just occasion to think that all government in the world is the product only of force and violence, and that men live together by no other rules but that of beasts, where the strongest carries it, and so lay a foundation for perpetual disorder and mischief, tumult, sedition, and rebellion (things that the followers of that hypothesis so loudly cry out against)[2] must

---

[1] "前面的讨论"指的是《政府论（上篇）》。中译本：［英］洛克：《政府论（上篇）》，叶启芳、瞿菊农译，北京，商务印书馆，2005。关于《政府论（上篇）》与《政府论（下篇）》之间的关系，参见本书的"导读"与本章的"导读"。

[2] 许多人认为这里的假设是在影射霍布斯的观点，但也可能是洛克在回忆费尔默对霍布斯的自然状态学说的批判。费尔默是霍布斯最早的批判者。洛克早在1667年就阅读了费尔默的这篇批判文章：*Observations Concerning the Original of Government, upon Mr. Hobs Leviathan, Mr. Milton Against Salmasius, H. Grotius De Jure Belli* (1652)，见［英］菲尔默：《"父权制"及其他著作》，184—234，北京，中国政法大学出版社，2003。

of necessity find out another rise of government, another original of political power, and another way of designing and knowing the persons that have it, than what Sir Robert Filmer[1] hath taught us.

## § 2.

To this purpose, I think it may not be amiss to set down what I take to be political power; that the power of a magistrate over a subject may be distinguished from that of a father over his children, a master over his servants, a husband over his wife, and a lord over his slave. All which distinct powers happening sometimes together in the same man, if he be considered under these different relations,

---

[1] 罗伯特·费尔默爵士（1588—1653）。费尔默出生于肯特郡一个颇有声望的绅士家族。他于1604年进入剑桥大学三一学院。1605年进入林肯律师学院，8年后获得律师从业资格。1618年，费尔默与伊利主教的女儿安妮结婚，住在威斯敏斯特大教堂。费尔默从17世纪20年代开始进行写作。内战时期，费尔默因年事已高没有为国王效力，在肯特郡的家中修养。费尔默的王权著作使得他在战后被迫捐献了大量的财产，并于1643年至1647年被关入大牢。出狱后，受到当时政治论辩风气的影响，费尔默在1648年接连匿名出版了几部小册子。它们是：2月出版的关于英格兰宪政史的《自由持有人大审讯》(*The Freeholder Grand Inquest*)，4月出版的反驳混合与有限君主学说的《混合或有限君主制的混乱》(*The Anarchy of a Mixed or Limited Monarchy*)，夏天出版的主张君主绝对主义的《所有过往的绝对权力的必要性》(*Necessity of the Absolute Power of All Kings*)。到了1648年下半年，包括费尔默在内的王权支持者们不再出声了。1649年1月查理一世被砍头。此后几年，费尔默远离尘嚣，闭门读书。1652年，费尔默出版了《论政府的起源》(*Observations Concerning the Original of Government, upon Mr. Hobs Leviathan, Mr. Milton Against Salmasius, H. Grotius De Jure Belli*) 一书，批判了霍布斯、弥尔顿与格劳秀斯的学说。费尔默最后一本政治著作是1652年5月出版的《对于亚里士多德的政治形势的评论》(*Observations upon Aristotle's Politiques Concerning Forms of Government, Together with Directions for Obedience to Governors in Dangerous and Doubtful Times*)。一年后，费尔默去世。

《父权制》这部作品写于1631年左右，由于各种原因，费尔默一直没有将其出版。尽管如此，《父权制》是费尔默最重要的政治著作，因为它包含了费尔默所有的主要观点，是他后来的几部作品的基础。费尔默的作品在17世纪60年代与70年代都有一定的读者，并获得了一定的关注，但是直到1679年到1680年的"排除危机"时期，他的作品才获得了广泛的关注。托利党想要利用费尔默的著作来为绝对王权辩护，因此费尔默的所有作品在1679年至1680年间都被重印出版。《父权制》也终于出现在市面上了。

it may help us to distinguish these powers one from another, and show the difference betwixt a ruler of a commonwealth, a father of a family, and a captain of a galley.

§ 3.

Political power, then, I take to be a right of making laws with penalties of death, and consequently all less penalties for the regulating and preserving of property, and of employing the force of the community, in the execution of such laws, and in the defence of the commonwealth from foreign injury; and all this only for the public good.

# Chapter II
## Of the State of Nature

### 导　读

　　近代思想史是自然法学说主导的一段思想史，而洛克是其中的代表。近代自然法学家们通过界定"自然法"来解释人的道德行动准则，从而为人间基本秩序确立原则。在具体的论证中，"自然状态"这个概念是他们共同的逻辑起点。在这些思想家看来，如果我们想要知道人自然而然地受到的道德法则是什么，我们首先需要知道人自然而然地所处的状态是什么。也就是说，当我们试图分析自然法时，我们必须要了解人的自然状态是什么。只有说明了人的自然状态，才能说明人在自然状态中遵循（或应当遵循）的法则是什么。这两个概念相互关联，不可分割。

　　就一种政治学说而言，考察自然状态是为我们反思政治状态的正当性提供一个基点。在现实生活中，人类处于各种特定的道德、经济、政治关系之中。不同的国家与种族的人往往处于不同现状中，拥有不同的伦理秩序、经济制度与政治架构。这一当下状态是一个事实状态，大部分人都无意识地生活于其中并认为"存在即是合理"。但是，如果想要反思这一事实状态的合理性，反思不同的事实状态的共通性，我们就需要超越这一当下状态，考察人的自然状态。通过将人还原到最原初的状

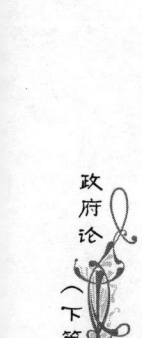

态之中，来看看人最基本的行为准则是什么，人与人之间的最基本的关系是什么。还原的方法可以是追寻人类早期的状态（或重构一种人类的发展史），也可以是人类的历史之外找到一个基点来提供评判的标尺。前一种被称为历史性的进路，后一种被称为哲学性的进路。

考察自然状态是所有近代自然法学家的共同做法，洛克也不例外。洛克将"论自然状态"作为《政府论（下篇）》立论的第一章。显然，它是洛克政治学说的起点。洛克首先指出，自然状态有两个规范性维度，一个是自然自由，一个是自然平等。对此我们可以追问，人凭什么享有自然自由与自然平等？自然自由与自然平等之间的关系是什么？两者是否有价值序列上的高低之分？对此，我们还需要与费尔默的主张进行比较，因为费尔默认为，人天生就处于一种服从上级权威的状态，人与人之间也不可能是平等的。

洛克接着说明了自然自由与自然法的关系。他着重指出，自然自由不是绝对自由，而是自然法范围内的自由。洛克在第6段具体说明了自然法的三点限制。对此，我们可以将其与霍布斯的自然自由论进行比较，因为霍布斯认为人的自然自由是一种绝对自由。此外，自然法这个概念在此显得十分关键，但是洛克却没有为自然法的性质与内涵提供具体的论证。人们是如何知晓自然法的，或者说自然法是如何被公布的呢？人们为何会遵守自然法，或者说为何应当遵守自然法呢？洛克回避了这些基本问题。他的理由是："深入自然法的细节超出了我这里要谈论的问题。"问题在于，洛克在《政府论两篇》中都没有"深入自然法的细节"。难道这个问题与《政府论两篇》所有主题都没有直接的关系吗？

既然自然法为自然自由设置了限制，接下来的问题就是：是否所有人都会遵守这个限制？这涉及自然状态中的暴力问题。违反自然法是一种暴力，制止违法者同样需要一种暴力。洛克区分了这两种暴力行为，前者是不合法的暴力，后者是合法的暴力，是对"自然法的执行权"的运用。洛克花了很大的篇幅来阐述自然法的执行权。我们需要明确洛克是如何来说明这种权力的性质、目的、界限以及运用方式的。此外还有一个重要的问题是：违反自然法以及自然法的执行权是否构成一个融贯的说法。洛克似乎认为，许多人都不会自觉地遵守自然法，如果是这样的话，自然法是否就是一个空洞的说辞呢？另一方面，洛克赋予人类以执行自然法的权力，但同时又指出："心地不良、感情用事和报复心理都会使他们过分地惩罚别人，结果只会发生混乱与无秩序。"似乎执行自然法的权力在实际运用过程中会转变为一种无法无天的暴力行为。如果大部分人都不会自觉地遵守自然法，而执行自然法的权力又具有自我消解的倾向，那么洛克所言的自然状态是否与霍布斯所说的战争状态一样呢？

自然状态这个概念在一般人来看是一个很抽象的概念。它似乎无法直接对应我们真实生活中的某一处境。洛克意识到人们可能会产生以下这一疑问："现在哪里有或曾经有过处在这种自然状态中的人呢？"自然状态的真实性问题是洛克自己提出的问题，他想必认为这是一个很重要的问题，但是洛克却仅仅在本章结束的地方提供了一些例证就将此问题打发掉了。在洛克这里，自然状态究竟是一个道德哲学层面上的假设，还是人类曾经真实经历过的一个历史阶段呢？洛克究竟是在采取一种历史性的进路，还是哲学性的进路呢？如果自然状态是一种道德假设，那么这种假设的人性基础是什么呢？它是否具有某些前提性的预设呢？如果自然状态是一种历史重构，那么它的重构是否具有足够的说服力呢？它如何具有规范性力量呢？这些都是我们需要去进一步思考的问题。

**延伸阅读材料：**

1. 洛克在《人类理解论》中对"自由"的分析：[英]洛克：《人类理解论》，关文运译，北京，商务印书馆，1997，第二卷第二十一章"能力"。

2. 霍布斯对自然自由的分析：[英]霍布斯：《利维坦》，黎思复、黎廷弼译，杨昌裕校，北京，商务印书馆，1997，第一部分第十四章"论第一与第二自然律以及契约法"。

3. 休谟对自然状态学说的批判：[英] 休谟：《人性论》，关文运译，郑之骧校，北京，商务印书馆，2005，第三卷第二章"论正义与非义"。

4. 杰里米·沃尔德伦专门研究洛克平等学说的著作：Jeremy Waldron, *God, Locke, and Equality: Christian Foundations in Locke's Political Thought*, Cambridge University Press (December 23, 2002).

5. 洛克在《自然法辩难》中对自然法问题的讨论：John Locke: *Essays on the Law of Nature*, edited by W. von Leyden, Clarendon Press, 1954.

6. 研究洛克"自然状态"概念的论文：

——Philip Vogt, *Locke,* Eden and Two States of Nature: The Fortunate Fall Revisited, *Journal of the History of Philosophy*, Volume 35, Number 4, October 1997, pp. 523–544.

——Robert A. Goldwin, Locke's State of Nature in Political Society, *The Western Political Quarterly*, Vol. 29, No. 1 (Mar., 1976), pp. 126–135.

——Barry Hindess, Locke's State of Nature, History of the Human Sciences, Vol. 20 No. 3; A. John Simmons, Locke's State of Nature, *Political Theory*, Vol. 17, No. 3 (Aug., 1989), pp. 449–470.

——John Anglim, On Locke's State of Nature, *Political Studies* (UK), 26 (1978), pp. 78–90.

——Richard Ashcraft, Locke's State of Nature: Historical Fact or Moral Fiction?, *The American Political Science Review*, Vol. 62, No. 3 (Sep., 1968), pp. 898–915.

7. 设有专章研究洛克的"自然状态"概念的著作：

——John Dunn, *The Political Thought of John Locke*, Cambridge University Press, 1969.

——Peter. C. Myers, *Our Only Star and Compass: Locke and the Struggle for Political Rationality*, Rowman & Littlefield, 1998.

——Richard H. Cox, *Locke on War and Peace*, Rowman & Littlefield (August 31, 1982).

## § 4.

To understand political power right, and derive it from its original, we must consider what state all men are naturally in, and that is, a state of perfect freedom to order their actions and dispose of their possessions and persons, as they think fit, within the bounds of the law of nature; without asking leave, or depending upon the will of any other man.

A state also of equality, wherein all the power and jurisdiction is reciprocal, no one having more than another; there being nothing more evident, than that creatures of the same species and rank, promiscuously born to all the same advantages of nature, and the use of the same faculties, should[1] also be equal one amongst another without subordination or subjection: unless the lord and master of them all should, by any manifest declaration of his will, set one above another, and confer on him, by an evident and clear appointment, an undoubted right to dominion and sovereignty.

## § 5.

This equality of men by nature, the judicious Hooker[2] looks upon as so evident in itself, and beyond all question, that he makes it the foundation of that obligation to mutual love amongst men, on which he builds the duties we owe one another, and from whence he derives the great maxims of justice and charity. His words are,

"The like natural inducement hath brought men to know, that it is no less their duty to love others than themselves; for seeing

---

[1] should 一词说明洛克这里是在一种应然层面而非事实层面上主张人的自由。洛克在《理解能力指导散论》与《政府论》中都承认人在身体构造与心智能力方面事实上都存在着差异。

[2] 理查德·胡克尔（Richard Hooker, 1553—1660），英国宗教改革时期的神学思想家和政治思想家，著有《教会政体的法律》（Laws of Ecclesiastica Polity）一书。胡克尔的学说在英国被广泛接受，所以洛克在《政府论（下篇）》中经常引用胡克尔的观点以获得教会人士的接受，但是两人的学说其实存在着很大的差异。

those things which are equal, must needs all have one measure; if I cannot but wish to receive good, even as much at every man's hands, as any man can wish unto his own soul, how should I look to have any part of my desire herein satisfied, unless myself be careful to satisfy the like desire, which is undoubtedly in other men, being of one and the same nature? To have any thing offered them repugnant to this desire, must needs in all respects grieve them as much as me; so that if I do harm, I must look to suffer, there being no reason that others should show greater measure of love to me, than they have by me showed unto them: my desire therefore to be loved of my equals in nature, as much as possibly may be, imposeth upon me a natural duty of bearing to them-ward fully the like affection: from which relation of equality between ourselves and them that are as ourselves, what several rules and canons natural reason hath drawn, for direction of life, no man is ignorant."

## § 6.

But though this be a state of liberty, yet it is not a state of licence: though man in that state have an uncontrolable liberty to dispose of his person or possessions, yet he has not liberty to destroy himself, or so much as any creature in his possession, but where some nobler use than its bare preservation calls for it. The state of nature has a law of nature to govern it, which obliges every one: and reason, which is that law, teaches all mankind, who will but consult it, that being all equal and independent, no one ought to harm another in his life, health, liberty, or possessions: for men being all the workmanship of one omnipotent and infinitely wise Maker; all the servants of one sovereign master, sent into the world by his order, and about his business; they are his property, whose workmanship they are, made to last during his, not another's pleasure: and being furnished with like faculties, sharing all in one community of nature, there cannot be supposed any such subordination among us, that may authorize us to destroy another, as if we were made for one another's uses, as the inferior ranks of creatures are for ours. Every one, as he is bound to preserve himself, and not to quit his station wilfully, so by the like reason, when his own preservation comes not in competition, ought he, as much as he can, to preserve the rest of mankind, and may not, unless it be to do justice to an offender, take away or impair the life, or what tends to the preservation of life, the liberty, health, limb, or goods of another.

§ 7.

And that all men may be restrained from invading others rights, and from doing hurt to one another, and the law of nature be observed, which willeth the peace and preservation of all mankind, the execution of the law of nature is, in that state, put into every man's hands, whereby every one has a right to punish the transgressors of that law to such a degree as may hinder its violation: for the law of nature would, as all other laws that concern men in this world, be in vain, if there were nobody that in the state of nature had a power to execute that law, and thereby preserve the innocent and restrain offenders. And if any one in the state of nature may punish another for any evil he has done, every one may do so: for in that state of perfect equality, where naturally there is no superiority or jurisdiction of one over another, what any may do in prosecution of that law, every one must needs have a right to do.

§ 8.

And thus, in the state of nature, "one man comes by a power over another;" but yet no absolute or arbitrary power, to use a criminal, when he has got him in his hands, according to the passionate heats, or boundless extravagancy of his own will; but only to retribute to him, so far as calm reason and conscience dictate, what is proportionate to his transgression; which is so much as may serve for reparation and restraint: for these two are the only reasons, why one man may lawfully do harm to another, which is that we call punishment. In transgressing the law of nature, the offender declares himself to live by another rule than that of reason and common equity, which is that measure God has set to the actions of men, for their mutual security; and so he becomes dangerous to mankind, the tye, which is to secure them from injury and violence, being slighted and broken by him. Which being a trespass against the whole species, and the peace and safety of it, provided for by the law of nature; every man upon this score, by the right he hath to preserve mankind in general, may restrain, or, where it is necessary, destroy things noxious to them, and so may bring such evil on any one, who hath transgressed that law, as may make him repent the doing of it, and thereby deter him, and by his example others, from doing the like mischief. And in this case, and upon this ground, "every man hath a right to punish the offender, and be executioner of the law of nature."

### § 9.

I doubt not but this will seem a very strange doctrine to some men: but before they condemn it, I desire them to resolve me, by what right any prince or state can put to death, or punish any alien, for any crime he commits in their country. It is certain their laws, by virtue of any sanction they receive from the promulgated will of the legislative, reach not a stranger: they speak not to him, nor, if they did, is he bound to hearken to them. The legislative authority, by which they are in force over the subjects of that commonwealth, hath no power over him. Those who have the supreme power of making laws in England, France, or Holland, are to an Indian but like the rest of the world, men without authority: and therefore, if by the law of nature every man hath not a power to punish offences against it, as he soberly judges the case to require, I see not how the magistrates of any community can punish an alien of another country; since, in reference to him, they can have no more power than what every man naturally may have over another.

## § 10.

Besides the crime which consists in violating the law, and varying from the right rule of reason, whereby a man so far becomes degenerate, and declares himself to quit the principles of human nature, and to be a noxious creature, there is commonly injury done to some person or other, and some other man receives damage by his transgression: in which case he who hath received any damage, has, besides the right of punishment common to him with other men, a particular right to seek reparation from him that has done it: and any other person, who finds it just, may also join with him that is injured, and assist him in recovering from the offender so much as may make satisfaction for the harm he has suffered.

## § 11.

From these two distinct rights, the one of punishing the crime for restraint, and preventing the like offence, which right of punishing is in every body; the other of taking reparation, which belongs only to the injured party; comes it to pass that the magistrate, who by being magistrate hath the common right of punishing put into his hands, can often, where the public good demands not the execution of the law, remit the punishment of criminal offences by his own authority, but yet cannot remit the satisfaction due to any private man for the damage he has received. That, he who has suffered the damage has a right to demand in his own name, and he alone can remit: the damnified person has this power of appropriating to himself the goods or service of the offender, by right of self-preservation, as every man has a power to punish the crime, to prevent its being committed again, "by the right he has of preserving all mankind;" and doing all reasonable things he can in order to that end: and thus it is, that every man, in the state of nature, has a power to kill a murderer, both to deter others from doing the like injury, which no reparation can compensate, by the example of the punishment that attends it from every body; and also to secure men from the attempts of a criminal, who having renounced reason, the common rule and measure God hath given to mankind, hath, by the unjust violence and slaughter he hath committed upon one, declared war against all mankind; and therefore may be destroyed as a lion or a tiger, one of those wild savage beasts, with whom men can have no society nor security: and upon this is grounded that great law of nature, "Whoso sheddeth man's blood, by man shall his blood be shed."[1] And Cain[2] was so fully convinced, that every one had a right to destroy such a criminal, that after the murder of his brother, he cries out, "Every one that findeth me, shall slay me;" so plain was it writ in the hearts of mankind.

### § 12.

By the same reason may a man in the state of nature punish the lesser breaches of that law. It will perhaps be demanded, with death? I answer, each transgression may be punished to that degree, and with so much severity, as will suffice to make it an ill bargain to the offender, give him cause to repent, and terrify others from doing the like. Every offence, that can be committed in the state of nature, may in the state of nature be also punished equally, and as far forth, as it may in a commonwealth: for though it would be beside my present purpose, to enter here into the particulars of the law of nature, or its measures of punishment, yet it is certain there is such a law, and that too as intelligible and plain to a rational creature, and a studier of that law, as the positive laws of commonwealths: nay, possibly plainer, as much as reason is easier to be understood, than the fancies and intricate contrivances of men, following contrary and hidden interests put into words; for so truly are a great part of the municipal laws of countries, which are only so far right, as they are founded on the law of nature, by which they are to be regulated and interpreted.

---

[1] 这句话的中文意思是："谁使人流血的，人亦必使他流血。"出自《旧约·创世纪》第九章第六句。

[2] 该隐（Cain）是《圣经》中的一个重要人物。他是亚当与妻子夏娃所生的两个儿子之一，因为嫉妒弟弟亚伯而把亚伯杀害。

## § 13.

To this strange doctrine, viz. That "in the state of nature every one has the executive power" of the law of nature, I doubt not but it will be objected, that it is unreasonable for men to be judges in their own cases, that self love will make men partial to themselves and their friends; and on the other side, that ill-nature, passion, and revenge will carry them too far in punishing others; and hence nothing but confusion and disorder will follow: and that therefore God hath certainly appointed government to restrain the partiality and violence of men. I easily grant, that civil government is the proper remedy for the inconveniencies of the state of nature, which must certainly be great, where men may be judges in their own case; since it is easy to be imagined, that he who was so unjust as to do his brother an injury, will scarce be so just as to condemn himself for it: but I shall desire those who make this objection, to remember, that absolute monarchs are but men; and if government is to be the remedy of those evils, which necessarily follow from men's being judges in their own cases, and the state of nature is therefore not to be endured; I desire to know what kind of government that is, and how much better it is than the state of nature, where one man commanding a multitude, has the liberty to be judge in his own case, and may do to all his subjects whatever he pleases, without the least liberty to any one to question or control those who execute his pleasure? and in whatsoever he doth, whether led by reason, mistake or passion, must be submitted to? much better it is in the state of nature, wherein men are not bound to submit to the unjust will of another: and if he that judges, judges amiss in his own, or any other case, he is answerable for it to the rest of mankind.

## § 14.

It is often asked as a mighty objection, "where are, or ever were there any men in such a state of nature?" To which it may suffice as an answer at present, that since all princes and rulers of independent governments, all through the world, are in a state of nature, it is plain the world never was, nor ever will be, without numbers of men in that state. I have named all governors of independent communities, whether they are, or are not, in league with others: for it is not every compact that puts an end to the state of nature between men, but only this one of agreeing together mutually to enter into one community, and make one body politic; other promises and compacts men may make one with another, and yet still be in the state of nature. The promises and bargains for truck, &c. between the two men in the desert island, mentioned by Garcilasso de la Vega[1], in his history of Peru; or between a Swiss and an Indian, in the woods of America; are binding to them, though they are perfectly in a state of nature, in reference to one another: for truth and keeping of faith belongs to men as men, and not as members of society.

§ 15.

To those that say, there were never any men in the state of nature, I will not only oppose the authority of the judicious Hooker, Eccl. Pol. lib. 1. sect. 10, where he says, "The laws which have been hitherto mentioned," i. e. the laws of nature, "do bind men absolutely, even as they are men, although they have never any settled fellowship, never any solemn agreement amongst themselves what to do, or not to do; but forasmuch as we are not by ourselves sufficient to furnish ourselves with competent store of things, needful for such a life as our nature doth desire, a life fit for the dignity of man; therefore to supply those defects and imperfections which are in us, as living singly and solely by ourselves, we are naturally induced to seek communion and fellowship with others. This was the cause of men's uniting themselves at first in politic societies."

---

[1] 加西拉梭（Garcilaso de la Vega, 1539—1616），历史学家、作家。加西拉梭出生于西班牙殖民统治的西属美洲的秘鲁总督区。他的父亲是一位西班牙征服者，母亲是秘鲁的一位印加公主。加西拉梭写了许多关于印加的生活、历史以及西班牙征服者的文字。这些文字以 Comentarios Reales de los Incas 为名于1617年出版。英文全译本以《论印加》（The Incas）为名于1961年出版。

But I moreover affirm, that all men are naturally in that state, and remain so, till by their own consents they make themselves members of some politic society; and I doubt not in the sequel of this discourse to make it very clear.

# Chapter III
## Of the State of War

### 导 读

第一位对自然状态做出深入分析的现代思想家是托马斯·霍布斯。霍布斯将自然状态描述为一种战争状态。他认为,由于人的竞争、猜疑与对荣誉的追逐,人的原初状态就是一种所有人对所有人的战争状态。他对战争状态的概括令人印象深刻:"人们不断处于暴力死亡的恐惧和危险中,人的生活孤独、贫困、卑污、残忍而短寿。"

有一些学者认为,洛克所界定的自然状态其实与霍布斯所讲的战争状态没有什么实质性的区别。但是在《政府论(下篇)》的第三章"论战争状态"中,洛克似乎非常重视这两者的区别。因此,这一章的首要问题,就是洛克是否有效地区分了自然状态与战争状态。

首先一个问题是战争状态的含义。洛克从三个角度说明了战争状态的内涵。

1. 在本章开头,他指出,造成战争状态是"用语言或行动表示对另一个人的生命有沉着的、确定的企图,而不是一时的意气用事"。

2. 在第 17 段,洛克又指出:"谁企图将另一个人置于自己的绝对权力之下,谁就同那人处于战争状态。"

3. 在第19段，洛克又指出："不基于权利以强力加诸别人，不论有无共同裁判者，都造成一种战争状态。"

就这些定义本身，我们需要进一步追问以下这些问题：首先，如何区分"沉着的、确定的企图"与"一时的意气用事"？我们如何能够确定行为的心理意图是什么？其次，"绝对权力"是一种什么性质的权力？具有哪些特征的行为表明行为人"企图将另一个人置于自己的绝对权力之下"？再次，"不基于权利以强力加诸别人"中的"权利"指的是哪些权利？此外，我们还可以追问，战争状态究竟是个体与个体之间的关系（即特定"侵犯者"与"无辜者"之间的关系），还是一个人与所有人之间的关系，还是所有人与所有人之间的整体关系？战争状态究竟是个体之间的偶发事件所造成的状态，还是一种人类的普遍状态？

这一章的第二个关键问题是，自然状态、战争状态与公民社会之间的关系。这三个状态是否是三种完全不同、截然对立、相互排斥的不同状态？还是说它们之间存在着重叠的地方？还是说，某个状态是一般性状态，其他状态是特殊性状态？比如说，自然状态与公民社会下是否会出现局部的战争状态呢？公民社会中，是否在某些时刻，就某些特定关系而言，存在某种自然状态呢？

公民社会的问题我们需要结合后面的章节才能加以回答，就目前而言，我们首先需要明确自然状态与战争状态之间的关系。如果说自然状态是一种遵守自然法的状态，战争状态是一种违反自然法的状态，那么自然状态与战争状态就是对立的状态。如果是这样的话，人的原初状态究竟是人的自然状态还是人的战争状态呢？按照这个思路，人的原初状态要么是自然状态要么是战争状态，而不可能同时是自然状态与战争状态。这样一来，似乎有一个概念就是多余的了。这好像不符合逻辑。那么，我们是否可以将战争状态理解为自然状态之下的一个子概念？也就是说，战争状态也许是潜藏在自然状态之中的一个潜在状态，一个非常状态。这样一来，自然状态就可以将战争状态纳入自己的范畴中。当我们试图去理解自然状态这个概念的内涵时，我们需要牢记，对自然状态的定义取决于我们如何看待人的本质与人在这个世界中的处境,而不是没有理论基础的主张。如果第二种解释是合理的,那么我们就需要追问,如此具有弹性的自然状态概念背后究竟是怎样一种对人的自然或本性、人获得道德知识的方式与能力、人实施道德行为的理解呢?

**延伸阅读材料:**

1. 霍布斯对"战争状态"的分析:[英]霍布斯:《利维坦》,黎思复、黎廷弼译,杨昌裕校,北京,商务印书馆,1997,第一部分第十三章"论人类幸福与苦难的自然状况"。

2. 对霍布斯的自然状态学说的研究:

——孔新峰:《从自然之人到公民:霍布斯政治思想新诠》,北京,国家行政学院出版社,2011,第三章"'质料':自然之人与自然状态"。

——Thornton, Helen, *State of Nature or Eden? : Thomas Hobbes and His Contemporaries on the Natural Condition of Human Beings*, Rochester, NY: University of Rochester Press, 2005.

——R. E. Ewin, *Virtues and Rights: The Moral Philosophy of Thomas Hobbes*, Chapter 5 "The Natural Condition of Mankind", Westview Press, 1991.

3. 普芬道夫(Samuel Baron von Pufendorf, 1632—1694)的自然状态学说及其对霍布斯的"战争状态"的批判:*Samuel Pufendorf's On the Natural State of Men*. The 1678 Latin edition and English, translated, annotated, and introduced by Michael Seidler, Lewiston, N.Y. : E. Mellen Press, c1990. 相关分析参见塞德勒为此书写的"导论"。

4. 参见上一章的"延伸阅读材料"。

有许多人认为，洛克的《政府论（下篇）》矛头指向的是英国17世纪的另一位伟大的思想家：托马斯·霍布斯（Thomas Hobbes, 1588—1679）。左图为霍布斯最为出名的一幅肖像画，由约翰·迈克尔·赖特（John Michael Wright）画于大约1669年—1670年间。右图为霍布斯最为重要的政治学著作《利维坦》（*Leviathan*, 1651）封面的一幅插图，形象地描绘出霍布斯所构想的主权者的形象。

## § 16.

The state of war is a state of enmity and destruction: and therefore declaring by word or action, not a passionate and hasty, but a sedate settled design upon another man's life, puts him in a state of war with him against whom he has declared such an intention, and so has exposed his life to the other's power to be taken away by him, or any one that joins with him in his defence, and espouses his quarrel; it being reasonable and just, I should have a right to destroy that which threatens me with destruction; for, by the fundamental law of nature, man being to be preserved as much as possible, when all cannot be preserved, the safety of the innocent is to be preferred: and one may destroy a man who makes war upon him, or has discovered an enmity to his being, for the same reason that he may kill a wolf or a lion; because such men are not under the ties of the common law of reason, have no other rule, but that of force and violence, and so may be treated as beasts of prey, those dangerous and noxious creatures, that will be sure to destroy him whenever he falls into their power.

## § 17.

And hence it is, that he who attempts to get another man into his absolute power, does thereby put himself into a state of war[1] with him; it being to be understood as a declaration of a design upon his life: for I have reason to conclude, that he who would get me into his power without my consent, would use me as he pleased when he got me there, and destroy me too when he had a fancy to it; for nobody can desire to have me in his absolute power, unless it be to compel me by force to that which is against the right of my freedom, i. e. make me a slave. To be free from such force is the only security of my preservation; and reason bids me look on him, as an enemy to my preservation, who would take away that freedom which is the fence

---

[1] 这句话很可能是洛克在 1689 年加进去的。影射英国国王詹姆斯二世与全体英国人处于"战争状态"。

to it; so that he who makes an attempt to enslave me, thereby puts himself into a state of war with me. He that, in the state of nature, would take away the freedom that belongs to any one in that state, must necessarily be supposed to have a design to take away every thing else, that freedom being the foundation of all the rest; as he that, in the state of society, would take away the freedom belonging to those of that society or commonwealth, must be supposed to design to take away from them every thing else, and so be looked on as in a state of war.

## § 18.

This makes it lawful for a man to kill a thief, who has not in the least hurt him, nor declared any design upon his life, any farther than, by the use of force, so to get him in his power, as to take away his money, or what he pleases, from him; because using force, where he has no right, to get me into his power, let his pretence be what it will, I have no reason to suppose, that he, who would take away my liberty, would not, when he had me in his power, take away every thing else. And therefore it is lawful for me to treat him as one who has put himself into a state of war with me, i. e. kill him if I can; for to that hazard does he justly expose himself, whoever introduces a state of war, and is aggressor in it.

## § 19.

And here we have the plain "difference between the state of nature and the state of war," which however some men[1] have confounded, are as far distant, as a state of peace, good-will, mutual assistance and preservation, and a state of enmity, malice, violence and mutual destruction, are one from another. Men living together according to reason, without a common superiour on earth, with authority to judge between them, is properly the state of nature. But force, or a declared design of force, upon the person of another, where

---

[1] 这里的"有些人"（men）是指霍布斯主义者，即持有霍布斯观点的人。

there is no common superiour on earth to appeal to for relief, is the state of war: and it is the want of such an appeal gives a man the right of war even against an aggressor, though he be in society and a fellow-subject. Thus a thief, whom I cannot harm, but by appeal to the law, for having stolen all that I am worth, I may kill, when he sets on me to rob me but of my horse or coat; because the law, which was made for my preservation, where it cannot interpose to secure my life from present force, which, if lost, is capable of no reparation, permits me my own defence, and the right of war, a liberty to kill the aggressor, because the aggressor allows not time to appeal to our common judge, nor the decision of the law, for remedy in a case where the mischief may be irreparable. Want of a common judge with authority, puts all men in a state of nature: force without right, upon a man's person, makes a state of war, both where there is, and is not, a common judge.

### § 20.

But when the actual force is over, the state of war ceases between those that are in society, and are equally on both sides subjected to the fair determination of the law; because then there lies open the remedy of appeal for the past injury, and to prevent future harm: but where no such appeal is, as in the state of nature, for want of positive laws, and judges with authority to appeal to, the state of war once begun, continues with a right to the innocent party to destroy the other whenever he can, until the aggressor offers peace, and desires reconciliation on such terms as may repair any wrongs he has already done, and secure the innocent for the future: nay, where an appeal to the law, and constituted judges, lies open, but the remedy is denied by a manifest perverting of justice, and a barefaced wresting of the laws to protect or indemnify the violence or injuries of some men, or party of men; there it is hard to imagine any thing but a state of war: for wherever violence is used, and injury done, though by hands appointed to administer justice, it is still violence and injury, however coloured with the name, pretences, or forms of law, the end whereof being to protect and redress the innocent, by an unbiassed application of it, to all who are under it; wherever that is not bona fide done, war is made upon the sufferers, who having no appeal on earth to right them, they are left to the only remedy in such cases, an appeal to heaven.[1]

## § 21.

To avoid this state of war (wherein there is no appeal but to heaven, and wherein every the least difference is apt to end, where there is no authority to decide between the contenders) is one great reason of men's putting themselves into society, and quitting the state of nature: for where there is an authority, a power on earth, from which relief can be had by appeal, there the continuance of the state of war is excluded, and the controversy is decided by that power. Had there been any such court, any superior jurisdiction on earth, to determine the right between Jephthah[2] and the Ammonites, they had never come to a state of war: but we see he was forced to appeal to heaven: "The Lord the Judge," says he, "be judge this day, between the children of Israel and the children of Ammon," Judg. xi. 27, and then prosecuting, and relying on his appeal, he leads out his army to battle: and therefore in such controversies, where the question is

---

[1] 这段话很可能是 1689 年加进去的，直接指向英国的光荣革命。
[2] 耶弗他（Jephthah）是《圣经·旧约》中的人物。耶弗他出生于基列阿得地区，是其父亲与一名妓女所生。他的兄弟们怕他继承家产，就将他逐出家门。耶弗他出走后成为匪帮的领袖。后来，亚扪人攻打以色列，基列的长老就请耶弗他回来带兵出战。耶弗他在他的要求被接受的情况下出任元帅。这个要求是：做以色列人的领袖。随后，耶弗他派使者与亚扪人谈判，但是亚扪人并不接受其说辞。由于双方对于谁是谁非根本无法达成一致看法，耶弗他准备与亚扪人开战。开战前耶弗他与耶和华达成一个约定：如果他打败亚扪人并从亚扪人那里平安回来，他将把先出门迎接他的任何人作为燔祭敬献上主。耶弗他最终取得了胜利，但是这个先出门迎接他的人却是他的独生女儿，耶弗他只能将其献给耶和华作为燔祭。《政府论》中有多处对耶弗他这一事例的引用：如《政府论（上篇）》的第 163 段、《政府论（下篇）》的第 109、176、241 段。

put, who shall be judge? it cannot be meant, who shall decide the controversy; every one knows what Jephthah here tells us, that "the Lord the Judge" shall judge. Where there is no judge on earth, the appeal lies to God in heaven. That question then cannot mean, who shall judge, whether another hath put himself in a state of war with me, and whether I may, as Jephthah did, appeal to heaven in it? of that I myself can only be judge in my own conscience, as I will answer it, at the great day, to the supreme judge of all men.

## Chapter IV
## Of Slavery

### 导 读

　　第四章"论奴役"非常简短，只有三段内容。一直以来，这一章的内容并没有得到学者们的重视。到20世纪90年代，当部分学者在关注洛克的政治学说与英国的殖民活动之间的关系时，这一章的内容才开始被深入地研究。奴役的英文是slavery，其词根是奴隶（slave）。当时英国对美洲的殖民活动以及非洲奴隶贸易活动都关系到一个核心问题：奴隶的合法性。后来美洲的独立活动也涉及一个相关问题：美洲的人民到底处于奴役状态还是自由状态。考虑到洛克对这些政治事件的参与，许多人试图提炼出洛克对这些问题的看法。

　　洛克于1667年离开牛津大学，开始作为沙夫茨伯里伯爵私人医生兼秘书，参与了一系列重大的社会政治活动。1671年至1675年，洛克是英属卡罗来纳殖民地的五位领主（沙夫茨伯里伯爵是其中之一）的秘书。1673年至1674年，洛克是贸易与海外种植园委员会（Council of Trade and Foreign Plantations）的秘书。在这段时间里，洛克还与沙夫茨伯里伯爵一起投资了皇家非洲公司（Royal African Company）。此外，洛克藏有大量有关海外殖民地的书籍，对这一问题表现出了极大的关注。显然，洛克对殖民地的情况是非常了解的。

更为重要的是，洛克对《卡罗来纳基本法》（Fundamental Constitutions of Carolina）的起草做出了一定的贡献。《卡罗来纳基本法》中有两条涉及奴隶问题。第107条规定，奴隶也可以像自由人一样选择自己的教会，但是"这并没有解除主人对他的民事支配"。第108条规定："卡罗来纳的每个自由人都对他的黑人奴隶享有绝对的权力与权威。"洛克如此深入而广泛地参与到当时的殖民活动与奴隶贸易活动中。从现代人的眼光来看，洛克的双手无疑是肮脏的。人们不禁要问，《政府论两篇》是否为《卡罗来纳基本法》中的奴隶条款提供了某些理论支持。这一问题引发了学界的关注，相关讨论集中于《政府论（下篇）》的第四章"论奴役"与第十六章"论征服"。相比较而言，第十六章的论述更为全面与详细，与我们这里所讲的政治实践问题关系更为直接，而第四章仅仅为此提供了一个理论起点。让我们先来看看洛克在第四章中的分析。

亚里士多德在《政治学》中曾提出一种"自然奴隶"的概念。他认为，某些人因为理性能力的有限，天生适合做奴隶，由他人来加以管理与培养。包括洛克在内的近代自然法学家都多少赞同某种奴隶制，但是他们并不赞同"自然奴隶"的说法，而是将奴役与奴隶建立在正义战争的基础上。也就是说，如果一个人（或一个国家）对另一个人（或国家）实施了侵害，那么后者向前者发动的战争就是正义的。如果后者获得了胜利，后者就可以正当地对前者加以奴役，将其作为自己的奴隶。问题的关键在于，这种奴役究竟为何种程度的奴役，其性质与界限在哪儿。在格劳秀斯看来，这种奴役是绝对的、完全的、永久的，而且它包括对他人的生命、财产以及妻儿的奴役权。但是，洛克却反对这种传统的看法，为这种奴役设置了诸多限制。

第一个限制，是人不能自愿地卖身为奴。奴役是对一个人的自由的限制，所以谈论奴役问题就需要结合自由问题。在洛克看来，由于一个人的自由是有限度的，所以另一个人对他的奴役也是有限度的。洛克将人的自由分为两种：人的自然自由与处在社会中的人的自由。两者的共同点在于：首先，他们都意味着以某种共同律法作为唯一的行为准绳，前者是自然法，后者是受人民委托去制定法律的立法机构（而非任何个体或团体）颁布的实定法。其次，除了这种共同律法外，这两种自由都意味着不受任何其他意志或其他律法的约束。

洛克所界定的自由显然不是绝对的自由，而是法律限度内的自由。洛克为何如此强调法律与自由，特别是自然法与自然自由的内在关系呢？原因在于，如果人享有绝对的自然自由，那么人就可以任意支配自己，甚至可以将自己交由他人来奴役，成为他人的奴隶。这里的一个关键问题是，人是否对自己的生命享有完整的支配权。格劳秀斯、普芬道夫、霍布斯都倾向于认为人享有这种支配权。因此，在他们那里，人可以通过社会契约将自己的所有权利、权力与自由让渡给主权者。这个逻辑就使得"不可让渡的权利"成为不可能。针对这种观点，洛克强调:"一个人既然没有创造自己生命的能力，就不能用契约或通过同意把自己交由任何人奴役，或置身于别人绝对的、任意的权力之下，任其夺去生命。"洛克之所以能够持这样一种观点，是因为他坚持人是上帝的财产，而上帝为人的生命状态设定了具体的要求，即不可被奴役。人必须要保存自己的自由状态，这是自然法的要求。

自然法所保护的这种生命状态只有在一种情况下会被打破，即战争状态的发生。"最完备的奴役状态，就是合法征服者与被征服者之间的战争状态的持续。"基于此，洛克在本章最后一段指出，某些人所谓的"卖身为奴"并不是将自己作为他人的奴隶，任由他人处置，而仅仅是出卖自己的劳动。原因在于，这里并不存在正义战争，因而不会使得某人成为另一个人的奴隶。洛克对奴役与奴隶还设置了其他一些限定，我们将在第十四章看到。

**延伸阅读材料：**

1.《卡罗来纳基本法》，载［英］洛克:《政治论文集》，北京，中国政法大学出版社，2003，第160–181页。

2. 对洛克思想中的奴役问题的相关研究：

——Jennifer Welchman, Locke on Slavery and Inalienable Rights,

*Canadian Journal of Philosophy*, Vol. 25, No. 1 (Mar., 1995), pp. 67–81.

——James Farr, Locke, Natural Law, and New World Slavery, *Political Theory*, Volume 36, Number 4, August 2008, pp. 495–522.

——James Farr, "So Vile and Miserable an Estate": The Problem of Slavery in Locke's Political Thought, *Political Theory*, Vol. 14, No. 2 (May, 1986), pp. 263–289.

——Wayne Glausser, Three Approaches to Locke and the Slave Trade, *Journal of the History of Ideas*, Vol. 51, No. 2 (Apr. - Jun., 1990), pp. 199–216.

英国上议院议员安东尼·阿什利·库珀（Anthony Ashley Cooper，1621—1683），又被称为 Lord Ashley，即后来的沙夫茨伯里第一伯爵（First Earl of Shaftesbury）。洛克与沙夫茨伯里于牛津大学相遇，洛克后来跟随其闯荡英国政界，伴其左右，荣辱与共。

## § 22.

The natural liberty of man is to be free from any superior power on earth, and not to be under the will or legislative authority of man, but to have only the law of nature for his rule. The liberty of man, in society, is to be under no other legislative power, but that established, by consent, in the commonwealth; nor under the dominion of any will, or restraint of any law, but what that legislative shall enact, according to the trust put in it. Freedom then is not what Sir Robert Filmer tells us, O, A.[1] 55. "a liberty for every one to do what he lists, to live as he pleases, and not to be tied by any laws:" but freedom of men under government is, to have a standing rule to live by, common to every one of that society, and made by the legislative power erected in it; a liberty to follow my own will in all things, where the rule prescribes not; and not to be subject to the inconstant, uncertain, unknown, arbitrary will of another man: as freedom of nature is, to be under no other restraint but the law of nature.

## § 23.

This freedom from absolute, arbitrary power, is so necessary to, and closely joined with a man's preservation, that he cannot part with it, but by what forfeits his preservation and life together: for a man, not having the power of his own life, cannot, by compact, or his own consent, enslave himself to any one, nor put himself under the absolute, arbitrary power of another, to take away his life, when he pleases. Nobody can give more power than he has himself; and he that cannot take away his own life, cannot give another power over it. Indeed, having by his fault forfeited his own life, by some act that deserves death; he, to whom he has forfeited it, may (when he has him in his power) delay to take it, and make use of him to

---

[1] O.A. 是指费尔默的《对亚里士多德政府形式的评论》(*Observations upon Aristotle's Politiques Touching Forms of Government*) 一文。参见：［英］菲尔默：《"父权制"及其他著作》，中国政法大学出版社 2003 年版（影印本），第 235–286 页。这是《政府论（下篇）》中唯一直接引用费尔默著作书名的地方。

his own service, and he does him no injury by it: for, whenever he finds the hardship of his slavery outweigh the value of his life, it is in his power, by resisting the will of his master, to draw on himself the death he desires.

## § 24.

This is the perfect condition of slavery, which is nothing else, but "the state of war continued, between a lawful conqueror and a captive:" for, if once compact enter between them, and make an agreement for a limited power on the one side, and obedience on the other, the state of war and slavery ceases, as long as the compact endures: for, as has been said, no man can, by agreement, pass over to another that which he hath not in himself, a power over his own life.

I confess, we find among the jews, as well as other nations, that men did sell themselves; but, it is plain, this was only to drudgery, not to slavery: for it is evident, the person sold was not under an absolute, arbitrary, despotical power; for the master could not have power to kill him, at any time, whom, at a certain time, he was obliged to let go free out of his service; and the master of such a servant was so far from having an arbitrary power over his life, that he could not, at pleasure, so much as maim him, but the loss of an eye, or tooth, set him free, Exod. xxi[1].

---

[1] Exod. xxi. 是《旧约·出埃及记》的第 21 章。这一章所记载的是耶和华通过摩西向以色列人所立的关于"对待奴仆的条例",包括以下两段内容:

"你若买希伯来人作奴仆,他必服侍你六年,第七年他可以自由,白白地出去。他若孤身来,就可以孤身去;他若有妻,他的妻就可以同他出去。他主人若给他妻子,妻子给他生了儿子或是女儿,妻子和儿女要归主人,他要独自出去。倘若奴仆明说:'我爱我的主人和我的妻子儿女,不愿意自由出去。'他的主人就要带他到审判官那里("审判官"或作"神"。下同),又要带他到门前,靠近门框,用锥子穿他的耳朵,他就永远服侍主人。

"人若卖女儿作婢女,婢女不可像男仆那样出去。主人选定她归自己,若不喜欢她,就要许她赎身;主人既然用诡计待她,就没有权柄卖给外邦人。主人若选定她给自己的儿子,就当待她如同女儿。若另娶一个,那女子的吃食、衣服、并好合的事,仍不可减少。若不向她行这三样,她就可以不用钱赎,白白地出去。"

# Chapter V
## Of Property

### 导 读

在近代早期的政治生活与思想理念中,"财产"日益成为一个关键词。在早期资本主义的发展中,私有财产权无疑是最为重要的一个制度发明。在政治学说中,财产权日益成为解释个体与国家的关系以及国家税收等宪法问题的关键。长久以来,洛克在《政府论(下篇)》(特别是其中的第五章"论财产")中的财产学说,被人们认为是洛克对思想史最为重要的一个贡献。为人十分谦虚的洛克也在信件中称,《政府论(下篇)》提供了当时对财产问题最好的分析。此外,洛克的财产学说也是他的政治学说的支柱。人的自由与平等地位、政治社会与政府的内涵、人民的反抗权等核心命题都建立在人的财产权的基础上。财产问题贯穿于《政府论(下篇)》的始终,它是我们理解《政府论(下篇)》的重中之重。

从近代早期开始,思想家开始从财产这个角度来分析整个人类世界。这是非常现代的视角。在古典时代与基督教主导的中世纪,人的德性与人的救赎是我们理解人在这个世界中的位置的角度。在近代早期,随着宗教改革、商品经济的发展带来的世俗化、个人化浪潮,财产或者说财产所表征的权利开始成为人们思考人与世界、人与人、人与国家的基本关系的基点。

在进入洛克的财产学说之前，我们需要牢记在心的一点是：在洛克等思想家的经典著作中，财产权问题并不是一个具体的经济关系问题，并不是现代民商法律体系中的财产权问题，而是政治学说的一个根本问题。洛克多次指出，自己所讲的财产包括人的生命、地产、自由等，即一切能够被人所有的东西。财产权问题其实就是权利问题。

权利这个概念现在已经成为道德哲学、法律哲学与政治哲学的一个基本概念，但是这个概念在近代早期还仅仅处于萌发期。当时，人们主要是从地方性习俗、宗教神学关系、封建臣属关系来定位各种社会角色的性质，判断其行为的对错。权利概念试图从权利主体、权利义务关系来重新界定这一切，因此它具有革命性的意义。就洛克来说，他的财产权学说最终是为了说明人的权利问题。他关心的问题是，我们是否可以谈论一种个体权利，是否可以用个体权利来解释人与人的基本关系、人与国家的基本关系。

第五章关于财产权的论述可以粗略地分为三个问题：财产权的起源问题、财产权的限度问题（或者说财产权与自然法的关系问题）和货币问题。

关于财产权的起源问题，我们需要注意两个问题。第一个问题是上帝的创世与人类的财产权的关系。现代的权利哲学理论基本上已经摆脱了神学的束缚，但是洛克的年代仍然是一个神学的时代，任何道德学说与政治学说仍然受到神学的限制。上帝与人的关系不仅是不可回避的问题，而且是一个前提性问题。就财产问题而言，起点必须是上帝的创世行为这一无可辩驳的真理。这里需要澄清的问题有：上帝创造世间万物供人类使用，这是否意味着人类拥有对万物的某种权利？如果是的话，这种权利是亚当独有并传承给后来的统治者的权利，还是所有人类共有的权利？第二个问题是，人类共有权与个人财产权之间的关系。洛克认为上帝将世界赐予人类共有。如果是这样的话，个人财产权是如何突破人类共有权而产生的呢？个人财产权的正当性基础是什么呢？

关于财产权的限度问题，我们首先需要明确，洛克所讲的个人财产权虽然具有某种正当性基础,但它并不是绝对的、无限制的。为了理解这个问题,我们首先需要了解洛克是如何为个人财产权设定界限的,这种限制的理由何在,其具体要求是什么。其次,我们需要反思洛克为何要通过自然法为个人财产权设定界限。洛克的理论目的是什么?这与他的政治社会概念、社会契约论以及革命学说有何内在的联系?

第三个问题是关于货币的问题。洛克在第五章的后半部分提到了货币制度。货币的出现改变了人与外物的关系。其中一个重要的结果是,它使得人们可以无限地积累财富。这是否与洛克之前所设置的对个人财产权的限制相冲突呢?如果货币制度具有正当性,那么它所带来的财富的不平等是否也具有正当性呢?

若要从思想史上定位洛克的财产权学说,我们需要辨析洛克的财产权学说与格劳秀斯、普芬道夫等人的财产学说的关系。比较这些思想家对上述问题的不同看法。对于洛克的财产权学说,现代学者争议最大的一个实际问题是,洛克究竟是绝对私有财产权的提倡者,还是按需占有、公平分配的财产制度的提倡者。用意识形体的话语来说就是,洛克究竟站在资本主义一边,还是社会主义一边。还是说,我们不可以用这种现代的范畴来简单地定位洛克的财产权学说。

**延伸阅读材料:**

1. 格劳秀斯的财产学说:[荷]格劳秀斯:《海洋自由论》,宇川译,上海三联书店 2005 年版。[荷]格劳秀斯:《战争与和平法》,A. C. 坎贝尔英译,何勤华等译,上海人民出版社。此中文版为节译版,英文完整版参见: Hugo Grotius, *The Rights of War and Peace,* edited and with an introduction by Richard Tuck, from the edition by Jean Barbeyrac, Indianapolis, Liberty Fund, 2005. 重点是第一卷第一章、第二卷第一章至第三章。相关的研究(另可参见本章的"延伸阅读材料 4"以及对格劳秀斯的"权利"概念的研究):

——John Salter, Hugo Grotius: Property and Consent, *Political Theory,* Vol. 29, No. 4 (Aug., 2001), pp. 537–555.

——John Salter, Adam Smith and the Grotian Theory of Property, *The British Journal of Politics & International Relations*, Volume 12, Issue 1, pp. 3–21, February 2010.

——Brian Tierney, *The Idea of Natural Rights, Natural Law and Church Law, 1150–1625*, Chapter XIII, William B. Eerdmans Publishing Co; Reprint edition (10 Oct. 2000).

2. 普芬道夫的财产学说：

——［德］塞缪尔·普芬道夫：《人和公民的自然法义务》，鞠成伟译，北京，商务印书馆，2009，第一卷第十二章至第十四章。

——Samuel Pufendorf, *On the Law of Nature and Nations in Eight Books*, 1672, in Samuel Pufendorf, *The Political Writings of Samuel Pufendorf*, edited by Craig L. Carr, translated by Michael J. Seidler, Book iv, Oxford University Press, 1994.

——相关研究（另可参考"延伸阅读材料4"）：王铁雄：《普芬道夫的自然财产权理论》，载《前沿》，2010（07）。

3. 对洛克财产学说的研究：

——霍伟岸：《洛克权利理论研究》，北京，法律出版社，2011，第五章"财产权"。

——James Tully, *A Discourse on Property*, Cambridge University Press, 1980.

——C. B. Macpherson, *The Political Theory of Possessive Individualism*, Chapter V, Oxford University Press, 1962.

——Michael P. Zuckert, *Natural Rights and the New Republicanism*, Chapter Nine, Princeton University Press, 1994.

——Gopal Sreenivasan, *The Limits of Lockean Rights in Property*, OUP USA (14 Dec. 1995).

——Jeremy Waldron, *The Right to Private Property*, Chapter 6, Clarendon Press; New Ed edition (8 Nov. 1990).

——A. John Simmons, *The Lockean Theory of Rights*, Princeton University Press; New Ed edition (5 July 1994).

——Andrzej Rapaczynski, *Nature and Politics: Liberalism in the Philosophies of Hobbes, Locke, and Rousseau*, Chapter iv, Cornell University Press, 1987.

4. 对西方近代财产与自然权利学说的研究：

——[英]彼得·甘西：《反思财产：从古代到革命时代》，陈高华译，第六章"自然状态与私有财产的起源：从格劳秀斯到黑格尔"，北京，北京大学出版社，2011。

——[美]理查德·塔克：《战争与和平的权利：从格劳秀斯到康德的政治思想与国际秩序》，罗炯等译，南京，译林出版社2009年版。

——James Tully, *A Discourse on Property*, Cambridge University Press, 1980.

——Richard Tuck, *Natural Rights Theories: Their Origin and Development*, Chapter 3–8, Cambridge University Press; New Ed edition (2 July 1981).

——Stephen Buckle, *Natural Law and the Theory of Property: Grotius to Hume*, Clarendon Press; New Ed edition (2 Sep. 1993).

## § 25.

Whether we consider natural reason, which tells us, that men, being once born, have a right to their preservation, and consequently to meat and drink, and such other things as nature affords for their subsistence; or revelation, which gives us an account of those grants God made of the world to Adam, and to Noah, and his sons; it is very clear, that God, as king David says, Psal. cxv. 16, "has given the earth to the children of men;" given it to mankind in common. But this being supposed, it seems to some a very great difficulty how any one should ever come to have a property in any thing: I will not content myself to answer, that if it be difficult to make out property, upon a supposition, that God gave the world to Adam, and his posterity in common, it is impossible that any man, but one universal monarch, should have any property upon a supposition, that God gave the world to Adam, and his heirs in succession, exclusive of all the rest of his posterity. But I shall endeavour to show, how men might come to have a property in several parts of that which God gave to mankind in common, and that without any express compact of all the commoners.[1]

## § 26.

God, who hath given the world to men in common, hath also given them reason to make use of it to the best advantage of life, and convenience. The earth, and all that is therein, is given to men for the support and comfort of their being. And though all the fruits it naturally produces, and beasts it feeds, belong to mankind in common, as they are produced by the spontaneous hand of nature; and nobody has originally a private dominion, exclusive of the rest of mankind, in any of them, as they are thus in their natural state; yet being given for the use of men, there must of necessity be a means to appropriate them some way or other, before they can be of any use, or at all beneficial to any particular man. The fruit, or

---

[1] 洛克这里所讲的这个难题是费尔默提出的。费尔默认为，如果没有所有人的一致同意，原初的共有状态无法合法地转化为个人享有私有财产权的状态。

venison, which nourishes the wild Indian, who knows no enclosure, and is still a tenant in common, must be his, and so his, i. e. a part of him, that another can no longer have any right to it, before it can do him any good for the support of his life.

### § 27.

Though the earth, and all inferiour creatures, be common to all men, yet every man has a property in his own person: this nobody has any right to but himself. The labour of his body, and the work of his hands, we may say, are properly his. Whatsoever then he removes out of the state that nature hath provided, and left it in, he hath mixed his labour with, and joined to it something that is his own, and thereby makes it his property. It being by him removed from the common state nature hath placed it in, it hath by this labour something annexed to it, that excludes the common right of other men. For this labour being the unquestionable property of the labourer, no man but he can have a right to what that is once joined to, at least where there is enough, and as good, left in common for others.

### § 28.

He that is nourished by the acorns he picked up under an oak, or the apples he gathered from the trees in the wood, has certainly appropriated them to himself. Nobody can deny but the nourishment is his. I ask then, when did they begin to be his? when he digested? or when he eat? or when he boiled? or when he brought them home? or when he picked them up? and it is plain, if the first gathering made them not his, nothing else could. That labour put a distinction between them and common: that added something to them more than nature, the common mother of all, had done; and so they became his private right. And will any one say he had no right to those acorns or apples he thus appropriated, because he had not the consent of all mankind to make them his? was it a robbery thus to assume to himself what belonged to all in common? If such a consent as that was necessary, man had starved, notwithstanding the plenty God had given him. We see in commons, which remain so by compact, that it is the taking any part of what is common, and removing it out of the state nature leaves it in, which begins the property; without which the common is of no use. And the taking of this or that part does not depend on the express consent of all the commoners. Thus the grass my horse has bit; the turfs my servant has cut; and the ore I have digged in any place, where I have a right to them in common with others; become my property, without the assignation or consent of any body. The labour that was mine, removing them out of that common state they were in, hath fixed my property in them.[1]

### § 29.

By making an explicit consent of every commoner necessary to any one's appropriating to himself any part of what is given in common, children or servants could not cut the meat, which their father or master had provided for them in common, without assigning to every one his peculiar part. Though the water running in the fountain be every one's, yet who can doubt, but that in the pitcher is his only who drew it out? His labour hath taken it out of the hands of nature, where it was common, and belonged equally to all her children, and hath thereby appropriated it to himself.

### § 30.

Thus this law of reason makes the deer that Indian's who hath killed it; it is allowed to be his goods, who hath bestowed his labour upon it, though before it was the common right of every one. And amongst those who are counted the civilized part of mankind, who have made and multiplied positive laws to determine property, this original law of nature, for the beginning of property, in what was before common, still takes place; and by virtue thereof, what fish any

---

[1] 在这一段的后半部分，洛克借用了英国圈地运动的话语与逻辑来说明私占共有之物的合理性。

one catches in the ocean, that great and still remaining common of mankind: or what ambergrise any one takes up here, is by the labour that removes it out of that common state nature left it in, made his property, who takes that pains about it. And even amongst us, the hare that any one is hunting, is thought his who pursues her during the chace: for being a beast that is still looked upon as common, and no man's private possession; whoever has employed so much labour about any of that kind, as to find and pursue her, has thereby removed her from the state of nature, wherein she was common, and hath begun a property.

§ 31.

It will perhaps be objected to this, that "if gathering the acorns, or other fruits of the earth, &c. makes a right to them, then any one may engross as much as he will." To which I answer, Not so. The same law of nature, that does by this means give us property, does also bound that property too. "God has given us all things richly," I Tim. vi. 17, is the voice of reason confirmed by inspiration. But how far has he given it us? To enjoy. As much as any one can make use of to any advantage of life before it spoils, so much he may by his labour fix a property in: whatever is beyond this, is more than his share, and belongs to others. Nothing was made by God for man to spoil or destroy. And thus, considering the plenty of natural provisions there was a long time in the world, and the few spenders; and to how small a part of that provision the industry of one man could extend itself, and engross it to the prejudice of others; especially keeping within the bounds, set by reason, of what might serve for his use; there could be then little room for quarrels or contentions about property so established.

§ 32.

But the chief matter of property being now not the fruits of the earth, and the beasts that subsist on it, but the earth itself; as that which takes in, and carries with it all the rest; I think it is plain, that property in that too is acquired as the former. As much land as a man tills, plants, improves, cultivates, and can use the product of, so much is his property. He by his labour does, as it were, enclose it from the common. Nor will it invalidate his right, to say every body else has an equal title to it, and therefore he cannot appropriate, he cannot enclose, without the consent of all his fellow commoners, all mankind. God, when he gave the world in common to all mankind, commanded man also to labour, and the penury of his condition required it of him. God and his reason commanded him to subdue the earth, i. e. improve it for the benefit of life, and therein lay out something upon it that was his own, his labour. He that, in obedience to this command of God, subdued, tilled, and sowed any part of it, thereby annexed to it something that was his property, which another had no title to, nor could without injury take from him.

§ 33.

Nor was this appropriation of any parcel of land, by improving it, any prejudice to any other man, since there was still enough, and as good left; and more than the yet unprovided could use. So that, in effect, there was never the less left for others because of his enclosure for himself: for he that leaves as much as another can make use of, does as good as take nothing at all. Nobody could think himself injured by the drinking of another man, though he took a good draught, who had a whole river of the same water left him to quench his thirst; and the case of land and water, where there is enough for both, is perfectly the same.

§ 34.

God gave the world to men in common; but since he gave it them for their benefit, and the greatest conveniences of life they were capable to draw from it, it cannot be supposed he meant it should always remain common and uncultivated. He gave it to the use of the industrious and rational, (and labour was to be his title to it) not to the fancy or covetousness of the quarrelsome and contentious. He that had as good left for his improvement, as was already taken up, needed not complain, ought not to meddle with what was already improved by another's labour: if he did, it is plain he desired the benefit of another's pains, which he had no right to, and not the ground which God had given him in common with others to labour on, and whereof there was as good left, as that already possessed, and more than he knew what to do with, or his industry could reach to.

### § 35.

It is true, in land that is common in England, or any other country, where there is plenty of people under government, who have money and commerce, no one can enclose or appropriate any part, without the consent of all his fellow-commoners; because this is left common by compact, i. e. by the law of the land, which is not to be violated. And though it be common, in respect of some men, it is not so to all mankind, but is the joint property of this country, or this parish. Besides, the remainder, after such enclosure, would not be as good to the rest of the commoners, as the whole was when they could all make use of the whole; whereas in the beginning and first peopling of the great common of the world, it was quite otherwise. The law man was under, was rather for appropriating. God commanded, and his wants forced him to labour. That was his property which could not be taken from him wherever he had fixed it. And hence subduing or cultivating the earth, and having dominion, we see are joined together. The one gave title to the other. So that God, by commanding to subdue, gave authority so far to appropriate: and the condition of human life, which requires labour and materials to work on, necessarily introduces private possessions.

## § 36.

The measure of property nature has well set by the extent of men's labour, and the conveniences of life: no man's labour could subdue or appropriate all; nor could his enjoyment consume more than a small part; so that it was impossible for any man, this way, to intrench upon the right of another, or acquire to himself a property, to the prejudice of his neighbour, who would still have room for as good, and as large a possession (after the other had taken out his) as before it was appropriated. This measure did confine every man's possession to a very moderate proportion, and such as he might appropriate to himself, without injury to any body, in the first ages of the world, when men were more in danger to be lost, by wandering from their company, in the then vast wilderness of the earth, than to be straitened for want of room to plant in. And the same measure may be allowed still without prejudice to any body, as full as the world seems: for supposing a man, or family, in the state they were at first peopling of the world by the children of Adam, or Noah; let him plant in some inland, vacant places of America, we shall find that the possessions he could make himself, upon the measures we have given, would not be very large, nor, even to this day, prejudice the rest of mankind, or give them reason to complain, or think themselves injured by this man's encroachment; though the race of men have now spread themselves to all the corners of the world, and do infinitely exceed the small number was at the beginning. Nay, the extent of ground is of so little value, without labour, that I have heard it affirmed, that in Spain itself a man may be permitted to plough, sow, and reap, without being disturbed, upon land he has no other title to, but only his making use of it. But, on the contrary, the inhabitants think themselves beholden to him, who by his industry on neglected, and consequently waste land, has increased the stock of corn, which they wanted.[1] But be this as it will, which I lay no

---

[1] 以这种方式私占荒地的做法在洛克时代的西班牙普遍存在。在阿拉贡（Aragon），只有当山区的荒地在60天内被开垦出来，这些地才变成开垦者的财产。在加泰罗尼亚（Catalonia），只要某小块地开始被开垦，这块地就属于开垦人了。在卡斯蒂利亚（Castile），开垦者只能通过劳动占有维持自己及其家庭所需的土地量。

stress on; this I dare boldly affirm, that the same rule of propriety, (viz.) that every man should have as much as he could make use of, would hold still in the world, without straitening any body; since there is land enough in the world to suffice double the inhabitants, had not the invention of money, and the tacit agreement of men to put a value on it, introduced (by consent) larger possessions, and a right to them; which, how it has done, I shall by and by show more at large.

### § 37.

This is certain, that in the beginning, before the desire of having more than man needed had altered the intrinsic value of things, which depends only on their usefulness to the life of man; or had agreed, that a little piece of yellow metal, which would keep without wasting or decay, should be worth a great piece of flesh, or a whole heap of corn; though men had a right to appropriate, by their labour, each one to himself as much of the things of nature as he could use: yet this could not be much, nor to the prejudice of others, where the same plenty was still left to those who would use the same industry. To which let me add, that he who appropriates land to himself by his labour, does not lessen, but increase the common stock of mankind: for the provisions serving to the support of human life, produced by one acre of enclosed and cultivated land, are (to speak much within compass) ten times more than those which are yielded by an acre of land of an equal richness lying waste in common. And therefore he that encloses land, and has a greater plenty of the conveniencies of life from ten acres, than he could have from an hundred left to nature, may truly be said to give ninety acres to mankind: for his labour now supplies him with provisions out of ten acres, which were by the product of an hundred lying in common. I have here rated the improved land very low, in making its product but as ten to one, when it is much nearer an hundred to one: for I ask, whether in the wild woods and uncultivated waste of America, left to nature, without any improvement, tillage, or husbandry, a thousand acres yield the needy and wretched inhabitants as many conveniencies of life, as ten acres equally fertile land do in Devonshire[1], where they are well cultivated.

Before the appropriation of land, he who gathered as much of the wild fruit, killed, caught, or tamed, as many of the beasts as he could; he that so employed his pains about any of the spontaneous products of nature, as any way to alter them from the state which nature put them in, by placing any of his labour on them, did thereby acquire a propriety in them: but if they perished, in his possession, without their due use; if the fruits rotted, or the venison putrified, before he could spend it; he offended against the common law of nature, and was liable to be punished: he invaded his neighbour's share, for he had no right, farther than his use called for any of them, and they might serve to afford him conveniencies of life.

## § 38.

The same measures governed the possession of land too: whatsoever he tilled and reaped, laid up and made use of, before it spoiled, that was his peculiar right; whatsoever he enclosed, and could feed, and make use of, the cattle and product was also his. But if either the grass of his inclosure rotted on the ground, or the fruit of his planting perished without gathering and laying up; this part of the earth, notwithstanding his inclosure, was still to be looked on as waste, and might be the possession of any other. Thus at the beginning, Cain might take as much ground as he could till, and make it his own land, and yet leave enough to Abel's sheep to feed on; a few acres would serve for both their possessions.[2]

[1] 德文郡，英格兰西南部的一个郡县。
[2] 该隐与亚伯的这一故事出自《旧约·创世纪》第 4 章。《政府论（上篇）》的第 76 段对此有更多的说明。

But as families increased, and industry enlarged their stocks, their possessions enlarged with the need of them; but yet it was commonly without any fixed property in the ground they made use of, till they incorporated, settled themselves together, and built cities; and then, by consent, they came in time to set out the bounds of their distinct territories, and agree on limits between them and their neighbours; and by laws within themselves settled the properties of those of the same society: for we see, that in that part of the world which was first inhabited, and therefore like to be best peopled, even as low down as Abraham's time, they wandered with their flocks, and their herds, which was their substance, freely up and down; and this Abraham did, in a country where he was a stranger. Whence it is plain, that at least a great part of the land lay in common: that the inhabitants valued it not, nor claimed property in any more than they made use of. But when there was not room enough in the same place, for their herds to feed together, they by consent, as Abraham and Lot did, Gen. xiii. 5, separated and enlarged their pasture, where it best liked them.[1] And for the same reason Esau went from his father, and his brother, and planted in Mount Seir, Gen. xxxvi. 6.[2]

---

[1] 《旧约·创世纪》第13章"亚伯兰与罗得分开"的原文为：亚伯兰带着他的妻子与罗得，并一切所有的，都从埃及上南地去。亚伯兰的金、银、牲畜极多。他从南地渐渐往伯特利去，到了伯特利和艾的中间，就是从前支搭帐棚的地方，也是他起先筑坛的地方，他又在那里求告耶和华的名。与亚伯兰同行的罗得也有牛群、羊群、帐棚。那地容不下他们，因为他们的财物甚多，使他们不能同居。当时，迦南人与比利洗人在那地居住。亚伯兰的牧人和罗得的牧人相争。亚伯兰就对罗得说："你我不可相争，你的牧人和我的牧人也不可相争，因为我们是骨肉（原文作"弟兄"）。遍地不都在你眼前吗？请你离开我。你向左，我就向右；你向右，我就向左。"罗得举目看见约旦河的全平原，直到琐珥，都是滋润的，那地在耶和华未灭所多玛，蛾摩拉以先，如同耶和华的园子，也像埃及地。于是罗得选择约旦河的全平原，往东迁移。他们就彼此分离了。亚伯兰住在迦南地，罗得住在平原的城邑，渐渐挪移帐棚，直到所多玛。

[2] 以扫（Esau）是以撒（亚伯拉罕与妻子撒拉所生的独子）和利百加所生的长子。《圣经》这一节的原文是："以扫带着他的妻子、儿女与家中一切的人口，并他的牛羊、牲畜和一切货财，就是他在迦南地所得的，往别处去，离了他兄弟雅各。"第七节的原文是："因为二人的财物群畜甚多，寄居的地方容不下他们，所以不能同居。"

## § 39.

And thus, without supposing any private dominion, and property in Adam, over all the world, exclusive of all other men, which can no way be proved, nor any one's property be made out from it; but supposing the world given, as it was, to the children of men in common, we see how labour could make men distinct titles to several parcels of it, for their private uses; wherein there could be no doubt of right, no room for quarrel.

## § 40.

Nor is it so strange, as perhaps before consideration it may appear, that the property of labour should be able to over-balance the community of land: for it is labour indeed that put the difference of value on every thing; and let any one consider what the difference is between an acre of land planted with tobacco or sugar, sown with wheat or barley, and an acre of the same land lying in common, without any husbandry upon it, and he will find, that the improvement of labour makes the far greater part of the value. I think it will be but a very modest computation to say, that of the products of the earth useful to the life of man, nine tenths are the effects of labour: nay, if we will rightly estimate things as they come to our use, and cast up the several expences about them, what in them is purely owing to nature, and what to labour, we shall find, that in most of them ninety-nine hundredths are wholly to be put on the account of labour.

## § 41.

There cannot be a clearer demonstration of any thing, than several nations of the Americans are of this, who are rich in land, and poor in all the comforts of life; whom nature having furnished as liberally as any other people, with the materials of plenty, i. e. a fruitful soil, apt to produce in abundance what might serve for food, raiment, and delight; yet for want of improving it by labour, have not one hundredth part of the conveniencies we enjoy: and a king of a large and fruitful territory there feeds, lodges, and is clad worse than a daylabourer in England.

### § 42.

To make this a little clear, let us but trace some of the ordinary provisions of life, through their several progresses, before they come to our use, and see how much of their value they receive from human industry. Bread, wine, and cloth, are things of daily use, and great plenty: yet notwithstanding, acorns, water, and leaves, or skins, must be our bread, drink, and cloathing, did not labour furnish us with these more useful commodities: for whatever bread is more worth than acorns, wine than water, and cloth or silk, than leaves, skins, or moss, that is wholly owing to labour and industry: the one of these being the food and raiment which unassisted nature furnishes us with: the other, provisions which our industry and pains prepare for us; which how much they exceed the other in value, when any one hath computed, he will then see how much labour makes the far greatest part of the value of things we enjoy in this world: and the ground which produces the materials, is scarce to be reckoned in, as any, or, at most, but a very small part of it: so little, that even amongst us, land that is left wholly to nature, that hath no improvement of pasturage, tillage, or planting, is called, as indeed it is, waste; and we shall find the benefit of it amount to little more than nothing.

This shows how much numbers of men are to be preferred to largeness of dominions; and that the increase of lands, and the right of employing of them, is the great art of government: and that prince, who shall be so wise and godlike, as by established laws of liberty to secure protection and encouragement to the honest industry of mankind, against the oppression of power and narrowness of party, will quickly be too hard for his neighbours: but this by the by. To return to the argument in hand.

## § 43.

An acre of land, that bears here twenty bushels of wheat, and another in America, which, with the same husbandry, would do the like, are, without doubt, of the same natural intrinsic value: but yet the benefit mankind receives from the one in a year, is worth 5l. and from the other possibly not worth a penny, if all the profit an Indian received from it were to be valued, and sold here; at least, I may truly say, not one thousandth. It is labour then which puts the greatest part of the value upon land, without which it would scarcely be worth any thing: it is to that we owe the greatest part of all its useful products; for all that the straw, bran, bread, of that acre of wheat, is more worth than the product of an acre of as good land, which lies waste, is all the effect of labour: for it is not barely the ploughman's pains, the reaper's and thresher's toil, and the baker's sweat is to be counted into the bread we eat; the labour of those who broke the oxen, who digged and wrought the iron and stones, who felled and framed the timber employed about the plough, mill, oven, or any other utensils, which are a vast number requisite to this corn, from its being seed to be sown, to its being made bread, must all be charged on the account of labour, and received as an effect of that: nature and the earth furnished only the almost worthless materials, as in themselves. It would be a strange "catalogue of things, that industry provided and made use of, about every loaf of bread," before it came to our use, if we could trace them; iron, wood, leather, bark, timber, stone, bricks, coals, lime, cloth, dyeing, drugs, pitch, tar, masts, ropes, and all the materials made use of in the ship, that brought any of the commodities used by any of the workmen, to any part of the work: all which it would be almost impossible, at least too long, to reckon up.

## § 44.

From all which it is evident, that though the things of nature are given in common, yet man, by being master of himself, and "proprietor of his own person, and the actions or labour of it, had still in himself the great foundation of property;" and that, which made up the greater part of what he applied to the support or comfort of his being, when invention and arts had improved the conveniencies of life, was perfectly his own, and did not belong in common to others.

### § 45.

Thus labour, in the beginning, gave a right of property, wherever any one was pleased to employ it upon what was common, which remained a long while the far greater part, and is yet more than mankind makes use of. Men, at first, for the most part, contented themselves with what unassisted nature offered to their necessities: and though afterwards, in some parts of the world, (where the increase of people and stock, with the use of money, had made land scarce, and so of some value) the several communities settled the bounds of their distinct territories, and by laws within themselves regulated the properties of the private men of their society, and so, by compact and agreement, settled the property which labour and industry began: and the leagues that have been made between several states and kingdoms, either expressly or tacitly disowning all claim and right to the land in the others possession, have, by common consent, given up their pretences to their natural common right, which originally they had to those countries, and so have, by positive agreement, settled a property amongst themselves, in distinct parts and parcels of the earth; yet there still are great tracts of ground to be found, which (the inhabitants thereof not having joined with the rest of mankind, in the consent of the use of their common money) lie waste, and are more than the people who dwell on it do, or can make use of, and so still lie in common; though this can scarce happen amongst that part of mankind that have consented to the use of money.

## § 46.

The greatest part of things really useful to the life of man, and such as the necessity of subsisting made the first commoners of the world look after, as it doth the Americans now, are generally things of short duration; such as, if they are not consumed by use, will decay and perish of themselves: gold, silver, and diamonds, are things that fancy or agreement hath put the value on, more than real use, and the necessary support of life. Now of those good things which nature hath provided in common, every one had a right, (as hath been said) to as much as he could use, and property in all that he could effect with his labour; all that his industry could extend to, to alter from the state nature had put it in, was his. He that gathered a hundred bushels of acorns or apples, had thereby a property in them, they were his goods as soon as gathered. He was only to look, that he used them before they spoiled, else he took more than his share, and robbed others. And indeed it was a foolish thing, as well as dishonest, to hoard up more than he could make use of. If he gave away a part to any body else, so that it perished not uselessly in his possession, these he also made use of. And if he also bartered away plums, that would have rotted in a week, for nuts that would last good for his eating a whole year, he did no injury; he wasted not the common stock; destroyed no part of the portion of the goods that belonged to others, so long as nothing perished uselessly in his hands. Again, if he would give his nuts for a piece of metal, pleased with its colour; or exchange his sheep for shells, or wool for a sparkling pebble or a diamond, and keep those by him all his life, he invaded not the right of others, he might heap as much of these durable things as he pleased; the exceeding of the bounds of his just property not lying in the largeness of his possession, but the perishing of any thing uselessly in it.[1]

---

[1] 关于货币的起源问题可参见：[英] 洛克：《论降低利息和提高货币价值的后果》，徐式谷译，北京，商务印书馆，1997。

## § 47.

And thus came in the use of money, some lasting thing that men might keep without spoiling, and that by mutual consent men would take in exchange for the truly useful, but perishable supports of life.

## § 48.

And as different degrees of industry were apt to give men possessions in different proportions, so this invention of money gave them the opportunity to continue and enlarge them: for supposing an island, separate from all possible commerce with the rest of the world, wherein there were but an hundred families, but there were sheep, horses, and cows, with other useful animals, wholesome fruits, and land enough for corn for a hundred thousand times as many, but nothing in the island, either because of its commonness, or perishableness, fit to supply the place of money; what reason could any one have there to enlarge his possessions beyond the use of his family and a plentiful supply to its consumption, either in what their own industry produced, or they could barter for like perishable, useful commodities with others? Where there is not something, both lasting and scarce, and so valuable to be hoarded up, there men will not be apt to enlarge their possessions of land, were it ever so rich, ever so free for them to take: for I ask, what would a man value ten thousand, or an hundred thousand acres of excellent land, ready cultivated and well stocked too with cattle, in the middle of the inland parts of America, where he had no hopes of commerce with other parts of the world, to draw money to him by the sale of the product? It would not be worth the enclosing, and we should see him give up again to the wild common of nature, whatever was more than would supply the conveniencies of life to be had there for him and his family.

## § 49.

Thus in the beginning all the world was America, and more so than that is now; for no such thing as money was any where known.

Find out something that hath the use and value of money amongst his neighbours, you shall see the same man will begin presently to enlarge his possessions.

### § 50.

But since gold and silver, being little useful to the life of man in proportion to food, raiment, and carriage, has its value only from the consent of men, whereof labour yet makes, in great part, the measure; it is plain, that men have agreed to a disproportionate and unequal possession of the earth, they having, by a tacit and voluntary consent, found out a way how a man may fairly possess more land than he himself can use the product of, by receiving in exchange for the overplus, gold and silver, which may be hoarded up without injury to any one; these metals not spoiling or decaying in the hands of the possessor. This partage of things in an inequality of private possessions, men have made practicable out of the bounds of society, and without compact; only by putting a value on gold and silver, and tacitly agreeing in the use of money: for in governments, the laws regulate the right of property, and the possession of land is determined by positive constitutions.

### § 51.

And thus, I think, it is very easy to conceive, "how labour could at first begin a title of property" in the common things of nature, and how the spending it upon our uses bounded it. So that there could then be no reason of quarrelling about title, nor any doubt about the largeness of possession it gave. Right and conveniency went together; for as a man had a right to all he could employ his labour upon, so he had no temptation to labour for more than he could make use of. This left no room for controversy about the title, nor for encroachment on the right of others; what portion a man carved to himself, was easily seen: and it was useless, as well as dishonest, to carve himself too much, or take more than he needed.

# Chapter VI
# Of Paternal Power

**导 读**

　　当我们去思考人类应该建立怎样的政治秩序模式时，我们常常会去想，是否有一种自然而然的秩序模式可加以参考。这时我们会发现，家庭似乎是一个很好的对照物。所有人都出生并成长于某一家庭中。在家庭中，子女听从父母（在近代早期主要是父亲）的教导与指令，父母关爱并照顾子女。古往今来，一直如此。我们有时候还会去考察人类的历史，看一看是否有一种自然而然发展出来的秩序模式可加以参考。这时我们会发现，在人类早期历史中，男性家长往往是一个家庭、家族或部落中的领导者，久而久之，他们还会成为一个王国的统治者。在这一王国中，臣民们服从国王的命令，国王享有安排各种事务的权力，如同慈父般关爱着所有臣民的安全与幸福。信仰基督教的人往往还会在《圣经》中寻找相关的线索。有些人发现上帝对人类的要求似乎是：子女应当生而服从父母的统治，臣民应当生而服从君主的统治。

　　主张父权制的人常常将这三种思考结论结合在一起，从而主张，君主的权力类似于父亲的权力，具有天然的正当性，而且这也符合《圣经》的教诲。而且，政治权力类似于（甚至等同于）父权，不仅包括命令与惩罚的权力，还包括道德与信仰方面的教导权力。洛克的论战对手费尔默就是这样一位主张父权制的思想家。这种父权制思想不仅否认人的自然自由与自然平等，而且赋予统治者以绝对的权力（包括生杀予夺的权力）。这无疑与洛克的自由平等思想，特别是他的个人权利学说相抵触。在第五章阐明了人的权利之后，洛克在第六章就开始着手批判这种父权制思想。

由于父权制将父亲的绝对权力与君主的绝对权力进行类比，所以洛克的首要任务就是消解父亲的绝对权力。由于洛克在第五章中赋予了所有人平等的权利主体地位，因此父亲的权力就随之受到了限制。父亲对子女的生命与财产并不享有支配的权力，不可对其加以侵害。这样一来，家庭内的权力从属关系就不复存在了。尽管如此，洛克并没有否认父母对子女的所有权力。由于孩童在年幼的时候缺乏生存能力与理性能力，他们需要父母的照顾与培养，因此父母对子女享有一定的权力。但是，这种权力具有几个重要的限制性特征。首先，它并不是一种"自然的权力"，也就是说父母并不当然地拥有这种权力。只有当他们履行了自己对子女的抚养责任时，他们才有资格享有这种权力（因此这种权力可以转移到养父母身上）。其次，它并不是一种绝对的权力，而是有限的权力。这种权力并不及于子女的生命或财产。再次，它并不是一种永久性的权力，而只是暂时的权力。当子女长大成人后，父母就不再享有这种权力了。

洛克对父权的这一重新定义依赖于他的个人权利学说，但是要彻底反驳父权制思想，他同时还需要反驳一个父权制的基本命题：父母给予子女生命，所以父母对子女享有绝对的权力。洛克的反驳理由是，人的生命最终是来自于上帝，父母仅仅是上帝创造生命过程中所借助的一个手段而已。我们需要注意的是，这一观点其实是非常反传统的观点。传统的基督教观点是，父母的生育行为以及生育行为带来的亲权都具有某种程度的神性，它们本身就体现了上帝的参与，而不仅仅是一个手段。

洛克对父权的重述带来的一个负面效果是，家庭的内部纽带会随之土崩瓦解。家庭成员之间，特别是父母与子女之间将不存在任何内在的道德关系。这显然不符合事实，也不是洛克想要的结果。因此,洛克为家庭重塑了一种内部纽带。这一纽带的内容是,子女应当永远尊敬、爱戴父母,父母应当关爱并照顾子女。深究起来,这里其实存在着一定的困难。首先,如果成年子女与父母都是平等的社会主体,那么子女为何要爱戴父母呢?洛克的回答是,因为父母曾经抚育了子女,所以子女应当加以报答。其次,在洛克看来,生育子女往往是父母性欲的产物,往往不是父母想要的结果,那么父母忽视子女的福利也并不当然是一种违背理性的做法。洛克甚至在《政府论(上篇)》中指出,遗弃甚至杀害子女的做法也大量存在。洛克无法从正面说明父母与子女之间的爱,无法充分证明他们之间的道德责任。洛克所倚重的理性与权利概念似乎仅仅只能在家庭内部建立起一种类似于契约的冰冷关系。洛克的家庭理论是否在瓦解父权的同时,也瓦解了家庭的亲情关系?如果是这样的话,这是我们在追求一个自由社会的同时必须要付出的代价吗?

如之前所说,当人们反观人类历史时,父权制的统治模式似乎是一种普遍现象。洛克并不否认这一点,但是他认为这仅仅是人类早期的一种实践,仅仅适用于人类社会的初级阶段。当这种简单的统治模式无法适应人性的败坏状态与社会的复杂性时,人们必然会通过理性来加以反思。他们反思的结果是,合法的政府必须建立在人民的同意的基础上。洛克在"论父权"的最后几段分析了这个问题,这已经开始触及社会与国家的起源问题了。这将是接下来几章的核心内容。

**延伸阅读材料:**

1.[英]菲尔默:《"父权制"及其他著作》,北京,中国政法大学出版社,2003。相关研究:赵万里:《罗伯特·菲尔默的政治思想研究》,中国人民大学2011年博士学位论文。

2.[英]洛克:《政府论(上篇)》,叶启芳、瞿菊农译,北京,商务印书馆,2005。

3.[英]洛克:《教育片论》,熊春文译,上海,上海人民出版社,2006。

4. 对洛克批判父权制的相关研究：

——吴增定:《家庭、政治与教育》，载《外国哲学》，2006（18）。

——吴增定:《利维坦的道德困境：早期现代政治哲学的问题与脉络》，第四篇"洛克政治哲学视野中的政治与教育"，北京，生活·读书·新知三联书店，2012。

——［英］纳坦·塔科夫:《为了自由：洛克的教育思想》，邓文正译，北京，生活·读书·新知三联书店，2001。特别是其中第一章"天赋自由与父权政治"。

——David Foster, Taming the Father: John Locke's Critique of Patriarchal Fatherhood, *The Review of Politics*, Vol. 56, No. 4 (Autumn, 1994), pp. 641–670.

——Jacqueline L. Pfeffer, The Family in John Locke's Political Thought, *Polity*, Vol. 33, No. 4 (Summer, 2001), pp. 593–618.

——Gordon J. Schochet, *Patriarchalism in Political Thought: The Authoritarian Family and Political Speculation and Attitudes Especially in Seventeenth-century England*, Wiley-Blackwell (5 May 1975).

洛克的《政府论两篇》主要批判了英国的另一位政治学者罗伯特·费尔默爵士（Sir Robert Filmer，1588—1653）的政治思想。左图为费尔默最重要的政治学著作《父权制》（Patriarcha，1680）在1680年出版时的封面。右图经常被人们认为是费尔默的画像，但其实它是费尔默的父亲爱德华爵士（Sir Edward）的画像。考虑到费尔默如此强调"父亲"这个概念的重要性，也许用一张他的父亲的照片来纪念他也是恰当的。

## § 52.

It may perhaps be censured as an impertinent criticism, in a discourse of this nature, to find fault with words and names, that have obtained in the world: and yet possibly it may not be amiss to offer new ones, when the old are apt to lead men into mistakes, as this of paternal power probably has done; which seems so to place the power of parents over their children wholly in the father, as if the mother had no share in it: whereas, if we consult reason or revelation, we shall find she hath an equal title. This may give one reason to ask, whether this might not be more properly called parental power? for whatever obligation nature and the right of generation[1] lays on children, it must certainly bind them equally to both concurrent causes of it. And accordingly we see the positive law of God every where joins them together without distinction, when it commands the obedience of children: "Honour thy father and thy mother," Exod. xx. 12. "Whosoever curseth his father or his mother," Lev. xx. 9. "Ye shall fear every man his mother and his father," Lev. xix. 5. "Children, obey your parents," &c. Eph. vi. 1, is the style of the Old and New Testament.[2]

## § 53.

Had but this one thing been well considered, without looking any deeper into the matter, it might perhaps have kept men from running into those gross mistakes they have made, about this power of parents; which, however it might, without any great harshness, bear the name of absolute dominion, and regal authority, when under the title of paternal power it seemed appropriated to the father, would yet have sounded but oddly, and in the very name shown the absurdity, if this supposed absolute power over

---

[1] 洛克对这种"基于生育而获得的权力"的批判参见:《政府论(上篇)》的第18、50、52段。

[2] 对母亲与父亲的同等权力的论述可参见:《政府论(上篇)》的第6、11、31、51段,而整个《政府论(上篇)》的第六章都涉及此问题。

children had been called parental; and thereby have discovered, that it belonged to the mother too: for it will but very ill serve the turn of those men, who contend so much for the absolute power and authority of the fatherhood, as they call it, that the mother should have any share in it; and it would have but ill supported the monarchy they contend for, when by the very name it appeared that that fundamental authority, from whence they would derive their government of a single person only, was not placed in one, but two persons jointly. But to let this of names pass.

### § 54.

Though I have said above, chap. ii. "That all men by nature are equal," I cannot be supposed to understand all sorts of equality; age or virtue may give men a just precedency: excellency of parts and merit may place others above the common level; birth may subject some, and alliance or benefits others, to pay an observance to those whom nature, gratitude, or other respects, may have made it due; and yet all this consists with the equality, which all men are in, in respect of jurisdiction or dominion one over another, which was the equality I there spoke of, as proper to the business in hand, being that equal right, that every man hath, to his natural freedom, without being subjected to the will or authority of any other man.

### § 55.

Children, I confess, are not born in this state of equality, though they are born to it. Their parents have a sort of rule and jurisdiction over them, when they come into the world, and for some time after; but it is but a temporary one. The bonds of this subjection are like the swaddling clothes they are wrapt up in, and supported by, in the weakness of their infancy: age and reason, as they grow up, loosen them, till at length they drop quite off, and leave a man at his own free disposal.

## § 56.

Adam was created a perfect man, his body and mind in full possession of their strength and reason, and so was capable from the first instant of his being to provide for his own support and preservation; and govern his actions according to the dictates of the law of reason which God had implanted in him. From him the world is peopled with his descendants, who are all born infants, weak and helpless, without knowledge or understanding: but to supply the defects of this imperfect state, till the improvement of growth and age hath removed them, Adam and Eve, and after them all parents were, by the law of nature, "under an obligation to preserve, nourish, and educate the children," they had begotten; not as their own workmanship, but the workmanship of their own maker, the Almighty, to whom they were to be accountable for them.

## § 57.

The law, that was to govern Adam, was the same that was to govern all his posterity, the law of reason. But his offspring having another way of entrance into the world, different from him, by a natural birth, that produced them ignorant and without the use of reason, they were not presently under that law; for nobody can be under a law, which is not promulgated to him; and this law being promulgated or made known by reason only, he that is not come to the use of his reason, cannot be said to be under this law; and Adam's children, being not presently as soon as born, under this law of reason, were not presently free: for law, in its true notion, is not so much the limitation, as the direction of a free and intelligent agent to his proper interest, and prescribes no farther than is for the general good of those under that law: could they be happier without it, the law, as a useless thing, would of itself vanish; and that ill deserves the name of confinement which hedges us in only from bogs and precipices. So that, however it may be mistaken, the end of law is not to abolish or restrain, but to preserve and enlarge freedom: for in all the states of created beings capable of laws, "where there is no law, there is no freedom;" for liberty is to be free from restraint and violence from others; which cannot be where there is not law: but freedom is not, as we are told[1], "a liberty for every man to do what he lists:" (for who could be free, when every other man's humour might domineer over him?) but a liberty to dispose, and order as he lists, his person, actions, possessions, and his whole property, within the allowance of those laws under which he is, and therein not to be subject to the arbitrary will of another, but freely follow his own.

§ 58.

The power, then, that parents have over their children, arises from that duty which is incumbent on them, to take care of their offspring during the imperfect state of childhood. To inform the mind, and govern the actions of their yet ignorant nonage, till reason shall take its place, and ease them of that trouble, is what the children want, and the parents are bound to: for God having given man an understanding to direct his actions, has allowed him a freedom of will, and liberty of acting, as properly belonging thereunto, within the bounds of that law he is under. But whilst he is in an estate, wherein he has not understanding of his own to direct his will, he is not to have any will of his own to follow: he that understands for him, must will for him too; he must prescribe to his will, and regulate his actions: but when he comes to the estate that made his father a freeman, the son is a freeman too.

§ 59.

This holds in all the laws a man is under, whether natural or civil. Is a man under the law of nature? What made him free of that

---

[1] 这里指的是费尔默。《政府论（下篇）》的第 22 段也引用了费尔默对自由的这一看法。

law? What gave him a free disposing of his property according to his own will, within the compass of that law? I answer, a state of maturity, wherein he might be supposed capable to know that law, that so he might keep his actions within the bounds of it. When he has acquired that state, he is presumed to know how far that law is to be his guide, and how far he may make use of his freedom, and so comes to have it; till then, somebody else must guide him, who is presumed to know how far the law allows a liberty. If such a state of reason, such an age of discretion made him free, the same shall make his son free too. Is a man under the law of England? What made him free of that law? that is, to have the liberty to dispose of his actions and possessions according to his own will within the permission of that law? A capacity of knowing that law; which is supposed by that law, at the age of one and twenty years, and in some cases sooner. If this made the father free, it shall make the son free too. Till then we see the law allows the son to have no will, but he is to be guided by the will of his father or guardian, who is to understand for him. And if the father die, and fail to substitute a deputy in his trust; if he hath not provided a tutor to govern his son, during his minority, during his want of understanding; the law takes care to do it; some other must govern him, and be a will to him, till he hath attained to a state of freedom, and his understanding be fit to take the government of his will. But after that, the father and son are equally free as much as tutor and pupil after nonage: equally subjects of the same law together, without any dominion left in the father over the life, liberty, or estate of his son, whether they be only in the state and under the law of nature, or under the positive laws of an established government.

### § 60.

But if, through defects that may happen out of the ordinary course of nature, any one comes not to such a degree of reason, wherein he might be supposed capable of knowing the law, and so living within the rules of it; he is never capable of being a free man, he is never let loose to the disposure of his own will (because he knows no bounds to it, has not understanding, its proper guide) but is continued under the tuition and government of others, all the time his own understanding is incapable of that charge. And so lunatics and idiots are never set free from the government of their parents. "Children, who are not as yet come unto those years whereat they may have; and innocents which are excluded by a natural defect from ever having; thirdly, madmen, which for the present cannot possibly have the use of right reason to guide themselves; have for their guide the reason that guideth other men, which are tutors over them, to seek and procure their good for them," says Hooker, Eccl. Pol. lib. i. sect. 7. All which seems no more than that duty which God and nature has laid on man, as well as other creatures, to preserve their offspring, till they can be able to shift for themselves, and will scarce amount to an instance or proof of parents regal authority.

## § 61.

Thus we are born free, as we are born rational; not that we have actually the exercise of either: age, that brings one, brings with it the other too. And thus we see how natural freedom and subjection to parents may consist together, and are both founded on the same principle. A child is free by his father's title, by his father's understanding, which is to govern him till he hath it of his own. The freedom of a man at years of discretion, and the subjection of a child to his parents, whilst yet short of that age, are so consistent, and so distinguishable, that the most blinded contenders for monarchy, by right of fatherhood, cannot miss this difference; the most obstinate cannot but allow their consistency: for were their doctrine all true, were the right heir of Adam now known, and by that title settled a monarch in his throne, invested with all the absolute unlimited power, Sir Robert Filmer talks of; if he should die as soon as his heir were born, must not the child, notwithstanding he were ever so free, ever so much sovereign, be in subjection to his mother and nurse, to tutors and governors, till age and education brought him reason and ability to govern himself and others? The necessities of his life, the health of his body, and the information of his mind, would require him to be directed by the will of others, and not his own; and yet will any one think, that this restraint and subjection were inconsistent with, or spoiled him of, that liberty or sovereignty he had a right to, or gave away his empire to those who had the government of his nonage? This government over him only prepared him the better and sooner for it. If any body should ask me when my son is of age to be free? I shall answer, just when his monarch is of age to govern. "But at what time," says the judicious Hooker, Eccl. Pol. lib. i. sect. 6. "a man may be said to have attained so far forth the use of reason, as sufficeth to make him capable of those laws whereby he is then bound to guide his actions: this is a great deal more easy for sense to discern, than for any one by skill and learning to determine."

### § 62.

Commonwealths themselves take notice of, and allow, that there is a time when men are to begin to act like freemen, and therefore till that time require not oaths of fealty, or allegiance, or other public owning of, or submission to, the government of their countries.

### § 63.

The freedom then of man, and liberty of acting according to his own will, is grounded on his having reason, which is able to instruct him in that law he is to govern himself by, and make him know how far he is left to the freedom of his own will. To turn him loose to an unrestrained liberty, before he has reason to guide him, is not the allowing him the privilege of his nature to be free; but to thrust him out amongst brutes, and abandon him to a state as wretched, and as much beneath that of a man, as theirs. This is that which puts the authority into the parents hands to govern the minority of their children. God hath made it their business to employ this care on their offspring, and hath placed in them suitable inclinations of tenderness and concern to temper this power, to apply it, as his wisdom designed it, to the children's good as long as they should need to be under it.

## § 64.

But what reason can hence advance this care of the parents due to their offspring into an absolute arbitrary dominion of the father, whose power reaches no farther than, by such a discipline as he finds most effectual, to give such strength and health to their bodies, such vigour and rectitude to their minds, as may best fit his children to be most useful to themselves and others: and, if it be necessary to his condition, to make them work, when they are able, for their own subsistence. But in this power the mother too has her share with the father.[1]

## § 65.

Nay, this power so little belongs to the father by any peculiar right of nature, but only as he is guardian of his children, that when he quits his care of them, he loses his power over them, which goes along with their nourishment and education, to which it is inseparably annexed; and it belongs as much to the foster-father of an exposed child, as to the natural father of another. So little power does the bare act of begetting give a man over his issue; if all his care ends there, and this be all the title he hath to the name and

---

[1] 洛克对教育问题的具体论述参见:［英］洛克:《教育片论》,熊春文译,上海,上海人民出版社,2006。

authority of a father. And what will become of this paternal power in that part of the world, where one woman hath more than one husband at a time? or in those parts of America, where, when the husband and wife part, which happens frequently, the children are all left to the mother, follow her, and are wholly under her care and provision? If the father die whilst the children are young, do they not naturally every where owe the same obedience to their mother, during their minority, as to their father were he alive; and will any one say, that the mother hath a legislative power over her children? that she can make standing rules, which shall be of perpetual obligation, by which they ought to regulate all the concerns of their property, and bound their liberty all the course of their lives? or can she enforce the observation of them with capital punishments? for this is the proper power of the magistrate, of which the father hath not so much as the shadow. His command over his children is but temporary, and reaches not their life or property: it is but a help to the weakness and imperfection of their nonage, a discipline necessary to their education: and though a father may dispose of his own possessions as he pleases, when his children are out of danger of perishing for want, yet his power extends not to the lives or goods, which either their own industry, or another's bounty has made theirs; nor to their liberty neither, when they are once arrived to the infranchisement of the years of discretion. The father's empire then ceases, and can from thenceforwards no more dispose of the liberty of his son, than that of any other man: and it must be far from an absolute or perpetual jurisdiction, from which a man may withdraw himself, having licence from divine authority to "leave father and mother, and cleave to his wife."

### § 66.

But though there be a time when a child comes to be as free from subjection to the will and command of his father, as the father himself is free from subjection to the will of any body else, and they are each under no other restraint but that which is common to them both, whether it be the law of nature, or municipal law of their country; yet this freedom exempts not a son from that honour which he ought, by the law of God and nature, to pay his parents. God having made the parents instruments in his great design of continuing the race of mankind, and the occasions of life to their children; as he hath laid on them an obligation to nourish, preserve, and bring up their offspring; so he has laid on the children a perpetual obligation of honouring their parents, which containing in it an inward esteem and reverence to be shown by all outward expressions, ties up the child from any thing that may ever injure or affront, disturb or endanger, the happiness or life of those from whom he received his; and engages him in all actions of defence, relief, assistance, and comfort of those, by whose means he entered into being, and has been made capable of any enjoyments of life: from this obligation no state, no freedom can absolve children. But this is very far from giving parents a power of command over their children, or authority to make laws and dispose as they please of their lives and liberties. It is one thing to owe honour, respect, gratitude, and assistance: another to require an absolute obedience and submission. The honour due to parents, a monarch in his throne owes his mother; and yet this lessens not his authority, nor subjects him to her government.

## § 67.

The subjection of a minor, places in the father a temporary government, which terminates with the minority of the child: and the honour due from a child, places in the parents perpetual right to respect, reverence, support and compliance too, more or less, as the father's care, cost, and kindness in his education, have been more or less. This ends not with minority, but holds in all parts and conditions of a man's life. The want of distinguishing these two powers, viz. that which the father hath in the right of tuition, during minority, and the right of honour all his life, may perhaps have caused a great part of the mistakes about this matter: for to speak properly of them, the first of these is rather the privilege of children, and duty of parents, than any prerogative of paternal power. The nourishment and education of their children is a charge so incumbent on parents for their children's good, that nothing can absolve them from taking care of it: and though the power of commanding and chastising them go along with it, yet God hath woven into the principles of human nature such a tenderness for their offspring, that there is little fear that parents should use their power with too much rigour; the excess is seldom on the severe side, the strong bias of nature drawing the other way. And therefore God Almighty, when he would express his gentle dealing with the Israelites, he tells them, that though he chastened them, "he chastened them as a man chastens his son," Deut. viii. 5, i. e. with tenderness and affection, and kept them under no severer discipline than what was absolutely best for them, and had been less kindness to have slackened. This is that power to which children are commanded obedience, that the pains and care of their parents may not be increased, or ill rewarded.

## § 68.

On the other side, honour and support, all that which gratitude requires to return for the benefits received by and from them, is the indispensable duty of the child, and the proper privilege of the parents. This is intended for the parents advantage, as the other is for the child's; though education, the parents duty, seems to have most power, because the ignorance and infirmities of childhood stand in need of restraint and correction; which is a visible exercise of rule, and a kind of dominion. And that duty which is comprehended in the word honour, requires less obedience, though the obligation be stronger on grown than younger children: for who can think the command, "Children, obey your parents," requires in a man that has children of his own the same submission to his father, as it does in his yet young children to him; and that by this precept he were bound to obey all his father's commands, if, out of a conceit of authority, he should have the indiscretion to treat him still as a boy.

## § 69.

The first part then of paternal power, or rather duty, which is education, belongs so to the father, that it terminates at a certain season; when the business of education is over, it ceases of itself, and is also alienable before: for a man may put the tuition of his son in other hands; and he that has made his son an apprentice[1] to another, has discharged him, during that time, of a great part of his obedience both to himself and to his mother. But all the duty of honour, the other part, remains nevertheless entire to them; nothing can cancel that: it is so inseparable from them both, that the father's authority cannot dispossess the mother of this right, nor can any man discharge his son from honouring her that bore him. But both these are very far from a power to make laws, and enforcing them with penalties that may reach estate, liberty, limbs, and life. The power of commanding ends with nonage; and though after that, honour and respect, support and defence, and whatsoever gratitude can oblige a man to, for the highest benefits he is naturally capable of, be always due from a son to his parents; yet all this puts no sceptre into the father's hand, no sovereign power of commanding. He has no dominion over his son's property, or actions; nor any right

---

[1] 通过订立契约，将自己的儿子交给某个师傅，在师傅的指导、影响下学得一定的手艺，并接受基本的读、写、算教育和职业道德教育。这种学徒制在17世纪的英国非常流行。

that his will should prescribe to his son's in all things, however it may become his son in many things not very inconvenient to him and his family, to pay a deference to it.

### § 70.

A man may owe honour and respect to an ancient, or wise man; defence to his child or friend; relief and support to the distressed; and gratitude to a benefactor, to such a degree, that all he has, all he can do, cannot sufficiently pay it: but all these give no authority, no right to any one, of making laws over him from whom they are owing. And it is plain, all this is due not only to the bare title of father; not only because, as has been said, it is owing to the mother too, but because these obligations to parents, and the degrees of what is required of children, may be varied by the different care and kindness, trouble and expense, which are often employed upon one child more than another.

### § 71.

This shows the reason how it comes to pass, that parents in societies, where they themselves are subjects, retain a power over their children, and have as much right to their subjection as those who are in the state of nature. Which could not possibly be, if all political power were only paternal, and that in truth they were one and the same thing: for then, all paternal power being in the prince, the subject could naturally have none of it. But these two powers, political and paternal, are so perfectly distinct and separate, are built upon so different foundations, and given to so different ends, that every subject that is a father, has as much a paternal power over his children, as the prince has over his: and every prince, that has parents, owes them as much filial duty and obedience, as the meanest of his subjects do to theirs; and cannot therefore contain any part or degree of that kind of dominion which a prince or magistrate has over his subjects.

### § 72.

Though the obligation on the parents to bring up their children, and the obligation on children to honour their parents, contain all the power on the one hand, and submission on the other, which are proper to this relation, yet there is another power ordinary in the father, whereby he has a tie on the obedience of his children; which though it be common to him with other men, yet the occasions of showing it almost constantly happening to fathers in their private families, and the instances of it elsewhere being rare, and less taken notice of, it passes in the world for a part of paternal jurisdiction. And this is the power men generally have to bestow their estates on those who please them best; the possession of the father being the expectation and inheritance of the children, ordinarily in certain proportions, according to the law and custom of each country; yet it is commonly in the father's power to bestow it with a more sparing or liberal hand, according as the behaviour of this or that child hath comported with his will and humour.

### § 73.

This is no small tie on the obedience of children: and there being always annexed to the enjoyment of land a submission to the government of the country, of which that land is a part; it has been commonly supposed, that a father could oblige his posterity to that government, of which he himself was a subject, and that his compact held them; whereas it being only a necessary condition annexed to the land, and the inheritance of an estate which is under that government, reaches only those who will take it on that condition, and so is no natural tic or engagement, but a voluntary submission:

for every man's children being by nature as free as himself, or any of his ancestors ever were, may, whilst they are in that freedom, choose what society they will join themselves to, what commonwealth they will put themselves under. But if they will enjoy the inheritance of their ancestors, they must take it on the same terms their ancestors had it, and submit to all the conditions annexed to such a possession. By this power indeed fathers oblige their children to obedience to themselves, even when they are past minority, and most commonly too subject them to this or that political power: but neither of these by any peculiar right of fatherhood, but by the reward they have in their hands to enforce and recompence such a compliance; and is no more power than what a Frenchman has over an Englishman, who, by the hopes of an estate he will leave him, will certainly have a strong tie on his obedience: and if, when it is left him, he will enjoy it, he must certainly take it upon the conditions annexed to the possession of land in that country where it lies, whether it be France or England.

## § 74.

To conclude then, though the father's power of commanding extends no farther than the minority of his children, and to a degree only fit for the discipline and government of that age; and though that honour and respect, and all that which the Latins called piety, which they indispensably owe to their parents all their life-time, and in all estates, with all that support and defence which is due to them, gives the father no power of governing, i. e. making laws and enacting penalties on his children; though by all this he has no dominion over the property or actions of his son; yet it is obvious to conceive how easy it was, in the first ages of the world, and in places still, where the thinness of people gives families leave to separate into unpossessed quarters, and they have room to remove or plant themselves in yet vacant habitations, for the father of the family to become the prince* of it; he had been a ruler from the beginning of the infancy of his children: and since without some government it would be hard for them to live together, it was likeliest it should, by the express or tacit consent of the children when they were grown up, be in the father, where it seemed without any change barely to continue; when indeed nothing more was required to it, than the permitting the father to exercise alone, in his family, that executive power of the law of nature, which every free man naturally hath, and by that permission resigning up to him a monarchical power, whilst they remained in it. But that this was not by any paternal right, but only by the consent of his children, is evident from hence, that nobody doubts, but if a stranger, whom chance or business had brought to his family, had there killed any of his children, or committed any other fact, he might condemn and put him to death, or otherwise punish him, as well as any of his children: which it was impossible he should do by virtue of any paternal authority over one who was not his child, but by virtue of that executive power of the law of nature, which, as a man, he had a right to: and he alone could punish him in his family, where the respect of his children had laid by the exercise of such a power, to give way to the dignity and authority they were willing should remain in him, above the rest of his family.

---

\* It is no improbable opinion, therefore, which the arch-philosopher was of, "That the chief person in every household was always, as it were, a king: so when numbers of households joined themselves in civil societies together, kings were the first kind of governors amongst them, which is also, as it seemeth, the reason why the name of fathers continued still in them, who, of fathers, were made rulers; as also the ancient custom of governors to do as Melchizedeck, and being kings, to exercise the office of priests, which fathers did at the first, grew perhaps by the same occasion. Howbeit, this is not the only kind of regiment that has been received in the world. The inconveniencies of one kind have caused sundry others to be devised; so that, in a word, all public regiment, of what kind soever, seemeth evidently to have risen from the deliberate advice, consultation, and composition between men, judging it convenient and behoveful; there being no impossibility in nature considered by itself, but that man might have lived without any public regiment." Hooker's Eccl. P. l. i. sect. 10.（注：此类注释为作者注。）

## § 75.

Thus it was easy, and almost natural for children, by a tacit, and scarce avoidable consent, to make way for the father's authority and government. They had been accustomed in their childhood to follow his direction, and to refer their little differences to him; and when they were men, who fitter to rule them? Their little properties, and less covetousness, seldom afforded greater controversies; and when any should arise, where could they have a fitter umpire than he, by whose care they had every one been sustained and brought up, and who had a tenderness for them all? It is no wonder that they made no distinction betwixt minority and full age; nor looked after one and twenty, or any other age that might make them the free disposers of themselves and fortunes, when they could have no desire to be out of their pupilage: the government they had been under during it, continued still to be more their protection than restraint: and they could no-where find a greater security to their peace, liberties, and fortunes, than in the rule of a father.

## § 76.

Thus the natural fathers of families by an insensible change became the politic monarchs of them too: and as they chanced to live long, and leave able and worthy heirs, for several successions, or otherwise; so they laid the foundations of hereditary, or elective kingdoms, under several constitutions and manners, according as chance, contrivance, or occasions happened to mould them. But if princes have their titles in their fathers right, and it be a sufficient proof of the natural right of fathers to political authority, because they commonly were those in whose hands we find, de facto, the exercise of government: I say, if this argument be good, it will as strongly prove, that all princes, nay princes only, ought to be priests, since it is as certain, that in the beginning, "the father of the family was priest, as that he was ruler in his own household."

# Chapter VII
## Of Political or Civil Society

### 导 读

在前几章中，洛克阐述了个体的基本道德与权利地位。但就人与人之间的关系而言，前几章仅仅从反面加以界定（例如不得违法自然法，父权的不合理）。从第七章开始，洛克开始从正面阐述人与人的共同生活秩序。首先是第七章至第十章，这一部分以"政治社会"这个概念为核心阐述了社会与国家的内涵。

在近代早期，人与人的共同生活秩序主要是奠定在封建关系与宗教关系的基础上。它们为人们在家庭、社会团体、国家等不同共同体中的具体身份与行动准则奠定了规范性基础。这种架构使得人们在不同共同体中的身份以及对不同共同体的政治义务交织在一起，成为导致欧洲各国大量社会冲突甚至战争（包括地方与中央之间、宗教权威与世俗统治者之间）的因素。这种多元分化的政治格局不仅无法维持一个稳定的政治结构，而且会带来内战。统一的民族国家越来越成为人们所期望的理想。

基于这一现实状况，阐明民族国家的内涵与基础是近代自然法学说一项历史使命。自然法学家首先将每一个个体从这些盘根交错的各种关系中解放出来，赋予它们平等自由的主体地位。但是，这仅仅是第一步。若要说明一种人类政治秩序原理，

就必须为人类设定一种共同体。这里就出现了不同的理论进路，即究竟是将"社会"作为基本范畴，还是将"国家"作为基本范畴。霍布斯通过国家与主权概念来说明政治共同体的秩序如何成为可能。其他的（严格意义上）近代自然法学家（例如格劳秀斯、普芬道夫）则是通过界定"社会"这个概念来完成这个任务的，洛克也是如此。关键的问题是，这个"社会"究竟是什么性质的社会。

如果我们仅仅将社会定义为某些人组成的具有某种内在纽带、享有某种共同目的的共同体，那么我们会发现，在实际生活中存在许多种不同性质的社会。例如，丈夫与妻子构成的"夫妻社会"、"父母与子女的社会"、主人与奴隶构成的"主奴社会"。在第七章的前半部分，洛克分别阐述了这几种社会各自不同的目的、约束关系以及范围。接着，洛克提出了一个"政治社会"的概念。在洛克看来，虽然前几种社会各不相同，但是却具有一个相同的地方，即这些社会都不具有立法权。立法权是指设定永久有效的法律来对人的财产与生命加以规定的权力。由于不具有立法权，这些社会往往不具有完整的独立性。当家庭内部、主奴之间发生纠纷时，有时候只能由外部权威（国家）来加以裁判。只有政治社会具有立法权，从而具有独立性与自足性。只有政治社会才能为政治权力与国家提供说明。

洛克的政治社会概念是在与自然状态概念（或者说"政治"（political）与"自然"（natural））对照的基础上提出的。政治社会的主要特征是约束所有人（包括君主）的共同法律与对所有人都享有权威的共同裁判者。基于此，洛克在本章的后半部分批判了绝对君主制。由于绝对君主制中的君主并不受法律的约束，因而它不是一种政治社会形态，而是自然状态。也就是说，绝对君主的权力地位与洛克所讲的"立法权"相抵触，所以绝对君主制并不是人类的政治生活形态。

洛克将立法权作为政治共同体（政治社会）的实质反映了现代国家学说的发展趋势。在中世纪，国家权力或者说君主的统治权最初建立在土地上。国家的本质就是一定范围的土地，这块土地是君主所有的，所以君主可以决定这块土地上的所有事情，从而拥有管理土地上的一切事务的最高权力。这也就是为什么基于土地的分封制与土地（以及土地作物）税收问题是国家的首要问题。后来，中世纪的统治者发现他们还可以通过另一种方式来建立自己的权力。这个方式就是司法。中世纪的人主要是生活在土地上的，土地是一切的基础。人们所关心的另一个问题，就是如何解决他们与他人发生的纠纷，包括关于土地的纠纷以及其他方面的纠纷。找谁解决纠纷就成了人们日常生活中的一件大事。国王通过皇室法庭、地方巡回法庭的建立，获取了司法权。国王除了是国土的拥有者外，还是正义的主持者。虽然中世纪的国王通过司法获得了政治权力，但是司法是法律的适用，而法律并不是全部由国王决定的。法庭所适用的法律包括古老的法律、地方性的习俗、宗教的教规等。国王虽然是司法的主持者，但他并不是立法者。

通过法律来统治比通过土地来统治更为有利，因为法律是普遍的，它不依赖于任何具体的人身关系，它对共同体的整合作用更为有力。君主们看到了这一点，思想家们也看到了这一点。在博丹与霍布斯所提出的主权概念中，立法权就是最高的权力。主权通过普遍立法这种形式来结合、捆绑一个政治共同体。这样的共同体就不再是封建共同体，而是具有现代色彩的法律共同体了。政治权力不再是一种财产权，而是一种抽象的规则制定权。尽管如此，在博丹与霍布斯那里，这一法律共同体并不涵盖所有人。君主超越于法律，享有立法者的超法律地位。有立法权必然要有立法者，而只有当立法者在法律之外（超越于法律），他才能够为法律的效力提供来源。这似乎是一个符合逻辑的说法，但是洛克却认为这是一个很大的问题。洛克认为立法权必须是共同约束包括立法者在内的所有人的权力。一种人间的权力如何能来自于人间的同时又约束人间的所有人呢？关于这个问题，我们需要结合后面的第九章来加以讨论。

**延伸阅读材料：**

1. 格劳秀斯对"人的社会性"的讨论：Hugo Grotius, *The Rights of War and Peace*, edited and with an introduction by Richard Tuck, from the edition by Jean Barbeyrac. Indianapolis, Liberty Fund, 2005, 特别是其中的"导论"（The Preliminary Discourse）。

2. 普芬道夫对"人的社会义务"的讨论：[德]塞缪尔·普芬道夫：《人和公民的自然法义务》，鞠成伟译，北京，商务印书馆，2009，特别是第一卷第一章至第八章。Samuel Pufendorf, *On the Law of Nature and Nations in Eight Books*, 1672, in Samuel Pufendorf, The Political Writings of Samuel Pufendorf, edited by Craig L. Carr, translated by Michael J. Seidler, Book ii & iii, Oxford University Press, 1994.

3. 博丹的国家主权学说：[法]博丹：《主权论》，[美]朱利安·H·富兰克林编，李卫海、钱俊文译，北京，北京大学出版社，2008。

4. 霍布斯对"公民社会"概念的批判及其国家主权学说：[英]霍布斯：《论公民》，应星、冯克利译，贵阳，贵州人民出版社，2003；[英]霍布斯：《利维坦》，黎思复、黎廷弼译，杨昌裕校，北京，商务印书馆，1997。

5. 关于中世纪国家的司法统治模式参见：[美]约瑟夫·R·斯特雷耶：《现代国家的起源》，华佳、王夏、宗福常译，王小卫校，上海，格致出版社2011年版；李栋：《通过司法限制权力：英格兰司法的成长与宪政的生长》，北京，北京大学出版社，2011。

## § 77.

God having made man such a creature, that in his own judgment, it was not good for him to be alone, put him under strong obligations of necessity, convenience, and inclination, to drive him into society, as well as fitted him with understanding and language to continue and enjoy it. The first society was between man and wife, which gave beginning to that between parents and children; to which, in time, that between master and servant came to be added: and though all these might, and commonly did meet together, and make up but one family, wherein the master or mistress of it had some sort of rule proper to a family; each of these, or all together, came short of political society, as we shall see, if we consider the different ends, ties, and bounds of each of these.

## § 78.

Conjugal society is made by a voluntary compact between man and woman; and though it consist chiefly in such a communion and right in one another's bodies as is necessary to its chief end, procreation; yet it draws with it mutual support and assistance, and a communion of interests too, as necessary not only to unite their care and affection, but also necessary to their common offspring, who have a right to be nourished and maintained by them, till they are able to provide for themselves.

## § 79.

For the end of conjunction between male and female being not barely procreation, but the continuation of the species; this conjunction betwixt male and female ought to last, even after procreation, so long as is necessary to the nourishment and support of the young ones, who are to be sustained by those that got them, till they are able to shift and provide for themselves. This rule, which the infinite wise Maker hath set to the works of his hands, we find the inferior creatures steadily obey. In those viviparous animals which feed on grass, the conjunction between male and female lasts no longer than the very act of copulation; because the teat of the dam being sufficient to nourish the young, till it be able to feed on grass, the male only begets, but concerns not himself for the female or young, to whose sustenance he can contribute nothing. But in beasts of prey the conjunction lasts longer: because the dam not being able well to subsist herself, and nourish her numerous offspring by her own prey alone, a more laborious, as well as more dangerous way of living, than by feeding on grass; the assistance of the male is necessary to the maintenance of their common family, which cannot subsist till they are able to prey for themselves, but by the joint care of male and female. The same is to be observed in all birds (except some domestic ones, where plenty of food excuses the cock from feeding, and taking care of the young brood), whose young needing food in the nest, the cock and hen continue mates, till the young are able to use their wing, and provide for themselves.

### § 80.

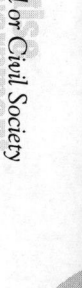

And herein I think lies the chief, if not the only reason, "why the male and female in mankind are tied to a longer conjunction" than other creatures, viz. because the female is capable of conceiving, and de facto is commonly with child again, and brings forth too a new birth, long before the former is out of a dependency for support on his parents help, and able to shift for himself, and has all the assistance that is due to him from his parents: whereby the father, who is bound to take care for those he hath begot, is under an obligation to continue in conjugal society with the same woman longer than other creatures, whose young being able to subsist of themselves before the time of procreation returns again, the conjugal bond dissolves of itself, and they are at liberty, till Hymen at his usual anniversary season summons them again to choose new mates. Wherein one cannot but admire the wisdom of the great Creator, who having given to man foresight, and an ability to lay up for the future, as well as to supply the present necessity, hath made it necessary, that society of man and wife should be more lasting, than of male and female amongst other creatures; that so their industry might be encouraged, and their interest better united, to make provision and lay up goods for their common issue, which uncertain mixture, or easy and frequent solutions of conjugal society, would mightily disturb.

## § 81.

But though these are ties upon mankind, which make the conjugal bonds more firm and lasting in man, than the other species of animals; yet it would give one reason to inquire, why this compact, where procreation and education are secured, and inheritance taken care for, may not be made determinable, either by consent, or at a certain time, or upon certain conditions, as well as any other voluntary compacts, there being no necessity in the nature of the thing, nor to the ends of it, that it should always be for life; I mean, to such as are under no restraint of any positive law, which ordains all such contracts to be perpetual.

## § 82.

But the husband and wife, though they have but one common concern, yet having different understandings, will unavoidably sometimes have different wills too; it therefore being necessary that the last determination, i. e. the rule, should be placed somewhere; it naturally falls to the man's share, as the abler and the stronger. But this reaching but to the things of their common interest and property, leaves the wife in the full and free possession of what by contract is her peculiar right, and gives the husband no more power over her life than she has over his; the power of the husband being so far from that of an absolute monarch, that the wife has in many cases a liberty to separate from him, where natural right or their contract allows it; whether that contract be made by themselves in the state of nature, or by the customs or laws of the country they live in; and the children upon such separation fall to the father's or mother's lot, as such contract does determine.

## § 83.

For all the ends of marriage being to be obtained under politic government, as well as in the state of nature, the civil magistrate doth not abridge the right or power of either naturally necessary to those ends, viz. procreation and mutual support and assistance whilst they are together; but only decides any controversy that may arise between man and wife about them. If it were otherwise, and that absolute sovereignty and power of life and death naturally belonged to the husband, and were necessary to the society between man and wife, there could be no matrimony in any of those countries where the husband is allowed no such absolute authority. But the ends of matrimony requiring no such power in the husband, the condition of conjugal society put it not in him, it being not at all necessary to that state. Conjugal society could subsist and attain its ends without it; nay, community of goods, and the power over them, mutual assistance and maintenance, and other things belonging to conjugal society, might be varied and regulated by that contract which unites man and wife in that society, as far as may consist with procreation and the bringing up of children till they could shift for themselves; nothing being necessary to any society, that is not necessary to the ends for which it is made.

## § 84.

The society betwixt parents and children, and the distinct rights and powers belonging respectively to them, I have treated of so largely, in the foregoing chapter, that I shall not here need to say any thing of it. And I think it is plain, that it is far different from a politic society.

## § 85.

Master and servant are names as old as history, but given to those of far different condition; for a freeman makes himself a servant to another, by selling him, for a certain time, the service he undertakes to do, in exchange for wages he is to receive: and though this commonly puts him into the family of his master, and under the ordinary discipline thereof: yet it gives the master but a temporary power over him, and no greater than what is contained in the contract between them. But there is another sort of servants, which by a peculiar name we call slaves, who being captives taken in a just war, are by the right of nature subjected to the absolute dominion and arbitrary power of their masters. These men having, as I say, forfeited their lives, and with it their liberties, and lost their estates; and being in the state of slavery, not capable of any property, cannot in that state be considered as any part of civil society; the chief end whereof is the preservation of property.

### § 86.

Let us therefore consider a master of a family with all these subordinate relations of wife, children, servants, and slaves, united under the domestic rule of a family; which, what resemblance soever it may have in its order, offices, and number too, with a little commonwealth, yet is very far from it, both in its constitution, power, and end: or if it must be thought a monarchy, and the paterfamilias the absolute monarch in it, absolute monarchy will have but a very shattered and short power, when it is plain by what has been said before, that the master of the family has a very distinct and differently limited power, both as to time and extent, over those several persons that are in it: for excepting the slave (and the family is as much a family, and his power as paterfamilias as great, whether there be any slaves in his family or no) he has no legislative power of life and death over any of them, and none too but what a mistress of a family may have as well as he. And he certainly can have no absolute power over the whole family, who has but a very limited one over every individual in it. But how a family, or any other society of men, differ from that which is properly political society, we shall best see by considering wherein political society itself consists.

## § 87.

Man being born, as has been proved, with a title to perfect freedom, and uncontrolled enjoyment of all the rights and privileges of the law of nature, equally with any other man, or number of men in the world, hath by nature a power, not only to preserve his property, that is, his life, liberty, and estate, against the injuries and attempts of other men; but to judge of and punish the breaches of that law in others, as he is persuaded the offence deserves, even with death itself, in crimes where the heinousness of the fact, in his opinion, requires it. But because no political society can be, nor subsist, without having in itself the power to preserve the property, and, in order thereunto, punish the offences of all those of that society; there and there only is political society, where every one of the members hath quitted his natural power, resigned it up into the hands of the community in all cases that excludes him not from appealing for protection to the law established by it. And thus all private judgment of every particular member being excluded, the community comes to be umpire by settled standing rules, indifferent, and the same to all parties; and by men having authority from the community, for the execution of those rules, decides all the differences that may happen between any members of that society concerning any matter of right; and punishes those offences which any member hath committed against the society, with such penalties as the law has established, whereby it is easy to discern, who are, and who are not, in political society together. Those who are united into one body, and have a common established law and judicature to appeal to, with authority to decide controversies between them, and punish offenders, are in civil society one with another: but those who have no such common appeal, I mean on earth, are still in the state of nature, each being, where there is no other, judge for himself, and executioner: which is, as I have before showed, the perfect state of nature.

## § 88.

And thus the commonwealth comes by a power to set down what punishment shall belong to the several transgressions which they think worthy of it, committed amongst the members of that society, (which is the power of making laws) as well as it has the power to punish any injury done unto any of its members, by any one that is not of it, (which is the power of war and peace,) and all this for the preservation of the property of all the members of that society, as far as is possible. But though every man who has entered into civil society, and is become a member of any commonwealth, has thereby quitted his power to punish offences against the law of nature, in prosecution of his own private judgment; yet with the judgment of offences, which he has given up to the legislative in all cases, where he can appeal to the magistrate, he has given a right to the commonwealth to employ his force, for the execution of the judgments of the commonwealth, whenever he shall be called to it; which indeed are his own judgments, they being made by himself, or his representative. And herein we have the original of the legislative and executive power of civil society, which is to judge by standing laws, how far offences are to be punished, when committed within the commonwealth; and also to determine, by occasional judgments founded on the present circumstances of the fact, how far injuries from without are to be vindicated; and in both these to employ all the force of all the members, when there shall be need.

## § 89.

Whenever therefore any number of men are so united into one society, as to quit every one his executive power of the law of nature, and to resign it to the public, there and there only is a political, or civil society. And this is done, wherever any number of men, in the state of nature, enter into society to make one people[1], one body politic, under one supreme government; or else when any one joins himself to, and incorporates with any government already made: for

---

[1] 这是 people 一词第一次在《政府论（下篇）》中出现。

hereby he authorizes the society, or, which is all one, the legislative thereof, to make laws for him, as the public good of the society shall require; to the execution whereof, his own assistance (as to his own degrees) is due. And this puts men out of a state of nature into that of a commonwealth, by setting up a judge on earth, with authority to determine all the controversies, and redress the injuries that may happen to any member of the commonwealth: which judge is the legislative, or magistrate appointed by it. And wherever there are any number of men, however associated, that have no such decisive power to appeal to, there they are still in the state of nature.

## § 90.

Hence it is evident, that absolute monarchy, which by some men[1] is counted the only governmen in the world, is indeed inconsistent with civil society, and so can be no form of civil government at all; for the end of civil society being to avoid and remedy these inconveniencies of the state of nature, which necessarily follow from every man being judge in his own case, by setting up a known authority, to which every one of that society may appeal upon any injury received, or controversy that may arise, and which every one of the society ought to obey;* wherever any persons are, who have not such an authority to appeal to for the decision of any difference between them, there those persons are still in the state of nature; and so is every absolute prince, in respect of those who are under his dominion.

## § 91.

For he being supposed to have all, both legislative and executive power in himself alone, there is no judge to be found, no

---

[1] 这里的"有些人"指的是费尔默及其追随者，不包括霍布斯。

\* "The public power of all society is above every soul contained in the same society; and the principal use of that power is, to give laws unto all that are under it, which laws in such cases we must obey, unless there be reason showed which may necessarily inforce, that the law of reason, or of God, doth enjoin the contrary." Hooker's. Eccl. Pol. l. i. sect. 16.

appeal lies open to any one, who may fairly, and indifferently, and with authority decide, and from whose decision relief and redress may be expected of any injury or inconveniency that may be suffered from the prince, or by his order: so that such a man, however intitled, czar, or grand seignior, or how you please, is as much in the state of nature, with all under his dominion, as he is with the rest of mankind: for wherever any two men are, who have no standing rule, and common judge to appeal to on earth, for the determination of controversies of right betwixt them, there they are still in the state of nature, and under all the inconveniencies of it,* with only this woful difference to the subject, or rather slave of an absolute prince; that whereas in the ordinary state of nature he has a liberty to judge of his right, and, according to the best of his power, to maintain it; now, whenever his property is invaded by the will and order of his monarch, he has not only no appeal, as those in society ought to have, but, as if he were degraded from the common state of rational creatures, is denied a liberty to judge of, or to defend his right; and so is exposed to all the misery and inconveniencies, that a man can fear from one, who being in the unrestrained state of nature, is yet corrupted with flattery, and armed with power.

---

\* "To take away all such mutual grievances, injuries and wrongs," i. e. such as attend men in the state of nature, "there was no way but only by growing into composition and agreement amongst themselves, by ordaining some kind of government public, and by yielding themselves subject thereunto, that unto whom they granted authority to rule and govern, by them the peace, tranquillity, and happy state of the rest might be procured. Men always knew that where force and injury was offered, they might be defenders of themselves; they knew that however men may seek their own commodity, yet if this were done with injury unto others, it was not to be suffered, but by all men, and all good means to be withstood. Finally, they knew that no man might in reason take upon him to determine his own right, and according to his own determination proceed in maintenance thereof, in as much as every man is towards himself, and them whom he greatly affects, partial; and therefore that strifes and troubles would be endless, except they gave their common consent, all to be ordered by some, whom they should agree upon, without which consent there would be no reason that one man should take upon him to be lord or judge over another." Hooker's Eccl. Pol. l. i. sect. 10.

## § 92.

For he that thinks absolute power purifies men's blood, and corrects the baseness of human nature, need read but the history of this or any other age, to be convinced of the contrary. He that would have been so insolent and injurious in the woods of America, would not probably be much better in a throne; where perhaps learning and religion shall be found out to justify all that he shall do to his subjects, and the sword presently silence all those that dare question it: for what the protection of absolute monarchy is, what kind of fathers of their countries it makes princes to be, and to what a degree of happiness and security it carries civil society, where this sort of government is grown to perfection; he that will look into the late relation of Ceylon[1], may easily see.

## § 93.

In absolute monarchies, indeed, as well as other governments of the world, the subjects have an appeal to the law, and judges to decide any controversies, and restrain any violence that may happen betwixt the subjects themselves, one amongst another. This every one thinks necessary, and believes he deserves to be thought a declared enemy to society and mankind, who should go about to take it away. But whether this be from a true love of mankind and society, and such a charity as we all owe one to another, there is reason to doubt: for this is no more than what every man, who loves his own power, profit, or greatness, may and naturally must do, keep those animals from hurting, or destroying one another, who labour and drudge only for his pleasure and advantage; and so are taken care of, not out of any love the master has for them, but love of himself, and the profit they bring him: for if it be asked, what security, what fence is there, in such a state, against the violence and oppression of this absolute ruler? The very question can scarce be borne. They

---

[1] 这个"对锡兰情况的新近阐述"是指以下这本书：Robert Knox, *An Historical Relation of the Island of Crylon*, 1680. 洛克在 1681 年 8 月 29 日购买了此书。"锡兰"是斯里兰卡共和国 1972 年之前的名字。

are ready to tell you, that it deserves death only to ask after safety. Betwixt subject and subject, they will grant, there must be measures, laws, and judges, for their mutual peace and security: but as for the ruler he ought to be absolute, and is above all such circumstances; because he has power to do more hurt and wrong, it is right when he does it. To ask how you may be guarded from harm, or injury, on that side where the strongest hand is to do it, is presently the voice of faction and rebellion: as if when men quitting the state of nature entered into society, they agreed that all of them but one should be under the restraint of laws, but that he should still retain all the liberty of the state of nature, increased with power, and made licentious by impunity. This is to think, that men are so foolish, that they take care to avoid what mischiefs may be done them by polecats, or foxes; but are content, nay think it safety, to be devoured by lions.

§ 94.

But whatever flatterers may talk to amuse people's understandings, it hinders not men from feeling; and when they perceive, that any man, in what station soever, is out of the bounds of the civil society which they are of, and that they have no appeal on earth against any harm they may receive from him, they are apt to think themselves in the state of nature, in respect of him whom they find to be so: and to take care, as soon as they can, to have that safety and security in civil society, for which it was instituted, and for which only they entered into it. And therefore, though perhaps at first, (as shall be showed more at large hereafter in the following part of this discourse) some one good and excellent man having got a pre-eminency amongst the rest, had this deference paid to his goodness and virtue, as to a kind of natural authority, that the chief rule, with arbitration of their differences, by a tacit consent devolved into his hands, without any other caution, but the assurance they had of his uprightness and wisdom; yet when time, giving authority, and (as some men would persuade us) sacredness to customs, which the negligent and unforeseen innocence of the first ages began, had brought in successors of another stamp; the people finding their properties not secure under the government, as then it was, (whereas government has no other end but the preservation of property)[1] could never be safe nor at rest, nor think themselves in civil society, till the legislature[2] was placed in collective bodies of men, call them senate, parliament, or what you please.* By which means every single person became subject, equally with other the meanest men, to those laws, which he himself, as part of the legislative, had established; nor could any one, by his own authority, avoid the force of the law, when once made; nor by any pretence of superiority plead exemption, thereby to license his own, or the miscarriages of any of his dependents. "No man in civil society can be exempted from the laws of it."** For if any man may do what he thinks fit, and there be no appeal on earth, for redress or security against any harm he shall do; I ask, whether he be not perfectly still in the state of nature, and so can be no part or member of that civil society: unless any one will say, the state of nature and civil society are one and the same thing, which I have never yet found any one so great a patron of anarchy as to affirm.

---

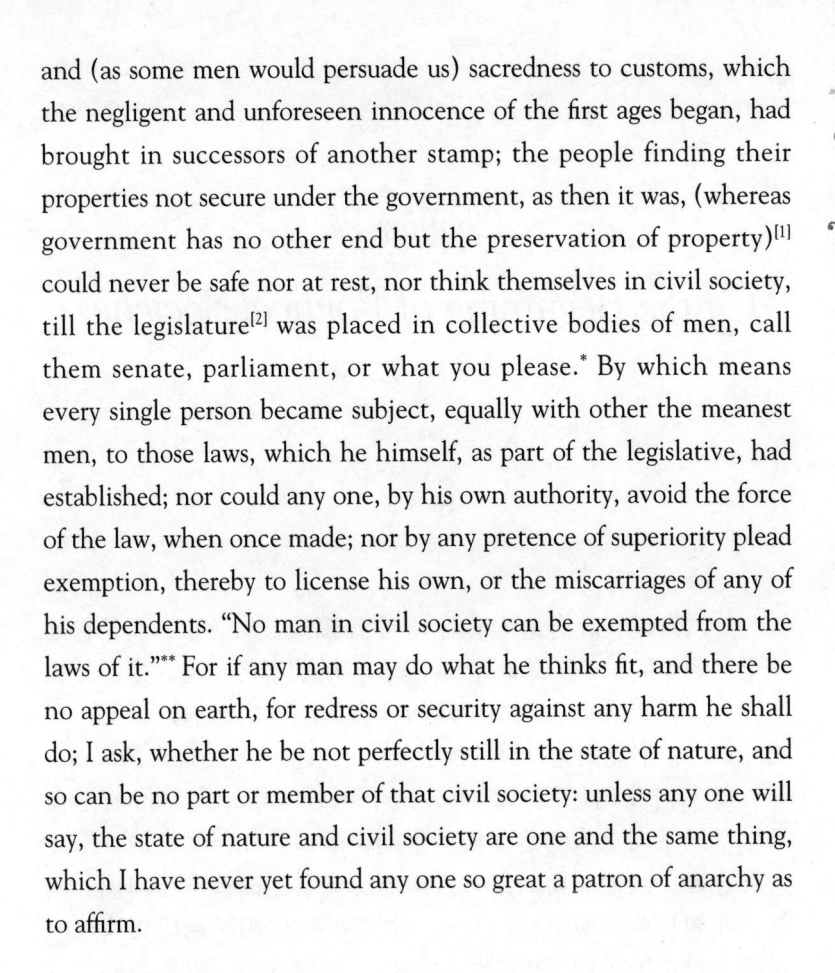

[1] 这句话是洛克对"政府的目的是保护财产"这一主张的最为强烈的表达。

[2] 洛克在之前几稿中使用的是 legislative 一词，而非 legislature。legislature 指的是制定法律的权力，而 legislative 指的是立法机构（如第 153、154 段）。

* "At the first, when some certain kind of regiment was once appointed, it may be that nothing was then farther thought upon for the manner of governing, but all permitted unto their wisdom and discretion, which were to rule, till by experience they found this for all parts very inconvenient, so as the thing which they had devised for a remedy, did indeed but increase the sore which it should have cured. They saw, that to live by one man's will became the cause of all men's misery. This constrained them to come into laws, wherein all men might see their duty beforehand, and know the penalties of transgressing them." Hooker's Eccl. P. lib. i. sect. 10.

** "Civil law, being the act of the whole body politic, doth therefore over-rule each several part of the same body." Hooker, ibid.

# Chapter VIII
## Of the Beginning of Political Societies

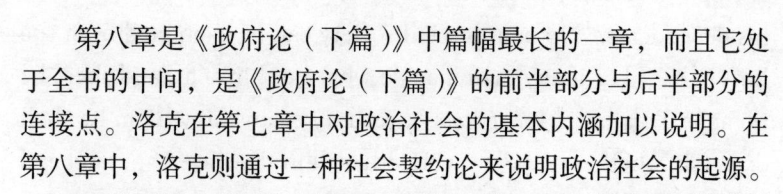

### 导 读

第八章是《政府论（下篇）》中篇幅最长的一章，而且它处于全书的中间，是《政府论（下篇）》的前半部分与后半部分的连接点。洛克在第七章中对政治社会的基本内涵加以说明。在第八章中，洛克则通过一种社会契约论来说明政治社会的起源。

通常当我们使用"起源"这个词的时候，我们指的是在发生学的意义上事物是如何产生的，事件是如何发生的。探究这种起源，我们需要的是考古学与历史学上的技术与知识。例如，我们想要说明美国的起源，就需要对美国早期历史遗迹的挖掘，对美国早期历史事件的分析。这种方法可以使我们了解特定事物与特定事件的起源，但是却无法获得一种规范性知识。即使我们知道了美国、法国、英国的不同起源，我们也仍然无法知道应该如何建立一个合法的国家，无法知道应该怎样去评述不同国家的合法性，而这才是洛克想要探究的东西。正是因为起源这个词的歧义性，现代政治学通常不用这个词。所以我们需要注意，洛克所说的起源并不是发生学上的起源，而是规范性知识意义上的起源。起源指的是事物的本质。洛克在这一章中想要探讨的是，政治社会应当是怎样形成的，应当具有哪些特征。

在本章前半部分的第 95—99 段，洛克对此给出了自己的答案。我们会发现，他的阐述完全是一种抽象的分析，不涉及任何历史分析。它是一种解释，而不是一种描述。就其内容而言，我们可以将他的解释称为以同意为核心的社会契约论。

社会契约论是每个近代自然法学家都会采用的分析工具，所以 17 到 18 世纪也可以被看做是社会契约论的一个高潮。其实早在中世纪，欧洲就已经出现了某种契约论。这种契约论主张，国王与臣民之间存在着一种契约关系，国王必须维护所有臣民的共同善。至于这种契约关系的基础是什么，臣民是否可以在国王破坏契约时加以反抗等一系列问题，则存在不同的解释。尽管如此，我们仍然能够区分这种传统契约理论与近代自然法学说中的契约论。后者与前者的不同在于，它具有鲜明的个人主义与理性主义色彩。由于自然状态概念将人类还原到某种个人状态，所以它具有个人主义色彩，而不像亚里士多德（或中世纪的亚里士多德主义）那样具有整体论色彩。由于这种契约并不仅仅建立在对上帝或人的意志的解释上，而是通过解释人的理性来加以说明，所以它具有理性主义色彩，而不像神授法权理论与父权制理论那样以超现实的神学基调为主。

洛克之所以采用社会契约论其实是他的理论前提的必然结果。如果我们以人的自然自由与平等以及人的自然权利为前提，那么一种共同体要能够在不违背这些前提的情况下产生，就只能通过以所有人的同意为基础的契约。只有当所有人自愿地将自己的部分权利与权力交出来，所有这些权利与权力才能够构成一个公共权威与公共权力，能够正当地限制人的自然自由与自然权利，为公共善服务。

这里涉及一个问题：如果社会契约能够将人们组成一个共同体，那么这个整体是依什么原则而行动，为共同体内的所有人立法？洛克在第 96 段提出了一个"大多数人的同意"原则。这一原则常常受到两种质疑。第一种质疑是：这一原则意味着以力量来取代权利。第二种质疑是：这一原则没有自然法上的正当基础，因为它意味着多数人可以否定其他人的主张。这两种质疑是否能够成立是值得我们思考的重要问题。

由于社会契约论的基本逻辑已经被后来的诸多政治理论与实践所接受，而且社会契约论也在政治哲学巨擘约翰·罗尔斯（John Rawls）的《正义论》中以某种更为哲学的方式得以在20世纪复兴，所以现代人还是比较能够理解与支持洛克的这种哲学分析方法。但是在17世纪，这种方法并不被普遍接受。例如在英国，人们总是通过对英国历史的考察（例如对大宪章的解释）来说明国王与议会的关系应当是怎样的。人们争论的问题是英国当初是怎么建立的、之前国王与议会的关系是怎样的等历史问题。洛克的《政府论》并不是写给少数哲学家看的，而是给广大英国读者看的，所以洛克从第100段开始回答了两种质疑。第一种质疑是：历史上从来没有发生过订立这种契约的事件。洛克花了很大的篇幅来重述人类的历史。这些具体的历史考察更容易说服一般的读者。但我们必须要注意到，洛克明确指出"国家也像个人一样，通常对自己的出生和幼年情况是不清楚的"。也就是说，通过考察人类社会的历史来获得确定的知识是徒劳无功的，甚至是缘木求鱼的做法。

公允地说，洛克并没有对社会契约的哲学基础进行充分的论证，这也是因为洛克并没有构建起一个完整的理论框架。在此情况下，洛克又急着去回应一般读者对历史真实性的质疑，这使得他分析显得有些混乱。这集中体现在他对第二个质疑的回答上。这个质疑是：所有人都是一出生就处于一个国家之中，一种统治关系中。也就是说，人在还没有表达过同意、订立过契约时，就已经处于一种政治服从状态中了。洛克对这一问题的回答引发了后来的思想家与学者的激烈争议，因为他在本章的第119段引入了一个"默示同意"的概念。对此，休谟就曾提出过尖锐的批评。究竟如何解决这个问题，也是我们可以进一步思考的问题。

**延伸阅读材料：**

1. 休谟对同意学说与社会契约论的批判：［英］休谟：《人性论》，关文运译，郑之骧校，北京，商务印书馆，2005，第三卷第二章"论正义与非义"。［英］休谟："论政府的起源"、"论原始契约"，载《休谟政治论文选》，张若衡译，北京，商务印书馆，1993。

2. 对西方社会契约论传统的研究：

——［英］迈克尔·莱斯诺夫等：《社会契约论》，刘训练、李丽红、张红梅译，南京，江苏人民出版社，2010。

——J. W. Gough, *The Social Contract: A Critical Study of Its Development*, Clarendon Press, 1957.

——Jean Hampton, *Hobbes and the Social Contract Tradition*, Cambridge University Press, 1986.

3. 对洛克的社会契约论的研究：

——Frederick Pollock, Hobbes and Locke: The Social Contract in English Political Philosophy, *Journal of the Society of Comparative Legislation*, New Series, Vol. 9, No. 1 (1908), pp. 107–112.

——E. Clinton Gardner, John Locke: Justice and the Social Compact, *Journal of Law and Religion*, Vol. 9, No. 2 (1992), pp. 347–371.

——Jeremy Waldron, John Locke: Social Contract versus Political Anthropology, *The Review of Politics*, Vol. 51, No. 1 (Winter, 1989), pp. 3–28.

——Patrick Riley, Locke on "Voluntary Agreement" and Political Power, *The Western Political Quarterly*, Vol. 29, No. 1 (Mar., 1976), pp. 136–145.

——Peter Hayes, Pirates, Privateers and the Contract Theories of Hobbes and Locke, *History of Political Thought*, Volume 29, Number 3, 2008 , pp. 461–484(24).

——James Tully, *A Discourse on Property*, Cambridge University Press 1980, 7. ⅰ. "Making a Polity".

4. 对洛克社会契约论中的"同意"概念的研究：

—— 王涛：《洛克思想中的"默示同意"概念》，载《华东政法学院学报》，2011年第2期。

——［美］汉娜·皮特金：《义务与同意》，载《政治义务：证成与反驳》，南京，江苏人民出版社，2007年。

——John Plamenatz , *Man and Society*, Longman Publishing Group, 1993, Chapter Eight 'Locke'.

——George Gale, John Locke on Territoriality: An Unnoticed Aspect of the Second Treatise, *Political Theory*, Vol. 1, No. 4 (Nov., 1973).

——John Dunn, Consent in the Political Theory of John Locke, *The Historical Journal*, X, 2(1967).

——Julian H. Franklin, Allegiance and Jurisdiction in Locke's Doctrine of Tacit Consent, *Political Theory*, Vol. 24, August 1996.

——Paul Russell, Locke on Express and Tacit Consent: Misinterpretations and Inconsistencies, *Political Theory*, Vol. 14, No. 2 (May, 1986).

——Iain W. Hampsher-Monk, Tacit Concept of Consent in Locke's Two Treatises of Government: A Note on Citizens, Travellers and Patriarchalism, *Journal of the History of Ideas*, Vol. 40, No. 1 (Jan. - Mar., 1979).

——G. A. den Hartogh, Express Consent and Full Membership in Locke, *Political Studies* ( March 1990), Volume 38, Issue 1.

——A. John Simmons, "Denisons" and "Aliens": Locke's Problem of Political Consent, *Social Theory and Practice*, Vol. 24, No. 2 (Summer 1998).

基督教会学院（Christ Church），由约瑟夫·马洛德·威廉·特纳（Joseph Mallord William Turner）画于1795年。洛克于1652年（20岁）进入牛津大学最好的学院——基督教会学院。除了中途短暂离开一年外，洛克一直到1667年都在这里学习、教书、写作。

### § 95.

Men being, as has been said, by nature, all free, equal, and independent, no one can be put out of this estate, and subjected to the political power of another, without his own consent. The only way, whereby any one divests himself of his natural liberty, and puts on the bonds of civil society, is by agreeing with other men to join and unite into a community, for their comfortable, safe, and peaceable living one amongst another, in a secure enjoyment of their properties, and a greater security against any, that are not of it. This any number of men may do, because it injures not the freedom of the rest; they are left as they were in the liberty of the state of nature. When any number of men have so consented to make one community or government, they are thereby presently incorporated, and make one body politic, wherein the majority have a right to act and conclude the rest.

### § 96.

For when any number of men have, by the consent of every individual, made a community, they have thereby made that community one body, with a power to act as one body, which is only by the will and determination of the majority: for that which acts any community, being only the consent of the individuals of it, and it being necessary to that which is one body to move one way; it is necessary the body should move that way whither the greater force carries it, which is the consent of the majority: or else it is impossible it should act or continue one body, one community, which the consent of every individual that united into it, agreed that it should; and so every one is bound by that consent to be concluded by the majority. And therefore we see, that in assemblies, impowered to act by positive laws, where no number is set by that positive law which impowers them, the act of the majority passes for the act of the whole, and of course determines; as having, by the law of nature and reason, the power of the whole.

## § 97.

And thus every man, by consenting with others to make one body politic under one government, puts himself under an obligation, to every one of that society, to submit to the determination of the majority, and to be concluded by it; or else this original compact, whereby he with others incorporate into one society, would signify nothing, and be no compact, if he be left free, and under no other ties than he was in before in the state of nature. For what appearance would there be of any compact? what new engagement if he were no farther tied by any decrees of the society, than he himself thought fit, and did actually consent to? This would be still as great a liberty, as he himself had before his compact, or any one else in the state of nature hath, who may submit himself, and consent to any acts of it if he thinks fit.

## § 98.

For if the consent of the majority shall not, in reason, be received as the act of the whole, and conclude every individual; nothing but the consent of every individual can make any thing to be the act of the whole: but such a consent is next to impossible ever to be had, if we consider the infirmities of health, and avocations of business, which in a number, though much less than that of a commonwealth, will necessarily keep many away from the public assembly. To which if we add the variety of opinions, and contrariety of interest, which unavoidably happen in all collections of men, the coming into society upon such terms would be only like Cato's coming into the theatre, only to go out again.[1] Such a constitution as this would make the mighty leviathan of a shorter duration, than the feeblest creatures, and not let it outlast the day it was born in: which cannot be supposed, till we can think, that rational creatures should desire and constitute societies only to be dissolved; for where the majority cannot conclude the rest, there they cannot act as one body, and

---

[1] 加图（Cato）全名为马尔库斯·波尔基乌斯·加图（Marcus Porcius Cato，公元前234年—公元前149年），罗马共和国时期的政治家、国务活动家、演说家。公元前195年,加图当选为罗马执政官。洛克这里引用的是一则关于加图的逸闻。

consequently will be immediately dissolved again.

### § 99.

Whosoever therefore out of a state of nature unite into a community, must be understood to give up all the power, necessary to the ends for which they unite into society, to the majority of the community, unless they expressly agreed in any number greater than the majority. And this is done by barely agreeing to unite into one political society, which is all the compact that is, or needs be, between the individuals, that enter into, or make up a commonwealth. And thus that, which begins and actually constitutes any political society, is nothing, but the consent of any number of freemen capable of a majority, to unite and incorporate into such a society. And this is that, and that only, which did, or could give beginning to any lawful government in the world.

### § 100.

To this I find two objections made.

First, "That there are no instances to be found in story, of a company of men independent and equal one amongst another, that met together, and in this way began and set up a government."

Secondly, "It is impossible of right, that men should do so, because all men being born under government, they are to submit to that, and are not at liberty to begin a new one."

### § 101.

To the first there is this to answer. That it is not at all to be wondered, that history gives us but a very little account of men, that lived together in the state of nature. The inconveniencies of that condition, and the love and want of society, no sooner brought any number of them together, but they presently united and incorporated, if they designed to continue together. And if we may not suppose men ever to have been in the state of nature, because we hear not much of them in such a state; we may as well suppose the armies of Salmanasser[1] or Xerxes[2] were never children, because we hear little of them, till they were men, and embodied in armies. Government is every where antecedent to records, and letters seldom come in amongst a people till a long continuation of civil society has, by other more necessary arts, provided for their safety, ease, and plenty: and then they begin to look after the history of their founders, and search into their original, when they have outlived the memory of it: for it is with commonwealths, as with particular persons, they are commonly ignorant of their own births and infancies: and if they know any thing of their original, they are beholden for it to the accidental records that others have kept of it. And those that we have of the beginning of any politics in the world, excepting that of the Jews, where God himself immediately interposed, and which favours not at all paternal dominion, are all either plain instances of such a beginning as I have mentioned, or at least have manifest footsteps of it.

## § 102.

He must show a strange inclination to deny evident matter of fact, when it agrees not with his hypothesis, who will not allow, that the beginnings of Rome and Venice were by the uniting together of several men free and independent one of another, amongst whom there was no natural superiority or subjection. And if Josephus Acosta's[3] word may be taken, he tells us, that in many parts of America there was no government at all. "There are great and apparent conjectures, says he, that these men, speaking of those of Peru, for a long time

---

[1] 萨玛那塞（Salmanasser）是公元前9世纪的一位古代亚述国王。
[2] 薛西斯（Xerxes）是指波斯国王薛西斯一世（公元前519年—公元前465年）。
[3] 阿科斯塔（Acosta，1540—1600）是西班牙传教士、博物学家。1590年，阿科斯塔出版了《印第安人的自然与道德史》(*Historia natural y moral de las Indias*)一书。这是第一本深入介绍南美洲的地理与文化的书籍。洛克这里引用的是爱德华·格瑞斯通（Edward Grimestone）1604年出版的英译本：*The Naturall and Morall Historie of the Indies*。

had neither kings nor commonwealths, but lived in troops, as they do this day in Florida, the Cheriquanas, those of Brasil, and many other nations, which have no certain kings, but as occasion is offered, in peace or war, they choose their captains as they please," l. i. c. 25. If it be said, that every man there was born subject to his father, or the head of his family; that the subjection due from a child to a father took not away his freedom of uniting into what political society he thought fit, has been already proved. But be that as it will, these men, it is evident, were actually free; and whatever superiority some politicians now would place in any of them, they themselves claimed it not, but by consent were all equal, till by the same consent they set rulers over themselves. So that their politic societies all began from a voluntary union, and the mutual agreement of men freely acting in the choice of their governors, and forms of government.

## § 103.

And I hope those who went away from Sparta with Palantus[1], mentioned by Justin[2], l. iii. c. 4, will be allowed to have been freemen, independent one of another, and to have set up a government over themselves, by their own consent. Thus I have given several examples out of history, of people free and in the state of nature, that being met together, incorporated and began a commonwealth. And if the want of such instances be an argument to prove that governments were not, nor could not be so begun, I suppose the contenders for paternal empire were better let it alone,

---

[1] 法兰托斯（Palantus）是斯巴达人的领袖，他于公元前8世纪在意大利建立了塔兰托（Tarentum）。

[2] 查士丁（Justin）是古罗马史学家，其拉丁名为 Marcus Junianius (or Junianus) Justinus。古罗马历史学家特洛古斯（Gnaeus Pompeius Trogus，活动于公元前1世纪前后）记载了法兰托斯建立塔兰托的事迹，而查士丁的《庞培乌斯·特洛古斯〈菲利浦史〉摘要》（*Epitome of Pompeius Trogus' "Philippic Histories"*）一书是我们知道特洛古斯的这一记载的唯一渠道。

than urge it against natural liberty: for if they can give so many instances out of history, of governments begun upon paternal right, I think (though at best an argument from what has been, to what should of right be, has no great force) one might, without any great danger, yield them the cause. But if I might advise them in the case, they would do well not to search too much into the original of governments, as they have begun de facto; lest they should find, at the foundation of most of them, something very little favourable to the design they promote, and such a power as they contend for.

### § 104.

But to conclude, reason being plain on our side, that men are naturally free, and the examples of history showing, that the governments of the world, that were begun in peace, had their beginning laid on that foundation, and were made by the consent of the people; there can be little room for doubt, either where the right is, or what has been the opinion, or practice of mankind, about the first erecting of governments.

### § 105.

I will not deny, that if we look back as far as history will direct us, towards the original of commonwealths, we shall generally find them under the government and administration of one man. And I am also apt to believe, that where a family was numerous enough to subsist by itself, and continued entire together, without mixing with others, as it often happens, where there is much land, and few people, the government commonly began in the father; for the father having, by the law of nature, the same power with every man else to punish, as he thought fit, any offences against that law, might thereby punish his transgressing children, even when they were men, and out of their pupilage; and they were very likely to submit to his punishment, and all join with him against the offender, in their turns, giving him thereby power to execute his sentence against any transgression, and so in effect make him the law maker, and governour over all that remained in conjunction with his family. He was fittest to be trusted; paternal affection secured their property and interest under his care; and the custom of obeying him, in their childhood, made it easier to submit to him, rather than to any other. If, therefore, they must have one to rule them, as government is hardly to be avoided amongst men that live together; who so likely to be the man as he that was their common father; unless negligence, cruelty, or any other defect of mind or body made him unfit for it? But when either the father died, and left his next heir, for want of age, wisdom, courage, or any other qualities, less fit for rule; or where several families met, and consented to continue together; there, it is not to be doubted, but they used their natural freedom to set up him whom they judged the ablest, and most likely to rule well over them. Conformable hereunto we find the people of America, who (living out of the reach of the conquering swords, and spreading domination of the two great empires of Peru and Mexico) enjoyed their own natural freedom, though, cæteris paribus, they commonly prefer the heir of their deceased king; yet, if they find him any way weak, or incapable, they pass him by, and set up the stoutest and bravest man for their ruler.

### § 106.

Thus, though looking back as far as records give us any account of peopling the world, and the history of nations, we commonly find the government to be in one hand; yet it destroys not that which I affirm, viz. that the beginning of politic society depends upon the consent of the individuals, to join into, and make one society; who, when they are thus incorporated, might set up what form of government they thought fit. But this having given occasion to men to mistake, and think, that by nature government was monarchical, and belonged to the father; it may not be amiss here to consider, why people in the beginning generally pitched upon this form; which though perhaps the father's preeminency might, in the first institution of some commonwealth give rise to, and place in the beginning the power in one hand; yet it is plain that the reason, that continued the form of government in a single person, was not any regard or respect to paternal authority; since all petty monarchies, that is, almost all monarchies, near their original, have been commonly, at least upon occasion, elective.

### § 107.

First then, in the beginning of things, the father's government of the childhood of those sprung from him, having accustomed them to the rule of one man, and taught them that where it was exercised with care and skill, with affection and love to those under it, it was sufficient to procure and preserve to men all the political happiness they sought for in society. It was no wonder that they should pitch upon, and naturally run into that form of government, which from their infancy they had been all accustomed to; and which, by experience, they had found both easy and safe. To which, if we add, that monarchy being simple, and most obvious to men, whom neither experience had instructed in forms of government, nor the ambition or insolence of empire had taught to beware of the encroachments of prerogative, or the inconveniencies of absolute power, which monarchy in succession was apt to lay claim to, and bring upon them; it was not at all strange, that they should not much trouble themselves to think of methods of restraining any exorbitancies of those to whom they had given the authority over them, and of balancing the power of government, by placing several parts of it in different hands. They had neither felt the oppression of tyrannical dominion, nor did the fashion of the age, nor their possessions, or way of living (which afforded little matter for covetousness or ambition) give them any reason to apprehend or provide against it; and therefore it is no wonder they put themselves into such a frame of government, as was not only, as I said, most obvious and simple, but also best suited to their present state and condition; which stood more in need of defence against foreign invasions and injuries, than of multiplicity of laws. The equality of a simple poor way of living, confining their desires within the narrow bounds of each man's small property, made few controversies, and so no need of many laws to decide them, or variety of officers to superintend the process, or look after the execution of justice, where there were but few trespasses, and few offenders. Since then those, who liked one another so well as to join into society, cannot but be supposed to have some acquaintance and friendship together, and some trust one in another; they could not but have greater apprehensions of others, than of one another: and therefore their first care and thought cannot but be supposed to be, how to secure themselves against foreign force. It was natural for them to put themselves under a frame of government which might best serve to that end, and choose the wisest and bravest man to conduct them in their wars, and lead them out against their enemies, and in this chiefly be their ruler.

### § 108.

Thus we see, that the kings of the Indians in America, which is still a pattern of the first ages in Asia and Europe, whilst the inhabitants were too few for the country, and want of people and money gave men no temptation to enlarge their possessions of land, or contest for wider extent of ground, are little more than generals of their armies; and though they command absolutely in war, yet at home and in time of peace they exercise very little dominion, and have but a very moderate sovereignty; the resolutions of peace and war being ordinarily either in the people, or in a council. Though the war itself, which admits not of plurality of governors, naturally devolves the command into the king's sole authority.

## § 109.

And thus, in Israel itself, the chief business of their judges, and first kings, seems to have been to be captains in war, and leaders of their armies; which (besides what is signified by "going out and in before the people," which was to march forth to war, and home again at the heads of their forces) appears plainly in the story of Jephthah. The Ammonites making war upon Israel, the Gileadites in fear sent to Jephthah, a bastard of their family whom they had cast off, and article with him, if he will assist them against the Ammonites, to make him their ruler; which they do in these words, "And the people made him head and captain over them," Judg. xi. 11, which was, as it seems, all one as to be judge. "And he judged Israel," Judg. xii. 7, that is, was their captain-general, "six years." So when Jotham upbraids the Shechemites with the obligation they had to Gideon, who had been their judge and ruler, he tells them, "He fought for you, and adventured his life far, and delivered you out of the hands of Midian," Judg. ix. 17. Nothing is mentioned of him, but what he did as a general: and indeed that is all is found in his history, or in any of the rest of the judges. And Abimelech particularly is called king, though at most he was but their general.[1] And when, being

---

[1] 根据《圣经》的记载，基甸（Gideon）是一位士师，他帮助以色列人打败了米甸人。基甸娶的一个妾住在示剑（Shechem），她给基甸生了一个儿子，名为亚比米勒（Abimelech）。后来，亚比米勒杀死了基甸的其他69个儿子，只剩下小儿子约旦（Jotham）。示剑人随后立亚比米勒为王。约旦得知此事后，向示剑人述说他们的不义。洛克所引的就是约旦的话的一部分。

weary of the ill conduct of Samuel's sons, the children of Israel desired a king, "like all the nations, to judge them, and to go out before them, and to fight their battles," 1 Sam. viii. 20. God granting their desire, says to Samuel, "I will send thee a man, and thou shalt anoint him to be captain over my people Israel, that he may save my people out of the hands of the Philistines," ix. 16. As if the only business of a king had been to lead out their armies, and fight in their defence; and accordingly Samuel, at his inauguration, pouring a vial of oil upon him, declares to Saul, that "the Lord had anointed him to be captain over his inheritance," x. 1. And therefore those who, after Saul's being solemnly chosen and saluted king by the tribes of Mispeh, were unwilling to have him their king, made no other objection but this, "How shall this man save us?" v. 27; as if they should have said, this man is unfit to be our king, not having skill and conduct enough in war to be able to defend us. And when God resolved to transfer the government to David, it is in these words, "But now thy kingdom shall not continue: the Lord hath sought him a man after his own heart, and the Lord hath commanded him to be captain over his people," xiii. 14. As if the whole kingly authority were nothing else but to be their general: and therefore the tribes who had stuck to Saul's family, and opposed David's reign, when they came to Hebron with terms of submission to them, they tell him, amongst other arguments, they had to submit to him as their king, that he was in effect their king in Saul's time, and therefore they had no reason but to receive him as their king now. "Also (say they,) in time past, when Saul was king over us, thou wast he that leddest out, and broughtest in Israel, and the Lord said unto thee, Thou shalt feed my people Israel, and thou shalt be a captain over

Israel."[1]

## § 110.

Thus, whether a family by degrees grew up into a commonwealth, and the fatherly authority being continue on to the elder son, every one in his turn growing up under it, tacitly submitted to it; and the easiness and equality of it not offending any one, every one acquiesced, till time seemed to have confirmed it, and settled a right of succession by prescription: or whether several families, or the descendants of several families, whom chance, neighbourhood, or business brought together, uniting into society: the need of a general, whose conduct might defend them against their enemies in war, and the great confidence the innocence and sincerity of that poor but virtuous age (such as are almost all those which begin governments, that ever come to last in the world), gave men of one another, made the first beginners of commonwealths generally put the rule into one man's hand, without any other express limitation or restraint, but what the nature of the thing and the end of government required: Whichever of those it was that at first put the rule into the hands of a single person, certain it is that nobody was entrusted with it but for the public good and safety, and to those ends, in the infancies of commonwealths, those who had it, commonly used it. And unless they had done so, young societies could not have subsisted;

---

[1] 洛克在本段的后半部分引用了《旧约·撒母耳记上》与《旧约·撒母耳记下》。撒母耳（Samuel）是以色列人的最后一位士师。当时，以色列人请求撒母耳为他们立王。随后，扫罗（Saul）受膏于撒母耳成为以色列第一位国王。再后来，由于扫罗做了许多违背上帝命令的事情，因此上帝就另外又挑选了一个国王人选，即大卫（David）。大卫起初在宫中为扫罗弹琴，后在与非利士人的战役中杀死挑战者歌利亚而受到人们的颂扬。此后，扫罗开始嫉妒大卫，并多次试图置其于死地，但都没有成功。即使大卫最终逃到荒野中，扫罗也没有停止对他的追杀。后来，扫罗在对非利士人的战役中战败并自尽。之后，大卫重返犹大，来到希伯仑并在那里受膏成为犹大王，而扫罗的儿子伊施波设成为以色列王。最终，大卫在与伊施波设的征战中获得胜利，最终成为统一的以色列王国的国王，定都耶路撒冷。

without such nursing fathers tender and careful of the public weal, all governments would have sunk under the weakness and infirmities of their infancy, and the prince and the people had soon perished together.

### § 111.

But though the golden age (before vain ambition, and "amor sceleratus habendi,"[1] evil concupiscence, had corrupted men's minds into a mistake of true power and honour) had more virtue, and consequently better governors, as well as less vicious subjects; and there was then no stretching prerogative on the one side, to oppress the people; nor consequently on the other, any dispute about privilege, to lessen or restrain the power of the magistrate;* and so no contest betwixt rulers and people about governors or government: yet when ambition and luxury in future ages would retain and increase the power, without doing the business for which it was given; and, aided by flattery, taught princes to have distinct and separate interests from their people; men found it necessary to examine more carefully the original and rights of government, and to find out ways to restrain the exorbitancies, and prevent the abuses of that power, which they having entrusted in another's hands only for their own good, they found was made use of to hurt them.

---

[1] 洛克附加的这个拉丁文也是"名誉，荣誉"的意思，出自古罗马诗人奥维德（Ovidius，Publius Naso；公元前 43 年 3 月 20 日—公元 18 年）的《变形记》（*Metamorphoseon libri*）第 1 卷第 131 行。

\* "At first, when some certain kind of regiment was once approved, it may be nothing was then farther thought upon for the manner of governing, but all permitted unto their wisdom and discretion, which were to rule, till by experience they found this for all parts very inconvenient, so as the thing which they had devised for a remedy, did indeed but increase the sore which it should have cured. They saw, that to live by one man's will, became the cause of all men's misery. This constrained them to come unto laws wherein all men might see their duty before-hand, and know the penalties of transgressing them." Hooker's Eccl. Pol. l. i. sect. 10.

## § 112.

Thus we may see how probable it is, that people that were naturally free, and by their own consent either submitted to the government of their father, or united together out of different families to make a government, should generally put the rule into one man's hands, and choose to be under the conduct of a single person, without so much as by express conditions limiting or regulating his power, which they thought safe enough in his honesty and prudence: though they never dreamed of monarchy being jure divino[1], which we never heard of among mankind, till it was revealed to us by the divinity of this last age; nor ever allowed paternal power to have a right to dominion, or to be the foundation of all government. And thus much may suffice to show, that, as far as we have any light from history, we have reason to conclude, that all peaceful beginnings of government have been laid in the consent of the people. I say peaceful, because I shall have occasion in another place to speak of conquest, which some esteem a way of beginning of governments.

The other objection I find urged against the beginning of polities, in the way I have mentioned, is this, viz.

## § 113.

"That all men being born under government, some or other, it is impossible any of them should ever be free, and at liberty to unite together, and begin a new one, or ever be able to erect a lawful government."

If this argument be good, I ask, how came so many lawful monarchies into the world? for if any body, upon this supposition, can show me any one man in any age of the world free to begin a lawful monarchy, I will be bound to show him ten other free men at liberty at the same time to unite and begin a new government

---

[1] jure divino 翻译为英文为 right of divine，即"神授法权"。

under a regal or any other form; it being demonstration, that if any one, born under the dominion of another, may be so free as to have a right to command others in a new and distinct empire, every one that is born under the dominion of another may be so free too, and may become a ruler, or subject of a distinct separate government. And so by this their own principle, either all men, however born, are free, or else there is but one lawful prince, one lawful government in the world. And then they have nothing to do, but barely to show us which that is; which when they have done, I doubt not but all mankind will easily agree to pay obedience to him.

### § 114.

Though it be a sufficient answer to their objection, to show that it involves them in the same difficulties that it doth those they use it against; yet I shall endeavour to discover the weakness of this argument a little farther.

"All men, say they, are born under government, and therefore they cannot be at liberty to begin a new one. Every one is born a subject to his father, or his prince, and is therefore under the perpetual tie of subjection and allegiance." It is plain mankind never owned nor considered any such natural subjection that they were born in, to one or to the other, that tied them, without their own consents, to a subjection to them and their heirs.

### § 115.

For there are no examples so frequent in history, both sacred and profane, as those of men withdrawing themselves, and their obedience from the jurisdiction they were born under, and the family or community they were bred up in, and setting up new governments in other places, from whence sprang all that number of petty commonwealths in the beginning of ages, and which always multiplied as long as there was room enough, till the stronger, or more fortunate, swallowed the weaker; and those great ones again breaking to pieces, dissolved into lesser dominions. All which are so many testimonies against paternal sovereignty, and plainly prove, that it was not the natural right of the father descending to his heirs, that made governments in the beginning, since it was impossible, upon that ground, there should have been so many little kingdoms; all must have been but only one universal monarchy, if men had not been at liberty to separate themselves from their families, and the government, be it what it will, that was set up in it, and go and make distinct commonwealths and other governments, as they thought fit.

## § 116.

This has been the practice of the world from its first beginning to this day; nor is it now any more hindrance to the freedom of mankind, that they are born under constituted and ancient polities, that have established laws, and set forms of government, than if they were born in the woods, amongst the unconfined inhabitants, that run loose in them: for those who would persuade us that, "by being born under any government, we are naturally subjects to it," and have no more any title or pretence to the freedom of the state of nature; have no other reason (bating that of paternal power, which we have already answered) to produce for it, but only, because our fathers of progenitors passed away their natural liberty, and thereby bound up themselves and their posterity to a perpetual subjection to the government which they themselves submitted to. It is true, that whatever engagement or promises any one has made for himself, he is under the obligation of them, but cannot, by any compact whatsoever, bind his children or posterity: for his son, when a man, being altogether as free as the father, any "act of the father can no more give away the liberty of the son," than it can of any body else: he may indeed annex such conditions to the land he enjoyed as a subject of any commonwealth, as may oblige his son to be of that community, if he will enjoy those possessions which were his father's; because that estate being his father's property, he may dispose, or settle it, as he pleases.

## § 117.

And this has generally given the occasion to mistake in this matter; because commonwealths not permitting any part of their dominions to be dismembered, nor to be enjoyed by any but those of their community, the son cannot ordinarily enjoy the possessions of his father, but under the same terms his father did, by becoming a member of the society; whereby he puts himself presently under the government he finds there established, as much as any other subject of that commonwealth. And thus "the consent of freemen, born under government, which only makes them members of it," being given separately in their turns, as each comes to be of age, and not in a multitude together; people take no notice of it, and thinking it not done at all, or not necessary, conclude they are naturally subjects as they are men.

## § 118.

But, it is plain, governments themselves understand it otherwise; they claim "no power over the son, because of that they had over the father;" nor look on children as being their subjects, by their fathers being so. If a subject of England have a child, by an English woman in France, whose subject is he? Not the king of England's; for he must have leave to be admitted to the privileges of it; nor the king of France's; for how then has his father a liberty to bring him away, and breed him as he pleases? and who ever was judged as a traitor or deserter, if he left, or warred against a country, for being barely born in it of parents that were aliens there? It is plain then, by the practice of governments themselves, as well as by the law of right reason, that "a child is born a subject of no country or government." He is under his father's tuition and authority, till he comes to age of discretion; and then he is a freeman, at liberty what government he will put himself under, what body politic he will unite himself to: for if an Englishman's son, born in France, be at liberty, and may do so, it is evident there is no tie upon him by his father's being a subject of this kingdom; nor is he bound up by any compact of his ancestors. And why then hath not his son, by the same reason, the same liberty, though he be born any where else? Since the power that a father hath naturally over his children is the same, wherever they be born, and the ties of natural obligations are not bounded by the positive limits of kingdoms and commonwealths.

### § 119.

Every man being, as has been showed, naturally free, and nothing being able to put him into subjection to any earthly power, but only his own consent; it is to be considered, what shall be understood to be a sufficient declaration of a man's consent, to make him subject to the laws of any government. There is a common distinction of an express and a tacit consent, which will concern our present case. Nobody doubts but an express consent, of any man entering into any society, makes him a perfect member of that society, a subject of that government. The difficulty is, what ought to be looked upon as a tacit consent, and how far it binds, i. e. how far any one shall be looked upon to have consented, and thereby submitted to any government, where he has made no expressions of it at all. And to this I say, that every man, that hath any possessions, or enjoyment of any part of the dominions of any government, doth thereby give his tacit consent, and is as far forth obliged to obedience to the laws of that government, during such enjoyment, as any one under it; whether this his possession be of land, to him and his heirs for ever, or a lodging only for a week; or whether it be barely travelling freely on the highway: and, in effect, it reaches as far as the very being of any one within the territories of that government.

## § 120.

To understand this the better, it is fit to consider, that every man, when he at first incorporates himself into any commonwealth, he, by his uniting himself thereunto, annexes also, and submits to the community, those possessions which he has, or shall acquire, that do not already belong to any other government: for it would be a direct contradiction, for any one to enter into society with others for the securing and regulating of property, and yet to suppose, his land, whose property is to be regulated by the laws of the society, should be exempt from the jurisdiction of that government, to which he himself, the proprietor of the land, is a subject. By the same act therefore, whereby any one unites his person, which was before free, to any commonwealth; by the same he unites his possessions, which were before free, to it also: and they become, both of them, person and possession, subject to the government and dominion of that commonwealth, as long as it hath a being. Whoever therefore, from thenceforth, by inheritance, purchase, permission, or otherways, enjoys any part of the land so annexed to, and under the government of that commonwealth, must take it with the condition it is under; that is, of submitting to the government of the commonwealth, under whose jurisdiction it is, as far forth as any subject of it.

## § 121.

But since the government has a direct jurisdiction only over the land, and reaches the possessor of it, (before he has actually incorporated himself in the society) only as he dwells upon, and enjoys that; the obligation any one is under, by virtue of such enjoyment, to "submit to the government, begins and ends with the enjoyment;" so that whenever the owner, who has given nothing but such a tacit consent to the government, will, by donation, sale, or otherwise, quit the said possession, he is at liberty to go and incorporate himself into any other commonwealth; or to agree with others to begin a new one, in vacuis locis, in any part of the world they can find free and unpossessed: whereas he, that has once, by actual agreement, and any express declaration, given his consent to be of any commonwealth, is perpetually and indispensably obliged to be, and remain unalterably a subject to it, and can never be again in the liberty of the state of nature; unless, by any calamity, the government he was under comes to be dissolved, or else by some public act cuts him off from being any longer a member of it.

## § 122.

But submitting to the laws of any country, living quietly, and enjoying privileges and protection under them, makes not a man a member of that society: this is only a local protection and homage due to and from all those, who, not being in a state of war, come within the territories belonging to any government, to all parts whereof the force of its laws extends. But this no more makes a man a member of that society, a perpetual subject of that commonwealth, than it would make a man a subject to another, in whose family he found it convenient to abide for some time, though, whilst he continued in it, he were obliged to comply with the laws, and submit to the government he found there. And thus we see, that foreigners, by living all their lives under another government, and enjoying the privileges and protection of it, though they are bound, even in conscience, to submit to its administration, as far forth as any denison; yet do not thereby come to be subjects or members of that commonwealth. Nothing can make any man so, but his actually entering into it by positive engagement, and express promise and compact. This is that, which I think, concerning the beginning of political societies, and that consent which makes any one a member of any commonwealth.

## Chapter IX

## *Of the Ends of Political Society and Government*

导 读

任何社会形态都具有特定的目的。例如，夫妻社会的目的是相互扶助、生儿育女；教会的目的是组织宗教活动，获得上帝的恩宠与救赎。那么，政治社会的目的是什么呢？我们如何来了解这一目的呢？首先，我们可以通过了解政治社会的必要性来了解其目的。如果我们明确了人类为什么要建立政治社会，我们就知道了人类建立政治社会是为了实现什么目的。其次，我们可以通过了解政治社会的构成方式来了解其目的。如果我们了解了政治社会的权力的来源，我们就知道了这种权力指向何处。这就是洛克在第九章中想要说明的问题。

政治社会是人类政治生活的形态。政治社会的目的取决于政治生活的目的。人类应当过怎样一种政治生活？在这个问题上，存在着一个古今之变。古代的思想家认为，政治生活是要追求卓越，包括人的卓越与共同体的卓越。通过政治生活，人会变得越来越完善，共同体变得越来越完美。政治生活是一种追求善的生活。现代思想家认为这种学说是不现实的，它为政治生活设定了过高的目的。一方面，这种理想型的共同体最多只能在一个很小的城邦中实现，而且它的实现还取决于许多偶然的因素（例如统治者的品格等）；另一方面，这种将某种道德

价值与政治目的关联的做法在现代世界已经无法实现了，因为并不存在一种单一的、普遍的价值目标。因此，现代思想家下降了政治生活的目的。下降并不是取消，而是为了寻找一个相对较低的但具有普遍性的价值目标。问题在于，究竟下降到什么程度，或者说究竟落在哪一种价值追求上。如果政治生活的目的是相安无事，那么这个价值目标就是和平。这是霍布斯的观点。他的逻辑是比较简单的，也是比较有力的。这个逻辑是：自然状态是战争状态，人们必须彻底摆脱这种状态才能在一种稳定的秩序中共同生活，所以人们需要一种绝对的公共权力来支配所有人，管理所有事务。只有每个人让渡自己所有的权利与权力，才能缔造出绝对的权力与绝对的秩序，人类才能过一种和平的政治生活。为了摆脱这个逻辑，洛克之前已经做出一些理论努力，例如重新定义自然状态、说明财产权等。在本章中，洛克又接着做了两件事。

一件事是将政治社会对自然状态的补救（即政治社会的必要性）解释为一种对自然秩序的改进而非对自然秩序的替换。霍布斯的逻辑的一个有力之处在于，它可以很好地解释政治的必要性（为什么一定要建立国家与政府），即克服战争状态。洛克并不认为自然状态是战争状态，这样的话，解释政治的必要性就成为一个难题。

在本章的前四段中，洛克指出了自然状态的三个不便之处。我们要注意，在洛克的分析中，自然状态本身并不具有内在的问题。也就是说，这种秩序并不是一个不具有正当性的秩序，并不是一个需要加以彻底摆脱的秩序，而仅仅是一个不稳定的秩序。它的问题仅仅在于，缺乏公共的律法以及共同的裁判者。所以，政治生活并不是对自然生活的彻底改造，政治规范并不是对自然规范的彻底转化，而仅仅是为它加上一个安全阀。

这个安全阀就是政治权威与政治权力。如何解释政治权威与政治权力的本质就是洛克要做的第二件事。洛克将自然状态到政治社会的契约过程拆分为两个不同的部分，并使得每个部分都与自然法保持关联。这两个部分是对两种权力的契约化。一是将保存自己与他人的权力交给政治社会。这个权力其实就是保护每个人的权利（财产）的权力。这构成了政治社会对所有人的权利通过普遍立法加以规范的正当性基础，也就是政治权威的基础。洛克将其称为"社会的立法权"。另一部分是将自然法的惩罚权交给政治社会。由于自然法的惩罚权并不是纯粹的暴力，而是维护人的权利而实施的暴力，所以它所构成的权力也不是纯粹的暴力，而是一种司法性质的暴力。它的目的是为了维护政治社会所制定的法律。了解这个契约理论的内涵是本章的重心。当然，我们还可以追问一个问题：我们是否必须将政治社会的目的降低到这么低的层面？我们是否必须将政治权力的内涵稀释到如此稀薄的程度？我们这里所说的从古到今的转变是否是现代人的必然选择呢？

### 延伸阅读材料：

1. 比较洛克与柏拉图、亚里士多德对政治共同体的目的的分析：[古希腊]柏拉图：《理想国》，郭斌和、张竹明译，北京，商务印书馆，1986；[古希腊]亚里士多德：《政治学》，吴寿彭译，北京，商务印书馆，2007。

2. 关于政治的目的上的"古今之变"参见：[美]列奥·施特劳斯：《自然权利与历史》，彭刚译，北京，生活·读书·新知三联书店，2006。

3. 比较洛克与霍布斯对政治共同体的目的以及契约论的具体内容的分析：[英]霍布斯：《利维坦》，黎思复、黎廷弼译，杨昌裕校，北京，商务印书馆，2007，第十四章至第十七章。

4. 对洛克的"政治社会"与"政治权力"概念的研究：

——John Dunn, The Contemporary Political Significance of John Locke's Conception of Civil Society, Iyyun (Jerusalem Philosophical Quarterly), 45, July 1996, pp. 103–124, reprinted in Sudipta Kaviraj and Sunil Khilnani (eds), *Civil Society: History and Possibilities*, CUP, 2001, pp. 39–57.

——Ruth W. Grant, *John Locke's Liberalism*, The University of Chicago Press, 1987, pp. 72–83.

——王涛：《洛克的政治社会概念与自然法学说》，载《清华法学》，2011年第6期。

5. 参考第七章与第八章的"延伸阅读材料4"。

## § 123.

If man in the state of nature be so free, as has been said; if he be absolute lord of his own person and possessions, equal to the greatest, and subject to nobody, why will he part with his freedom? why will he give up his empire, and subject himself to the dominion and control of any other power? To which it is obvious to answer, that though in the state of nature he hath such a right, yet the enjoyment of it is very uncertain, and constantly exposed to the invasion of others; for all being kings as much as he, every man his equal, and the greater part no strict observers of equity and justice, the enjoyment of the property he has in this state is very unsafe, very unsecure. This makes him willing to quit a condition, which, however free, is full of fears and continual dangers: and it is not without reason, that he seeks out, and is willing to join in society with others, who are already united, or have a mind to unite, for the mutual preservation of their lives, liberties, and estates, which I call by the general name, property.

## § 124.

The great and chief end, therefore, of men's uniting into commonwealths, and putting themselves under government, is the preservation of their property. To which in the state of nature there are many things wanting.

First, there wants an established, settled, known law, received and allowed by common consent to be the standard of right and wrong, and the common measure to decide all controversies between them: for though the law of nature be plain and intelligible to all rational creatures; yet men being biassed by their interest, as well as ignorant for want of studying it, are not apt to allow of it as a law binding to them in the application of it to their particular cases.

## § 125.

Secondly, in the state of nature there wants a known and indifferent judge, with authority to determine all differences according to the established law: for every one in that state being both judge and executioner of the law of nature, men being partial to themselves, passion and revenge is very apt to carry them too far, and with too much heat, in their own cases; as well as negligence, and unconcernedness, to make them too remiss in other men's.

## § 126.

Thirdly, in the state of nature, there often wants power to back and support the sentence when right, and to give it due execution. They who by any injustice offend, will seldom fail, where they are able, by force to make good their injustice; such resistance many times makes the punishment dangerous, and frequently destructive, to those who attempt it.

## § 127.

Thus mankind, notwithstanding all the privileges of the state of nature, being but in an ill condition, while they remain in it, are quickly driven into society. Hence it comes to pass that we seldom find any number of men live any time together in this state. The inconveniencies that they are therein exposed to, by the irregular and uncertain exercise of the power every man has of punishing the transgressions of others, make them take sanctuary under the established laws of government, and therein seek the preservation of their property. It is this makes them so willingly give up every one his single power of punishing, to be exercised by such alone, as shall be appointed to it amongst them; and by such rules as the community, or those authorized by them to that purpose, shall agree on. And in this we have the original right of both the legislative and executive power, as well as of the governments and societies themselves.

## § 128.

For in the state of nature, to omit the liberty he has of innocent delights, a man has two powers.

The first is to do whatsoever he thinks fit for the preservation of himself and others within the permission of the law of nature: by which law, common to them all, he and all the rest of mankind are one community, make up one society, distinct from all other creatures. And, were it not for the corruption and viciousness of degenerate men, there would be no need of any other; no necessity that men should separate from this great and natural community, and by positive agreements combine into smaller and divided associations.

The other power a man has in the state of nature, is the power to punish the crimes committed against that law. Both these he gives up, when he joins in a private, if I may so call it, or particular politic society, and incorporates into any commonwealth, separate from the rest of mankind.

## § 129.

The first power, viz. "of doing whatsoever he thought fit for the preservation of himself," and the rest of mankind, he gives up to be regulated by laws made by the society, so far forth as the preservation of himself and the rest of that society shall require; which laws of the society in many things confine the liberty he had by the law of nature.

## § 130.

Secondly, the power of punishing he wholly gives up, and engages his natural force, (which he might before employ in the execution of the law of nature, by his own single authority, as he thought fit) to assist the executive power of the society, as the law thereof shall require: for being now in a new state, wherein he is to enjoy many conveniencies, from the labour, assistance, and society of others in the same community, as well as protection from its whole strength; he is to part also, with as much of his natural liberty, in providing for himself, as the good, prosperity, and safety of the society shall require; which is not only necessary, but just, since the other members of the society do the like.

## § 131.

But though men, when they enter into society, give up the equality, liberty, and executive power they had in the state of nature, into the hands of the society, to be so far disposed of by the legislative, as the good of the society shall require; yet it being only with an intention in every one the better to preserve himself, his liberty and property; (for no rational creature can be supposed to change his condition with an intention to be worse) the power of the society, or legislative constituted by them, can never be supposed to extend farther, than the common good; but is obliged to secure every one's property, by providing against those three defects above mentioned, that made the state of nature so unsafe and uneasy. And so whoever has the legislative or supreme power of any commonwealth, is bound to govern by established standing laws, promulgated and known to the people, and not by extemporary decrees; by indifferent and upright judges, who are to decide controversies by those laws; and to employ the force of the community at home, only in the execution of such laws; or abroad to prevent or redress foreign injuries, and secure the community from inroads and invasion. And all this to be directed to no other end, but the peace, safety, and public good of the people.

# Chapter X
# *Of the Forms of a Commonwealth*

## 导 读

　　从政治学诞生之日起，政体问题就是其中的一个核心问题。洛克所讲的国家形式其实就是政体。政体指的是统治方式或者说政治权力的组织形式。简单地讲，就是由谁来通过什么方式为共同体做出最高决定。最常见的区分政体的方式是按照掌握权力的人数来进行划分。如果由一个人来做出决定，就是君主政体；如果由所有人来做出决定，就是民主政体；如果由少部分具有特定品质的人来做出决定就是贵族制。结合这三种方式来做出决定就是混合政体。

　　洛克将国家形式分为民主制、君主制（世袭的与选任的）、寡头制与混合制四种。洛克的划分与传统的划分是否完全相同呢？洛克倾向于哪种政体呢？当时的英国似乎并不属于前三种，那么洛克是倾向于混合制吗？要回答这个问题，我们需要对政体学说在17世纪（特别是17世纪的英国）的发展有所了解。

　　在古典时代，亚里士多德、西塞罗、波利比乌斯（Polybius, 200 BC—118 BC）等人都倾向于某种混合政体。到了中世纪，普遍盛行的政体则是君主制。到了近代早期，传统的混合政体学说得到了复兴，特别是在意大利的自治城市共和国（如威尼斯）。虽然混合政体学说有复兴的势头，但是在17世纪的欧洲

大陆，君主制却日趋繁荣。君主日益摆脱教皇与教会的控制，成为国家大部分事务的最高决定者。这一过程的产物就是绝对君主制（特别是在法国）。绝对君主制独尊王权，反对任何机构享有与君主平起平坐的地位，因此与混合政体相对立。

英国的情况则与此不同，英国是混合政体学说在17世纪发展的中心地。通过之前几个世纪的努力，英国的议会在国家政治舞台上已牢牢占据了与国王相抗衡的地位。议会对于立法、征税等重大国家事务都有发言权。"王在巴列门中"（King in Parliament）是英国独特宪制的核心。国王与上议院、下议院的相互合作是三者行使权力的唯一方式。虽然国王仍被认为是国家的唯一象征与统治者，但是国王必须通过议会来行使他的统治权。英国的这一宪政架构由来已久，但这并没有妨碍人们认为英国是君主制国家，但思想家们觉得仅仅用"君主制"这个概念已无法准确形容英国的政体，所以他们开始用"混合君主制"来形容英国的政体，将国王、下议院、上议院对应着政体的君主因素、民主因素与贵族因素（君主因素占主导），分别代表着不同的利益群体、不同的智慧与不同的作用。在15世纪到17世纪，这种混合政体学说在英国获得了极大的发展。1642年，查理一世在回应议会的《对国会十九条陈的回复》中就主动放弃了独尊王权的君权神授学说，采纳了混合政体学说。

但此后的英国内战书写了一段独特的英国史，也改变了英国人对政体的认知。人们目睹了国王（查理一世）被杀头，国家在没有国王与上议院的情况下由下议院与护国公克伦威尔来运行（1649年至1660年的共和政体），而独享大权的下议院却也不时成为专断的权力机构，并最终昙花一现。这一系列的政治变动使得混合政体学说丧失了生命力与解释力，因为它无法解释君主怎么可以被判死刑，无法解释上议院怎么可以被取消等一系列问题，更无法说明英国今后的政体应该如何建立。为了稳定大局，人们又夹道欢迎查理二世的归来，欢迎君主制的复辟以及上议院的恢复。权宜之计并非长久之计，道路通向何处呢？实施纯粹的君主制与纯粹的议会制显然都会导致暴政。必须找到一个起点来重新阐述政治权力的基本原理，并在此原理上来重新解释一种能够维护自由的政体。

这个新的起点是以民主（混合政体的一个要素）为基础的法律至上观，或者更准确地说是以民主为基础的"立法权"至上观。传统上，国王的一个主要职责是主持正义，即执行各种法律，维持王国的正义。这里的法律包括本朝的法律，还包括前朝的法律甚至更古老的法律、古老的习惯与风俗、宗教（包括教皇与罗马教会）的规范等。政治权力作为一个整体本质上是一种"司法权"，即适用各种各样的法律的权力。后来，随着王权的增强，王权越来越体现为直接的立法权，包括制定法律、适用法律、废止法律、改变法律、进行豁免与赦免的权力。这种"广义的立法权"日益成为政治权力的本质，而这里的"法"被认为是某一俗世主体发出的命令（而非传统、理性等其他东西）。这代表着对政治权力的本质以及对法律本质的重新理解。在此基础上，英国议会与国王为争夺此"广义立法权"展开了激烈的斗争。

人们发现，如果将"广义的立法权"完全赋予国王或议会，都会带来暴政。那该怎么办呢？我们可以舍弃"广义的立法权"这个高度抽象的概念，将其进行拆解，将其中不同性质的权力赋予不同的国家机构，这就是混合政体。但是这样的制度架构在英国内战中已经崩塌了。另一种思路是将"广义的立法权"放在人民身上，用人民的共同福利与共同利益来为"广义的立法权"奠定民主性的基础(这一思路符合当时的民主浪潮）。然后，再将"广义的立法权"划分为几大主要权力，分别赋予不同的国家机构，某一机构严格对应于某一职能。

在此方向上迈出实质性一步的第一位英国思想家就是洛克。洛克回答了以下这些问题："广义的立法权"从何而来？人民是如何形成的？如何将"广义的立法权"放在人民身上？在前几章中，洛克用社会契约论说明了所有个体如何形成一个政治社会（即"人民"），同时还说明了政治社会如何获得立法的权力。政治社会是一个具有对所有人进行普遍立法的抽象实体，洛克将它的立法产物称之为"社会的法律"。这个"社会的立法权"就是我们上面所说的"广义的立法权"，它基于每个人的自然权

利,是一个具有民主色彩的政治权力概念。"社会的立法权"的归属就决定了政体。

依据古典的混合政体学说,各个阶层的人通过不同的机构,以不同方式参与所有事务的决定。混合君主制借用了这个思路,试图以君主为主,将君主制、贵族制、民主制的要素相结合,从而防止某一要素握有独断的权力。分权学说与混合政体的目的是相同的,但困难在于君主制、贵族制、民主制并不对应于行政权、司法权与立法权。洛克的新学说摆脱了这个旧的思路,从"社会的立法权"的角度重新说明了政治权力的统一属性,并以此为基础界定了不同的政府权力与不同的政府机构。它将混合政体中的"民主"这一个要素作为基础,摧毁了混合政体以及其背后的阶层划分做法。表面上看,洛克是依据人数来划分政体的,但是这个划分的基础却是一种新的"立法权"概念。

洛克的这一学说基于对英国独特的政治传统与政治现实的反思,但其实在理论上还是存在另一种现代思想道路。例如霍布斯提出的绝对主权学说就用绝对主权概念回避了法律至上与民主。霍布斯之所以认为君主制是最好的(如果不是唯一的)的政体是基于以下这一逻辑:国家的本质在于一种绝对主权,主权是一种人格化的意志型权力,而若要保证这一拟制的意志权力落实到现实中仍保持高度的统一性,那么最好由一个人来代表这一意志,所以主权最好是落实在一个人身上。国王、主权、国家的关系类似于法人代表、公司最高决策权、公司的关系。霍布斯极力反对混合政体与分权制度,因为他认为这将会消解掉主权,导致国家的分裂与混乱。绝对主权思想在现实中其实从没有得到完全的实现,因为君主独享一切政治权力在现实中很难实现(在英国就尤为明显了)。但是,若要反驳绝对主权学说,就必须从理论上反驳主权的不可分割。洛克的学说之所以可以避开霍布斯的逻辑,是因为他的国家学说不是意志论,而是一种理性论。洛克认为,国家的实质是自然法为基础的"立法权",而不是共同意志为基础的主权。立法权具有形式上与内容上的特定内容,所以它不是一种可以人格化的权力。统一的意志是不可分割的,统一的理性却是可以通过某种分权的方式来实现。

**延伸阅读材料：**

1. 亚里士多德的政体学说：[古希腊]亚里士多德:《政治学》，吴寿彭译，第五卷，北京，商务印书馆，2007。

2. 西塞罗的政体学说：[古罗马]西塞罗:《国家篇·法律篇》，苏力、沈叔平译，北京，商务印书馆，1999。

3. 波利比乌斯的政体学说：F. W. Walbank, *A Historical Commentary on Polybius*, Clarendon Press, 1957.

4. 霍布斯的绝对主权学说：[英]霍布斯:《利维坦》，黎思复、黎廷弼译，杨昌裕校，北京，商务印书馆，1997。

5. 孟德斯鸠的政体学说：[法]孟德斯鸠:《论法的精神》，许明龙译，上卷第一编第二章至第八章，北京，商务印书馆，2009。

6. M. J. C. Vile, *Constitutionalism and the Separation of Powers*, Liberty Fund, 2 edition (March 1, 1998). 特别是其中的第二章与第三章对17世纪英国政体思想的分析。

洛克的一幅著名的肖像，由戈弗雷·内勒（Godfrey Kneller）画于 1698 年。

## § 132.

The majority having, as has been showed, upon men's first uniting into society, the whole power of the community naturally in them, may employ all that power in making laws for the community from time to time, and executing those laws by officers of their own appointing; and then the form of the government is a perfect democracy: or else may put the power of making laws into the hands of a few select men, and their heirs or successors; and then it is an oligarchy: or else into the hands of one man, and then it is a monarchy: if to him and his heirs, it is an hereditary monarchy: if to him only for life, but upon his death the power only of nominating a successor to return to them; an elective monarchy. And so accordingly of these the community may make compounded and mixed forms of government, as they think good. And if the legislative power be at first given by the majority to one or more persons only for their lives, or any limited time, and then the supreme power to revert to them again; when it is so reverted, the community may dispose of it again anew into what hands they please, and so constitute a new form of government: for the form of government depending upon the placing the supreme power, which is the legislative (it being impossible to conceive that an inferiour power should prescribe to a superiour, or any but the supreme make laws), according as the power of making laws is placed, such is the form of the commonwealth.

## § 133.

By commonwealth, I must be understood all along to mean, not a democracy, or any form of government; but any independent community, which the Latines signified by the word civitas; to which the word which best answers in our language, is commonwealth, and most properly expresses such a society of men, which community or city in English does not: for there may be subordinate communities in government; and city amongst us has quite a different notion from commonwealth: and therefore, to avoid ambiguity, I crave leave to use the word commonwealth in that sense, in which I find it used by king James the first: and I take it to be its genuine signification; which if any body dislike, I consent with him to change it for a better.

# Chapter XI
# Of the Extent of the Legislative Power

## 导 读

  我们在第十章的导读中指出，洛克的学说并不是一种传统的混合政体学说。洛克的基础是"统一"而非"混合"。那么这个高度抽象的"社会的立法权"如何落实？它以什么方式来运行呢？它如何得出一种分权呢？要回答这些问题，我们需要接着去看接下来的四章。从第十一章到第十四章，洛克通过分析几种不同的国家权力，提出了国家内部的分权架构。

  在第十章中洛克指出，"社会的立法权"的具体落实（即被谁掌握）就是政体的确立。这个过程并不是一个权力的转化，而是抽象的"社会的立法权"转化为由具体的机构实施的"立法权"。第十一章是对这个"立法权"的具体分析。在第一段（第134段）中洛克强调了立法权是"国家的最高权力"。在本章其他部分，洛克说明了"立法权"的四个限制。这里有几个问题值得我们注意。

  首先，洛克所讲的"立法权"究竟是什么？它从何而来？生活于现代社会中的人通常将立法权理解为与行政权、司法权相对等的一种政治权力，它通常掌握在代议制的立法机构中。这一理解基于西方现代成熟的三权分立制度。三种政府权力"分"的是它们背后的人民主权。人民主权作为国家的本质为三种政府权力提供效力来源。三权分立思想建立在国家与政府的区分、三种不同政府权力的区分的基础上。在洛克的时代，人们还没有清晰的人民主权概念，还没有明确地区分国家与政府并划分出三种政府权力，但是洛克的学说朝着这个方向迈出了实质性的一步。

洛克之所以在之前提出"政治社会"这个概念是想回答以下这个问题：国家权力究竟是一种什么性质的权力。它是一种更大规模的暴力，还是一种通过各种方式治理人群的管理性权力，还是一种依据习惯、教义等规范来解决纠纷的权力？洛克的回答是：国家权力是政治社会掌握的有暴力保障的"社会的立法权"。洛克几乎不用国家（state）这个词，是怕引起人们对当时的绝对主义国家概念的联想。政治社会并不是某个外在于国家的概念，不是异于国家的实体，它是国家的本质。洛克是在用"政治社会"这个概念代替"国家"这个概念。"社会的立法权"与"主权"都是可以终结自然状态、缔造政治状态的抽象权力。政治社会与国家都是对政治共同体的抽象描述。要从这一抽象层面落实到具体层面，就是将政治社会落实为政府以及不同的政府机构，将"社会的立法权"落实为政府的权力。在洛克看来，由于"社会的立法权"的独特属性，它的落实只能产生出"政府的立法权"这一种权力。也正因为如此，这个立法权是最高的权力。当然这个最高的权力还可以衍生出执行权，我们到下一章再来谈这个问题。

其次，"立法权"为何既具有最高性又具有有限性？"社会的立法权"是社会契约的唯一产物，服从"社会的立法权"是人民做出同意的唯一内容。政府的立法权是政治社会的"社会的立法权"的落实，因此"社会的立法权"的属性直接决定了立法权的属性。一方面，社会的立法权的最高性使得立法权具有最高性。最高性意味着立法权在政府范围内具有终极性，没有比立法权更高的权力。另一方面，它意味着所有政府权力与政府-臣民的关系最终都来自于立法权。立法权是政府整个规范体系的效力渊源。问题在于，既然立法权是最高的权力，怎么又能受到限制呢？这种限制的正当性基础在哪儿？

这第二个问题是这一章的核心问题。洛克想要提出一种法律至上学说，或者说法治学说。法治意味着所有类型的政府权力都不是无限的专断权力，所有政府机构都必须服从法律。这里悖论在于，如果没有一个最高权力，一个政府就没有统一的基础，实定法就没有来源，但如果存在一个最高权力，那么这个权力的拥有者会享有专断的绝对权力，从而高于法律。就洛克的学说来说，这个困难就是如何来为立法权设定限制。

一种简单的方法是将立法权分散到不同的机构中。但是这种传统的做法并不必然会提供坚实的保障。一方面，不同的机构可能会合谋以获得无限的专断权力；另一方面，一个机构可能通过某种方式架空其他的机构，从而获得无限的专断权力。更为有效的、根本的办法是为立法权本身设置界限。也就是说，如果能够从理论上说明立法权本身就不是任意立法的权力，而是一种具有特定界限、特定目的、特定形式的权力，那么无论哪个（或哪些）机构握有立法权都不会成为独断专行的机构。

在洛克这里，立法权既具有最高性，又具有有限性。这一双重属性首先是洛克之前的社会契约论所得出的"社会的立法权"的特定内涵的反映。例如它对人民的生命与财产不享有绝对的专断权力，立法权必须表现为正式公布的、经常有效的法律等。立法权的有限性还来自于洛克的"委托（trust）理论"。洛克将"社会的立法权"到政府的立法权的转化定位为一种人民委托。这个委托理论的逻辑内涵是：委托的发起人（委托人）和委托的受益人都是政治社会，接受委托的人（托管人）是政府（主要是立法机关和执行机关）。在这个委托关系中，委托人与托管人订立了一个需要他对第三方承担义务的契约，但第三方（即委托的受益人）与托管人之间是没有契约关系的，托管人仅仅是单方面地接受了一项义务。人们之前通常用契约来解释这个转化，洛克则不用契约而用委托来解释这个转化。这是比较新颖的做法。那么，契约与委托有什么不同？洛克为什么要用委托来加以解释？

**延伸阅读材料：**

1. 塔利对洛克的"社会的立法权"的分析：James Tully, A *Discourse on Property*, Cambridge University Press, 1980, pp. 157–163.

2. 邓恩对洛克的"委托"概念的研究：John Dunn, The Concept of "Trust" in the Politics of John Locke, in *Philosophy in History*, Cambridge University Press, 1984, pp. 270–302.

3. 高夫对洛克的"委托理论"的研究：J. W. Gough, *John Locke's Political Philosophy*, Oxford University Press, 1950.

4. 王涛：《洛克的宪政设计方案辨析》，载《政治与法律》，2011年第3期。

## § 134.

The great end of men's entering into society, being the enjoyment of their properties in peace and safety, and the great instrument and means of that being the laws established in that society; the first and fundamental positive law of all commonwealths is the establishing of the legislative power; as the first and fundamental natural law, which is to govern even the legislative itself, is the preservation of the society, and (as far as will consist with the public good) of every person in it. This legislative is not only the supreme power of the commonwealth, but sacred and unalterable in the hands where the community have once placed it; nor can any edict of any body else, in what form soever conceived, or by what power soever backed, have the force and obligation of a law, which has not its sanction from that legislative which the public has chosen and appointed; for without this the law could not have that, which is absolutely necessary to its being a law, the consent of the society; over whom nobody can have a power to make laws, but by their own consent,* and by authority received from them. And therefore all the obedience, which by the most solemn ties any one can be obliged to pay, ultimately terminates in this supreme

---

\* "The lawful power of making laws to command whole politic societies of men, belonging so properly unto the same entire societies, that for any prince or potentate of what kind soever upon earth, to exercise the same of himself, and not by express commission immediately and personally received from God, or else by authority derived at the first from their consent, upon whose persons they impose laws; it is no better than mere tyranny. Laws they are not therefore which public approbation hath not made so." Hooker's Eccl. Pol. l. i. sect. 10. "Of this point therefore we are to note, that sith men naturally have no full and perfect power to command whole politic multitudes of men, therefore utterly without our consent, we could in such sort be at no man's commandment living. And to be commanded we do consent, when that society, whereof we be a part, hath at any time before consented, without revoking the same by the like universal agreement.
"Laws therefore human, of what kind soever, are available by consent." Ibid.

power, and is directed by those laws which it enacts; nor can any oaths to any foreign power whatsoever, or any domestic subordinate power, discharge any member of the society from his obedience to the legislative, acting pursuant to their trust; nor oblige him to any obedience contrary to the laws so enacted, or farther than they do allow; it being ridiculous to imagine one can be tied ultimately to obey any power in the society, which is not supreme.

## § 135.

Though the legislative, whether placed in one or more, whether it be always in being, or only by intervals, though it be the supreme power in every commonwealth; yet,

First, it is not, nor can possibly be absolutely arbitrary over the lives and fortunes of the people: for it being but the joint power of every member of the society given up to that person, or assembly, which is legislator; it can be no more than those persons had in a state of nature before they entered into society, and gave up to the community: for nobody can transfer to another more power than he has in himself; and nobody has an absolute arbitrary power over himself, or over any other, to destroy his own life, or take away the life or property of another. A man, as has been proved, cannot subject himself to the arbitrary power of another; and having in the state of nature no arbitrary power over the life, liberty, or possession of another, but only so much as the law of nature gave him for the preservation of himself and the rest of mankind; this is all he doth, or can give up to the commonwealth, and by it to the legislative power, so that the legislative can have no more than this. Their power, in the utmost bounds of it, is limited to the public good of the society. It is a power, that hath no other end but preservation, and therefore can never have a right to destroy, enslave, or designedly to impoverish the subjects.* The obligations of the law of nature cease not in society, but only in many cases are drawn closer, and have by human laws known penalties annexed to them, to enforce their observation. Thus the law of nature stands as an eternal rule to all men, legislators as well as others. The rules that they make for other men's actions, must, as well as their own and other men's actions, be conformable to the laws of nature, i. e. to the will of God, of which that is a declaration; and the "fundamental law of nature being the preservation of mankind," no human sanction can be good or valid against it.

### § 136.

Secondly, the legislative or supreme authority cannot assume to itself a power to rule, by extemporary, arbitrary decrees;** but is bound to dispense justice, and to decide the rights of the subject,

---

\* "Two foundations there are which bear up public societies; the one a natural inclination, whereby all men desire sociable life and fellowship; the other an order, expressly or secretly agreed upon, touching the manner of their union in living together: the latter is that which we call the law of a commonwealth, the very soul of a politic body, the parts whereof are by law animated, held together, and set on work in such actions as the common good requireth. Laws politic, ordained for external order and regiment amongst men, are never framed as they should be, unless presuming the will of man to be inwardly obstinate, rebellious, and averse from all obedience to the sacred laws of his nature; in a word, unless presuming man to be, in regard of his depraved mind, little better than a wild beast, they do accordingly provide, notwithstanding, so to frame his outward actions, that they be no hindrance unto the common good, for which societies are instituted. Unless they do this, they are not perfect." Hooker's Eccl. Pol. l. i. sect. 10.

\*\* "Human laws are measures in respect of men whose actions they must direct, howbeit such measures they are as have also their higher rules to be measured by, which rules are two, the law of God, and the law of nature; so that laws human must be made according to the general laws of nature, and without contradiction to any positive law of scripture, otherwise they are ill made." Hooker's Eccl. Pol. l. iii. sect. 9.

"To constrain men to any thing inconvenient doth seem unreasonable." Ibid. l. i. sect.

by promulgated, standing laws, and known authorised judges. For the law of nature being unwritten, and so no-where to be found, but in the minds of men; they who through passion, or interest, shall miscite, or misapply it, cannot so easily be convinced of their mistake, where there is no established judge: and so it serves not, as it ought, to determine the rights, and fence the properties of those that live under it; especially where every one is judge, interpreter, and executioner of it too, and that in his own case: and he that has right on his side, having ordinarily but his own single strength, hath not force enough to defend himself from injuries, or to punish delinquents. To avoid these inconveniencies, which disorder men's properties in the state of nature, men unite into societies, that they may have the united strength of the whole society to secure and defend their properties, and may have standing rules to bound it, by which every one may know what is his. To this end it is that men give up all their natural power to the society which they enter into, and the community put the legislative power into such hands as they think fit: with this trust, that they shall be governed by declared laws, or else their peace, quiet, and property will still be at the same uncertainty, as it was in the state of nature.

### § 137.

Absolute arbitrary power, or governing without settled standing laws, can neither of them consist with the ends of society and government, which men would not quit the freedom of the state of nature for, and tie themselves up under, were it not to preserve their lives, liberties, and fortunes, and by stated rules of right and property to secure their peace and quiet. It cannot be supposed that they should intend, had they a power so to do, to give to any one, or more, an absolute arbitrary power over their persons and estates, and put a force into the magistrate's hand to execute his unlimited will arbitrarily upon them. This were to put themselves into a worse condition than the state of nature, wherein they had a liberty to defend their right against the injuries of others, and were upon equal terms of force to maintain it, whether invaded by a single man, or many in combination. Whereas by supposing they have given up themselves to the absolute arbitrary power and will of a legislator, they have disarmed themselves, and armed him, to make a prey of them when he pleases; he being in a much worse condition, who is exposed to the arbitrary power of one man, who has the command of 100,000, than he that is exposed to the arbitrary power of 100,000 single men; nobody being secure, that his will, who has such a command, is better than that of other men, though his force be 100,000 times stronger. And therefore, whatever form the commonwealth is under, the ruling power ought to govern by declared and received laws, and not by extemporary dictates and undetermined resolutions: for then mankind will be in a far worse condition than in the state of nature, if they shall have armed one or a few men with the joint power of a multitude, to force them to obey at pleasure the exorbitant and unlimited degrees of their sudden thoughts, or unrestrained, and till that moment unknown wills, without having any measures set down which may guide and justify their actions; for all the power the government has, being only for the good of the society, as it ought not to be arbitrary and at pleasure, so it ought to be exercised by established and promulgated laws; that both the people may know their duty, and be safe and secure within the limits of the law; and the rulers too kept within their bounds, and not be tempted, by the power they have in their hands, to employ it to such purposes, and by such measures, as they would not have known, and own not willingly.

## § 138.

Thirdly, the supreme power cannot take from any man part of his property without his own consent, for the preservation of property being the end of government, and that for which men enter into society, it necessarily supposes and requires, that the people should have property, without which they must be supposed to lose that, by entering into society, which was the end for which they entered into it; too gross an absurdity for any man to own. Men therefore in society having property, they have such right to the goods, which by the law of the community are their's, that no body hath a right to take their substance or any part of it from them, without their own consent; without this they have no property at all; for I have truly no property in that, which another can by right take from me, when he pleases, against my consent. Hence it is a mistake to think, that the supreme or legislative power of any commonwealth can do what it will, and dispose of the estates of the subject arbitrarily, or take any part of them at pleasure. This is not much to be feared in governments where the legislative consists, wholly or in part, in assemblies which are variable, whose members, upon the dissolution of the assembly, are subjects under the common laws of their country, equally with the rest. But in governments, where the legislative is in one lasting assembly always in being, or in one man, as in absolute monarchies, there is danger still, that they will think themselves to have a distinct interest from the rest of the community; and so will be apt to increase their own riches and power, by taking what they think fit from the people: for a man's property is not at all secure, though there be good and equitable laws to set the bounds of it between him and his fellow-subjects, if he who commands those subjects, have power to take from any private man, what part he pleases of his property, and use and dispose of it as he thinks good.

### § 139.

But government, into whatsoever hands it is put, being, as I have before showed, intrusted with this condition, and for this end, that men might have and secure their properties; the prince, or senate, however it may have power to make laws, for the regulating of property between the subjects one amongst another, yet can never have a power to take to themselves the whole, or any part of the subject's property, without their own consent: for this would be in effect to leave them no property at all. And to let us see, that even absolute power where it is necessary, is not arbitrary by being absolute, but is still limited by that reason, and confined to those ends, which required it in some cases to be absolute, we need look no farther than the common practice of martial discipline: for the preservation of the army, and in it of the whole commonwealth, requires an absolute obedience to the command of every superiour officer, and it is justly death to disobey or dispute the most dangerous or unreasonable of them; but yet we see, that neither the serjeant, that could command a soldier to march up to the mouth of a cannon, or stand in a breach, where he is almost sure to perish, can command that soldier to give him one penny of his money; nor the general, that can condemn him to death for deserting his post, or for not obeying the most desperate orders, can yet, with all his absolute power of life and death, dispose of one farthing of that soldier's estate, or seize one jot of his goods; whom yet he can command any thing, and hang for the least disobedience: because such a blind obedience is necessary to that end, for which the commander has his power, viz. the preservation of the rest; but the disposing of his goods has nothing to do with it.

### § 140.

It is true, governments cannot be supported without great charge, and it is fit every one who enjoys his share of the protection, should pay out of his estate his proportion for the maintenance of it. But still it must be with his own consent, i. e. the consent of the majority, giving it either by themselves, or their representatives chosen by them: for if any one shall claim a power to lay and levy taxes on the people, by his own authority, and without such consent of the people, he thereby invades the fundamental law of property, and subverts the end of government: for what property have I in that, which another may by right take when he pleases, to himself?

### § 141.

Fourthly, the legislative cannot transfer the power of making laws to any other hands: for it being but a delegated power from the people, they who have it cannot pass it over to others. The people alone can appoint the form of the commonwealth, which is by constituting the legislative, and appointing in whose hands that shall be. And when the people have said, we will submit to rules, and be governed by laws made by such men, and in such forms, nobody else can say other men shall make laws for them; nor can the people be bound by any laws, but such as are enacted by those whom they have chosen, and authorized to make laws for them. The power of the legislative being derived from the people by a positive voluntary grant and institution, can be no other than what that positive grant conveyed, which being only to make laws, and not to make legislators, the legislative can have no power to transfer their authority of making laws and place it in other hands.

### § 142.

These are the bounds which the trust, that is put in them by the society and the law of God and nature, have set to the legislative power of every commonwealth, in all forms of government.

First, they are to govern by promulgated established laws, not to be varied in particular cases, but to have one rule for rich and poor, for the favourite at court, and the countryman at plough.

Secondly, these laws also ought to be designed for no other end ultimately, but the good of the people.

Thirdly, they must not raise taxes on the property of the people, without the consent of the people, given by themselves or their deputies. And this properly concerns only such governments where the legislative is always in being, or at least where the people have not reserved any part of the legislative to deputies, to be from time to time chosen by themselves.

Fourthly, the legislative neither must nor can transfer the power of making laws to any body else, or place it any where, but where the people have.

# Chapter XII

## Of the Legislative, Executive, and Federative Power of the Commonwealth[1]

### 导 读

洛克在本章中划分了国家的三种权力，除了之前所讲的立法权，另两个权力是执行权与对外权。我们首先需要重视的是执行权。洛克指出，执行权是"一个经常存在的权力，负责执行被制定和继续有效的法律"。由于立法机构不可常设，所以需要一个常设的执行权来执行法律。由此可见，执行权的功能是协助和补充立法权的实现。

英国传统上的执行权涉及两个因素，一个是国王，一个是法院系统。执行权指的是在国王的领导下，法院系统适用法律的权力。这个权力作为一种特殊的王权，被归属到国王身上。让我们来看一下相关的古代史。通常（例如在中国），古代君王的权力主要是通过设置地方性行政机构来实现对整个国家的统治。由于英国独特的历史情况，英王在早期并没能成功地通过郡长、治安法官等行政性机构的设置来实现对地方的有效治理。从 12 世纪开始，英国国王开始采用司法的方式来实现对国家的控制。首先是流动性的巡回法庭，然后是设置在威斯敏斯特宫廷的普通诉讼法院、王室法院等中央法院等等一系列措施。国王的行政权力很大程度上是通过这种司法方式来实现的。英国

---

[1] 本章所讨论的分权问题在之前已有多次暗示：第 91、107、127 段。

的司法体系的建立与王权的发展密切相关。司法体系一方面有利于国王统治权的实现，另一方面司法技术的精细化、法律团体的职业化也使得司法系统与司法权获得了一定的自主地位。

12世纪的英国法学者格兰维尔的《论英格兰王国的法律和习惯》、13世纪的法学家布拉克顿的《论英格兰的法律和习惯》、15世纪的王座法院首席法官福蒂斯丘的《论英格兰的法律与政制》等经典法学著作都指出，王权虽然是至高的，但是它具有双重性。我们可以将其概括为国王的治理权与国王的执行权。前者是国王管理国家公共事务的权力，它是政治性的权力，不受任何限制；后者特指国王利用法律程序、通过司法机构来处理特定事务的权力，它是法律性的权力，受到相关法律规定的限制。历史上，国王总是试图扩大自己的治理权，使自己可以任意地干涉国家的任何事务。法律人则试图将更多的事务纳入法律程序，从而防止法院的运作与臣民的权利受到国王的任意干涉。这一冲突在历史中多次出现，而治理权与审判权的二元划分无法为其提供解决之道。按照这一传统的分类，国王在治理与审判上都保有最高权威，只不过他对审判权的行使受到普通法规范的限制。就审判权而言，其范围与界限本身就没有明确的规定。双方都通过援引先例来加以说明，而先例往往有利于国王，因为王权先于司法权出现（司法权起初是国王创设的）。另一方面，当法律人认为国王是在越权干涉审判事务时，他们并没有正当的法律理由与权力来制裁国王。

到了17后半叶世纪，人们越来越坚持法律至上的观点，希望将国王以及议会的一切权力都纳入到法律框架中。单纯的王权已经不是英格兰土地上的唯一最高权力。一方面，一些普通法学家不断强调司法权的独立。例如大法官柯克（Sir Edward Coke, 1552—1634）就认为，国王是靠不住的，议会也是靠不住，唯一持久存在、保障国民自由的就是自成体系的普通法。这种普通法司法理论的一个致命缺陷在于，它无法在宪法层面上对国王与议会提出挑战。如果要将法律至上观转化为一种法律主权学说或者说宪政学说的话，我们需要更为根本的政治学说来重新说明主要的政治权力的性质。

另一方面的演进提供了这种学说生长的背景，即直接代表人民的立法权开始独立出来，并由议会分享甚至主导。在17世纪，许多人（例如约翰·弥尔顿）从抽象的角度来区分法律的制定与法律的实施，将前者称为立法权，后者称为执行权。首先，国家的主要事务都需要通过立法来加以规定。其次，执行权则被认为是通过法院机制来适用法律的权力，国王是这个权力的源头。这个执行权包括对具体案件做出审判以及依据法律进行统治。所以它包括了我们今天所称的"行政权"与"司法权"。这带来了两个结果：一方面，不仅传统上所讲的国王的执行权与治理权都被纳入到这种新的执行权概念中，被解释为一种法律性权力；另一方面，国王治理国家的行为也要受到法院的审查和议会的制约。也就是说，国王对他的一切行为都要负责，他需要向法律与人民交代。

这种新的权力二分法的总的观点是立法权与执行权是不同性质的权力，应当由不同的机构掌握，才能保障自由。这体现了从职能混合到职能分离的发展。但是，这些说法仍然是在传统学说的阴影下展开的。立法权与执行权都来自于传统的国家权力概念：国家是履行一种司法职能的政治体。洛克的贡献在于他为权力的二分法提供了新的基础与融贯的解释。这个新的基础是一种新的国家观，即国家的本质是掌握"社会的立法权"的政治社会。在此基础上，立法权是政府的最高权力，执行权则是不同于立法权但隶属于立法权的政府权力。

在洛克这里，执行权总体上是一种司法性质的权力，而不是现代意义上的行政权。在17世纪上半叶的时候，已经有人发现仅仅从这种严格意义上的执行权来理解国王的权力是不充分的。乔治·劳尔森（George Lawson）、查尔斯·达利森（Charles Dallison）将此种执行权再进行二分：管理的权力与审判的权力。前者非常接近于现代的执行权。在英国内战时期，传统的二分法与这种新的三分法就已经并存。我们可以追问的一个问题是，为何洛克并没有做出这进一步的区分呢？

**延伸阅读材料：**

1. 关于英国早期通过司法治理国家的历史与意义参见：

——李栋：《通过司法限制权力：英格兰司法的成长与宪政的生长》，北京，北京大学出版社，2011，特别是其中的第二章与第五章。

——杨利敏：《亨利二世司法改革的国家构建意义》，载《比较法研究》，2012年第4期。

2. 格兰维尔的《论英格兰王国的法律和习惯》：*The Treatise on the Laws and Customs of the Realm of England Commonly Called Glanvill*, Clarendon Press; New Ed edition (16 Dec. 1993).

3. 布拉克顿的《论英格兰的法律和习惯》：Henry de Bracton, *Laws and Customs of England*, Belknap Press of Harvard University Press, 1968.

4. [英]福蒂斯丘：《论英格兰的法律与政制》，袁瑜琤译，北京，北京大学出版社，2008。

5. [英]劳尔森：《神圣政体和世俗政体》，北京，中国政法大学出版社，2003。

6. 富兰克林对劳尔森与洛克的主权学说的比较研究：Julian Franklin, *John Locke and the Theory of Sovereignty*, Cambridge University Press, 1978.

7. 麦基文对英国王权二重性的分析：[美]C. H. 麦基文：《宪政古今》，翟小波译，贵阳，贵州人民出版社，2004。

8. 彭斯对"执行权"概念的溯源：J. H. Burns, Regimen Medium: Executive Power in Early-modern Political Thought, *History of Political Thought*. – 29 (2008): 213–229.

9. 维尔对17世纪分权学说的分析：M. J. C. Vile, *Constitutionalism and the Separation of Powers*, Liberty Fund; 2 edition (March 1, 1998).

此图是目前我们所知的洛克最早的一幅肖像，由约翰·格林希尔（John Greenhill）画于大约 1672 年至 1676 年间。

## § 143.[1]

The legislative power is that, which has a right to direct how the force of the commonwealth shall be employed for preserving the community and the members of it. But because those laws which are constantly to be executed, and whose force is always to continue, may be made in a little time; therefore there is no need, that the legislative should be always in being, not having always business to do. And because it may be too great a temptation to human frailty, apt to grasp at power, for the same persons, who have the power of making laws, to have also in their hands the power to execute them; whereby they may exempt themselves from obedience to the laws they make, and suit the law, both in its making and execution, to their own private advantage, and thereby come to have a distinct interest from the rest of the community, contrary to the end of society and government: therefore in well ordered Commonwealths[2], where the good of the whole is so considered, as it ought, the legislative power is put into the hands of divers persons, who, duly assembled, have by themselves, or jointly with others, a power to make laws; which when they have done, being separated again, they are themselves subject to the laws they have made; which is a new and near tie upon them, to take care that they make them for the public good.

## § 144.

But because the laws, that are at once, and in a short time made, have a constant and lasting force, and need a perpetual execution, or an attendance thereunto: therefore it is necessary there should be a power always in being, which should see to the execution of the laws that are made, and remain in force. And thus the legislative and executive power come often to be separated.

---

[1] 本章所讨论的分权问题在之前已有多次暗示：第 91、107、127 段。
[2] 洛克这里所讲的 well ordered Commonwealths 指的是当时的英格兰。

## § 145.

There is another power in every commonwealth, which one may call natural, because it is that which answers to the power every man naturally had before he entered into society: for though in a commonwealth, the members of it are distinct persons still in reference to one another, and as such are governed by the laws of the society; yet in reference to the rest of mankind, they make one body, which is, as every member of it before was, still in the state of nature with the rest of mankind. Hence it is, that the controversies that happen between any man of the society with those that are out of it, are managed by the public; and an injury done to a member of their body engages the whole in the reparation of it. So that, under this consideration, the whole community is one body in the state of nature, in respect of all other states or persons out of its community.

## § 146.

This therefore contains the power of war and peace, leagues and alliances, and all the transactions, with all persons and communities without the commonwealth; and may be called federative, if any one pleases. So the thing be understood, I am indifferent as to the name.

## § 147.

These two powers, executive and federative, though they be really distinct in themselves, yet one comprehending the execution of the municipal laws of the society within itself, upon all that are parts of it; the other the management of the security and interest of the public without, with all those that it may receive benefit or damage from; yet they are always almost united. And though this federative power in the well or ill management of it be of great moment to the commonwealth, yet it is much less capable to be directed by antecedent, standing, positive laws, than the executive; and so must necessarily be left to the prudence and wisdom of those whose hands it is in, to be managed for the public good: for the laws that concern subjects one amongst another, being to direct their actions, may well enough precede them. But what is to be done in reference to foreigners, depending much upon their actions, and the variation of designs, and interests, must be left in great part to the prudence of those who have this power committed to them, to be managed by the best of their skill, for the advantage of the commonwealth.

### § 148.

Though, as I said, the executive and federative power of every community be really distinct in themselves, yet they are hardly to be separated, and placed at the same time in the hands of distinct persons; for both of them requiring the force of the society for their exercise, it is almost impracticable to place the force of the commonwealth in distinct, and not subordinate hands; or that the executive and federative power should be placed in persons that might act separately, whereby the force of the public would be under different commands: which would be apt some time or other to cause disorder and ruin.

# Chapter XIII
# Of the Subordination of the Powers of the Commonwealth

## 导 读

纯粹的分权学说是指：为了维护政治自由必须将政府划分为立法、行政和司法三部门。每个部门有相应的政府职能，即立法、行政和司法的职能。每个部门都只能限于行使自己的职能，不可侵蚀其他部门的职能。进而，组成这三个政府机构的人员一定要保持分离和不同，不允许任何个人同时是一个以上部门的成员。这样一来，每个部门将对其他部门都是一个制约，没有任何一群人将能控制国家的全部政治机器。我们可以将分权学说分为机构分离、职能分离与人员分离三部分。

分权原则仅仅是对政治自由的消极保障，它并没有说明如果发生越权现象该怎么办。因此，仅有分权制度还是不够的，必须要有某种制衡原则（check and balance）。制衡原则是指，必须赋予每个权力某种干预其他权力的有限权力，从而积极地对每个权力加以限制。

在前两章中我们看到，洛克提出了一种分权原则，即立法权、执行权与对外权的区分。洛克将立法权界定为最高权力。那么他是否是在提出立法权至上或者说立法机构至上呢？如果是这样的话，立法权就是一种不受制约的权力。另一个问题是，就当时的英国宪制而言，国王是执行权的最终拥有者，但国王同时还具有某种立法权以及召集与解散议会的权力，那国王是否也是某种最高权力者呢？在本章中，我们将看到，洛克不仅说明了对立法权、执行权的相互制衡机制，还突破制衡原则说明了一种宪法革命学说以制约立法权的最高性。

在本章的第一段，洛克首先说明了立法权被滥用的问题。他指出，立法权只是一种受委托的权力，因此当它背离其委托目的的时候，社会就获得了一种原初的最高权力来重新组织立法权的归属。这个问题涉及革命与政府解体问题，第十九章将有具体的分析。目前我们需要明确的一点是，立法权并不是在任何时候、任何情况下都是最高权力。

接下来，洛克说明了立法权与执行权的相互制衡关系。从权力序列上讲，立法权高于执行权，执行权必须严格地执行立法机构制定的法律。这是立法权对执行权的制约。但是，问题远没有这么简单。我将结合英国当时的宪法制度与历史来说明其中的复杂性。

首先，我们需要考虑一下最高执行权的问题。洛克指出，当执行权属于一个人，而他也有权参与立法时，这个人就是"至高无上的权力者"，拥有"最高的执行权"。原因在于，如果没有这个人的参与，所有的立法权与执行权都无法行使。显然，这个人就是指英国国王。在洛克之前，那些提出区分立法权与执行权的英国人曾指出，如果一定要确立一个最高权力者的话，那就只能是国王。原因在于，立法机构无法涉足执行权，而国王却可以同时涉足立法权与执行权。洛克的社会契约论使得他躲开了这个逻辑，因为这个逻辑预设了立法权与执行权的对等，而在洛克这里，执行权在权力体系上隶属于立法权。因此，洛克的这个最高执行者没有自己独立的意志，没有自足的权力，"有的只是法律的意志，法律的权力"。从英国的情况看，这一最高执行者（国王）在当时是无法回避的（除非英国人再次砍掉国王的头颅），国王享有对议会议案的否决权。但是洛克指出，这种最高执行者是"极少"出现的。也就是说，通常情况下，我们并不需要这样一个最高执行权。这是不是说明，洛克认为用一种无君的共和制来解决17世纪末的英国政治危机也可能是一条出路呢？

其次，就执行权对立法权的制约而言，新一届议会的召开与解散要么是按照法定的时间，要么是由执行机关根据局势定夺。这里涉及几个问题。首先，按照英国的传统，无论议会依何缘故召开，国王都具有召集权。这是一个法定程序。如果国王不召集议会怎么办呢？从历史上看，1258年的《牛津条例》使得英国的议会成为一个定期（三年）举行会议的国家机关。此后，议会的召开条件与期限多有变动，相关规定也并未得到国王的严格遵守。面对国王可能不召集议会从而使得议会被架空这个问题，一个极端的解决办法就是将相关的权力赋予议会。例如，1641年，查理一世被迫御准《三年期议会法》。该法规定，国王必须每三年召集一届议会（如果国王不召集，议会可自行开会），而解散、休会与推延的权力都必须遵照实定法或由议会来决定。这一做法无疑可以防止国王专制，但是洛克清醒地意识到，立法机构经常召开或长时间召开也是危险的，因为立法机构可能以此而获得专断的权力，成为一个专制的机构。例如，1640年的"长期议会"（1640—1660）就独掌大权，蜕变为一个专制机构。因此，洛克依然认为英国传统上赋予国王的召集与解散议会的权力仍然是非常必要的。而且，许多重大的国事是偶然发生的，如果刻板地依照法律规定来召集议会，则会为国家带来重大危机，因此必须赋予国王依据局势召集议会的权力。

另一个问题是如果国王享有召集与解散议会的权力，这一权力是可能被滥用的。在英国历史上，国王常常滥用权力，随心所欲地召集议会或阻碍议会的召开。查理一世在内战前就曾让议会休会了11年之久。在1680年与1681年，当议会通过《排除法案》后，查理二世两次解散议会，并随后迫害辉格党人，其中就包括沙夫茨伯里。洛克对此的回答是：此时，人民应当采取行动来反抗国王。这是第十九章将要讨论的问题。洛克的一个总的观点是，议会的召开与解散应当遵照法律规定，但是国王在极少数的特殊情况下可以自行召开与解散议会，其目的必须是维护公共利益。

上面所讲的是英国的具体情况。洛克是否对英国的这些具

体制度做出了最好的解释?此外,洛克是否在理论高度上为立法权、人民的革命权、执行权的复杂关系提供了一个融贯的解释,一个与他的《政府论(下篇)》的整个理论框架相一致的解释呢?

洛克在本章的最后两段指出,执行机关在实际情况发生重大变化的时候,享有改变议员席位分配制度的权力。这种权力完全是一种法律外的权力,即改变选举法的权力。如何能够证明这种权力的正当性?洛克诉诸一种法律体系外的理由:人民的福祉。这带出了一个非常重大的问题,即下一章将要讨论的国王特权问题。

**延伸阅读材料:**

1. 关于分权原则与制衡原则的基本内涵与相互关系参见:M. J. C. Vile, *Constitutionalism and the Separation of Powers*, Liberty Fund; 2 edition (March 1, 1998).

2. 对洛克所述的几种政治权力的内在关系的分析参见:

——王涛:《洛克的宪政设计方案辨析》,载《政治与法律》,2011 年第 3 期。

——John T. Scott, The Sovereignless State and Locke's Language of Obligation, *The American Political Science Review*, Vol. 94, No. 3 (Sep., 2000).

3. 关于英国 17 世纪议会与国王、立法权与执行权之间的相互斗争与制衡参见:

——阎照祥:《英国政治制度史》,第五章,北京,人民出版社,1999。

——程汉大:《英国政治制度史》,第五章,北京,中国社会科学出版社,1995。

——[英]梅特兰:《英格兰宪政史》,李红海译,"第四阶段:威廉三世驾崩时的公法概述",北京,中国政法大学出版社,2010。

——[美]哈德罗·J·伯尔曼:《法律与革命:新教改革对西方法律传统的影响》,袁瑜琤、苗文龙译,第二部分第七章"英国革命,1640—1689",北京,法律出版社,2008。

## § 149.

Though in a constituted commonwealth, standing upon its own basis, and acting according to its own nature, that is, acting for the preservation of the community, there can be but one supreme power, which is the legislative, to which all the rest are and must be subordinate; yet the legislative being only a fiduciary power to act for certain ends, there remains still "in the people a supreme power to remove or alter the legislative," when they find the legislative act contrary to the trust reposed in them: for all power given with trust for the attaining an end, being limited by that end; whenever that end is manifestly neglected or opposed, the trust must necessarily be forfeited, and the power devolve into the hands of those that gave it, who may place it anew where they shall think best for their safety and security. And thus the community perpetually retains a supreme power of saving themselves from the attempts and designs of any body, even of their legislators, whenever they shall be so foolish, or so wicked, as to lay and carry on designs against the liberties and properties of the subject: for no man, or society of men, having a power to deliver up their preservation, or consequently the means of it, to the absolute will and arbitrary dominion of another; whenever any one shall go about to bring them into such a slavish condition, they will always have a right to preserve what they have not a power to part with; and to rid themselves of those who invade this fundamental, sacred, and unalterable law of self-preservation, for which they entered into society. And thus the community may be said in this respect to be always the supreme power, but not as considered under any form of government, because this power of the people can never take place till the government be dissolved.

## § 150.

In all cases, whilst the government subsists, the legislative is the supreme power: for what can give laws to another, must needs be superiour to him; and since the legislative is no otherwise legislative of the society, but by the right it has to make laws for all the parts, and for every member of the society, prescribing rules to their actions, and giving power of execution, where they are transgressed; the legislative must needs be the supreme, and all other powers, in any members or parts of the society, derived from and subordinate to it.

§ 151.

In some commonwealths, where the legislative is not always in being, and the executive is vested in a single person, who has also a share in the legislative; there that single person in a very tolerable sense may also be called supreme; not that he has in himself all the supreme power, which is that of law-making; but because he has in him the supreme execution, from whom all inferiour magistrates derive all their several subordinate powers, or at least the greatest part of them: having also no legislative superiour to him, there being no law to be made without his consent, which cannot be expected should ever subject him to the other part of the legislative, he is properly enough in this sense supreme. But yet it is to be observed, that though oaths of allegiance and fealty are taken to him, it is not to him as supreme legislator, but as supreme executor of the law, made by a joint power of him with others: allegiance being nothing but an obedience according to law, which when he violates, he has no right to obedience, nor can claim it otherwise, than as the public person invested with the power of the law; and so is to be considered as the image, phantom, or representative of the commonwealth, acted by the will of the society, declared in its laws; and thus he has no will, no power, but that of the law. But when he quits this representation, this public will, and acts by his own private will, he degrades himself, and is but a single private person without power, and without will, that has no right to obedience; the members owing no obedience but to the public will of the society.

### § 152.

The executive power, placed any where but in a person that has also a share in the legislative, is visibly subordinate and accountable to it, and may be at pleasure changed and displaced; so that it is not the supreme executive power that is exempt from subordination: but the supreme executive power vested in one, who having a share in the legislative, has no distinct superior legislative to be subordinate and accountable to, farther than he himself shall join and consent; so that he is no more subordinate than he himself shall think fit, which one may certainly conclude will be but very little. Of other ministerial and subordinate powers in a commonwealth, we need not speak, they being so multiplied with infinite variety, in the different customs and constitutions of distinct commonwealths, that it is impossible to give a particular account of them all. Only thus much, which is necessary to our present purpose, we may take notice of concerning them, that they have no manner of authority, any of them, beyond what is by positive grant and commission delegated to them, and are all of them accountable to some other power in the commonwealth.

### § 153.

It is not necessary, no, nor so much as convenient, that the legislative should be always in being; but absolutely necessary that the executive power should; because there is not always need of new laws to be made, but always need of execution of the laws that are made. When the legislative hath put the execution of the laws they make into other hands, they have a power still to resume it out of those hands, when they find cause, and to punish for any male administration against the laws. The same holds also in regard of the federative power, that and the executive being both ministerial and subordinate to the legislative, which, as has been showed, in a constituted commonwealth is the supreme. The legislative also in this case being supposed to consist of several persons, (for if it be a single person, it cannot but be always in being, and so will, as supreme, naturally have the supreme executive power, together with the legislative) may assemble, and exercise their legislature, at the times that either their original constitution, or their own adjournment, appoints, or when they please; if neither of these hath appointed any time, or there be no other way prescribed to convoke them: for the supreme power being placed in them by the people, it is always in them, and they may exercise it when they please, unless by their original constitution they are limited to certain seasons, or by an act of their supreme power they have adjourned to a certain time; and when that time comes, they have a right to assemble and act again.

## § 154.

If the legislative, or any part of it, be made up of representatives chosen for that time by the people, which afterwards return into the ordinary state of subjects, and have no share in the legislature but upon a new choice, this power of choosing must also be exercised by the people, either at certain appointed seasons, or else when they are summoned to it; and in this latter case the power of convoking the legislative is ordinarily placed in the executive, and has one of these two limitations in respect of time: that either the original constitution requires their assembling and acting at certain intervals, and then the executive power does nothing but ministerially issue directions for their electing and assembling according to due forms; or else it is left to his prudence to call them by new elections, when the occasions, or exigencies of the public require the amendment of old, or making of new laws, or the redress or prevention of any inconveniencies, that lie on, or threaten the people.

### § 155.

It may be demanded here, what if the executive power, being possessed of the force of the commonwealth, shall make use of that force to hinder the meeting and acting of the legislative, when the original constitution, or the public exigencies require it? I say, using force upon the people without authority, and contrary to the trust put in him that does so, is a state of war with the people, who have a right to reinstate their legislative in the exercise of their power: for having erected a legislative, with an intent they should exercise the power of making laws, either at certain set times, or when there is need of it; when they are hindered by any force from what is so necessary to the society, and wherein the safety and preservation of the people consists, the people have a right to remove it by force. In all states and conditions, the true remedy of force without authority, is to oppose force to it. The use of force without authority, always puts him that uses it into a state of war, as the aggressor, and renders him liable to be treated accordingly.

### § 156.

The power of assembling and dismissing the legislative, placed in the executive, gives not the executive a superiority over it, but is a fiduciary trust placed in him for the safety of the people, in a case where the uncertainty and variableness of human affairs could not bear a steady fixed rule: for it not being possible that the first framers of the government should, by any foresight, be so much masters of future events as to be able to prefix so just periods of return and duration to the assemblies of the legislative, in all times to come, that might exactly answer all the exigencies of the commonwealth; the best remedy could be found for this defect was to trust this to the prudence of one who was always to be present, and whose business it was to watch over the public good. Constant frequent meetings of the legislative, and long continuations of their assemblies, without necessary occasion, could not but be burdensome to the people, and must necessarily in time produce more dangerous inconveniencies, and yet the quick turn of affairs might be sometimes such as to need their present help: any delay of their convening might endanger the public; and sometimes too their business might be so great, that the limited time of their sitting might be too short for their work, and rob the public of that benefit which could be had only from their mature deliberation. What then could be done in this case to prevent the community from being exposed some time or other to eminent hazard, on one side or the other, by fixed intervals and periods, set to the meeting and acting of the legislative; but to intrust it to the prudence of some, who being present, and acquainted with the state of public affairs, might make use of this prerogative for the public good? and where else could this be so well placed as in his hands, who was intrusted with the execution of the laws for the same end? Thus supposing the regulation of times for the assembling and sitting of the legislative not settled by the original constitution, it naturally fell into the hands of the executive, not as an arbitrary power depending on his good pleasure, but with this trust always to have it exercised only for the public weal, as the occurrences of times and change of affairs might require. Whether settled periods of their convening, or a liberty left to the prince for convoking the legislative, or perhaps a mixture of both, hath the least inconvenience attending it, it is not my business here to inquire; but only to show, that though the executive power may have the prerogative of convoking and dissolving such conventions of the legislative, yet it is not thereby superiour to it.

## § 157.

Things of this world are in so constant a flux, that nothing remains long in the same state. Thus people, riches, trade, power, change their stations, flourishing mighty cities come to ruin, and prove in time neglected desolate corners, whilst other unfrequented places grow into populous countries, filled with wealth and inhabitants. But things not always changing equally, and private interest often keeping up customs and privileges, when the reasons of them are ceased; it often comes to pass, that in governments, where part of the legislative consists of representatives chosen by the people, that in tract of time this representation becomes very unequal and disproportionate to the reasons it was at first established upon. To what gross absurdities the following of custom, when reason has left it, may lead, we may be satisfied, when we see the bare name of a town, of which there remains not so much as the ruins, where scarce so much housing as a sheepcote, or more inhabitants than a shepherd is to be found[1], sends as many representatives to the grand assembly of law-makers, as a whole county numerous in people, and powerful in riches. This strangers stand amazed at, and every one must confess needs a remedy; though most think it hard to find one; because the constitution of the legislative being the original and supreme act of the society, antecedent to all positive laws in it, and depending wholly on the people, no inferiour power can alter it. And therefore the people, when the legislative is once constituted, having, in such a government as we have been speaking of, no power to act as long as the government stands; this inconvenience is thought incapable of a remedy.

---

[1] 洛克在这里所指的是英国历史上所谓的"腐烂的城镇"（rotten boroughs），例如当时的塞勒姆（Sarum）。当时，工业的兴起与发展使得一些旧的城镇只剩下极少数的居民，但是根据原先的法律，它们还继续产生出与人口不成比例的下议院代表。

## § 158.

"Salus populi suprema lex"[1] is certainly so just and fundamental a rule, that he, who sincerely follows it, cannot dangerously err. If therefore the executive, who has the power of convoking the legislative, observing rather the true proportion than fashion of representation, regulates not by old custom, but true reason, the number of members in all places that have a right to be distinctly represented, which no part of the people, however incorporated, can pretend to, but in proportion to the assistance which it affords to the public; it cannot be judged to have set up a new legislative, but to have restored the old and true one, and to have rectified the disorders which succession of time had insensibly, as well as inevitably introduced; for it being the interest as well as intention of the people, to have a fair and equal representative; whoever brings it nearest to that, is an undoubted friend to, and establisher of the government, and cannot miss the consent and approbation of the community; prerogative being nothing but a power in the hands of the prince to provide for the public good, in such cases, which depending upon unforeseen and uncertain occurrences, certain and unalterable laws could not safely direct; whatsoever shall be done manifestly for the good of the people, and the establishing the government upon its true foundations, is, and always will be, just prerogative. The power of erecting new corporations, and therewith new representatives, carries with it a supposition that in time the measures of representation might vary, and those places have a just right to be represented which before had none; and by the same reason, those cease to have a right, and be too inconsiderable for such a privilege, which before had it. It is not a change from the present state, which perhaps corruption or decay has introduced, that makes an inroad upon the government; but the tendency of it to

---

[1] *Salus populi suprema lex* 这一拉丁文翻译为中文为"人们的福利是最高的法律"。

injure or oppress the people, and to set up one part or party, with a distinction from, and an unequal subjection of the rest. Whatsoever cannot but be acknowledged to be of advantage to the society, and people in general, upon just and lasting measures, will always, when done, justify itself; and whenever the people shall choose their representatives upon just and undeniably equal measures, suitable to the original frame of the government, it cannot be doubted to be the will and act of the society, whoever permitted or caused them so to do.[1]

---

[1] 对选举权以及选区划分的改革是沙夫茨伯里领导下的辉格党在詹姆斯二世时期试图在议会上提出的一项法案的主要内容（1679年3月）。

# Chapter XIV
## Of Prerogative

**导 读**

　　如何为人类的共同生活建立秩序？这是政治学最根本的一个问题。如果人类没有任何规范（包括习俗、道德、宗教与法律），那么人类的生活就必然是混乱的。人类之所以没有在混乱中灭亡，是因为人类通过各种方式建立起了秩序。从古到今，人类依赖于不同的秩序，如部落首领的家族式秩序、国王统治的封建等级秩序、自由平等基础上的法治秩序等。目前，法治社会已经成为最广为接受的一种秩序。这种秩序也许并不是效率最高的，也许并不是最温情脉脉的，但却被认为是唯一正当的。法治社会的一个根本信念是，只有当所有的政府权力都受到法律的限制时，人民的自由与幸福才能得到保障。也就是说，任何的政府行为都必须被纳入到法律框架中，不得超出法律的规定（更不用说违反法律）。

　　法治社会被认为是人类最重要的制度发明，洛克的《政府论（下篇）》也被认为是法治思想的经典著作。尽管人人都向往理想的法治社会，但是认为所有国家事务都可以纳入法治框架的想法却忽视了人类政治生活的复杂性与多变性。在面对突发的严重自然灾害时、在面对迫在眉睫的恐怖主义威胁时、在面对大规模的经济危机时，如果政府依然按照法定程序与手段来解决问题，那么可能会严重损害国家安全与人民的生命与财产。

原因在于：首先，法律不可能对所有突发的事件做出具体的规定，政府如果只能依法办事，那么此时就只能无所作为。其次，相关的法律规定可能会严重束缚政府去及时有效地解决危机。在这种非常时刻，严格遵从法治理念可能就会被人认为是天真幼稚的"法条主义"者。教条地遵守法律恰恰是在背离法律的目的：对人民的自由与安全的保障。

现实主义者对人类政治事务的这一观察无疑是具有启发性的。此外，从人类几千年的历史来看，这种危机时刻并不是非常罕见的。严重的国家安全事件不时地发生。即使在日常情况下，许多小规模的事件也往往需要政府突破法律，及时采取措施。例如洛克所举的例子：发生火灾时，为了避免火势蔓延，不顾法律的禁止，强制拆除旁边的房屋。通常情况下，这种危机处理权是交给执行机关（或者用现代的话来说是行政机关）的。洛克将这种权力称为"特权"，即"人民之许可他们的统治者，在法律没有规定的场合，按照他们的自由抉择来办理一些事情，甚至有时与法律的明文规定相抵触，来为公众谋福利"。除了上面我们所提到的原因外，洛克还指出，有效地行使特权是一个"贤明的君主"应当做的事情，不然的话，他就是昏庸的、无能的。

特权无疑是一种法外权力，它的正当性基础在于，它是"为公众谋福利"。如果洛克所讲的执行权包含这种特权的话，人们不禁要问，洛克的特权概念是否与前两章所讲的"执行权从属于立法权"的提法相矛盾。如果我们仅仅将洛克的国家学说限定为有限政府学说或法治政府学说，那么这个矛盾无疑是存在的，洛克的学说就不具有融贯性。但其实，特权完全可以被纳入到洛克的理论框架中。

洛克所想要阐述的是如何来维护一个自由社会，而一个自由社会不仅需要法律内的静态秩序，也需要法律外的动态秩序。一个自由社会不仅需要所有人与所有政府机构依法办事，还需要在特殊时刻采取政治行动。例如政府的特权行为，例如人民的革命行动等。这些行动不符合实定法，不具有合法性（legality），是法外行为（extralegal），但它们符合自然法，具有正当性（legitimacy），不是宪法外（extraconstitutional）行为。

虽然洛克认为特权是具有必要性与正当性的，但是他对特权也有严格的限定。首先，它必须是为了公共福利，而不是为了私人利益。为了谋求私人或少数人的利益而无视法律不是特权行为，而是暴政与独裁。因此，特权是非常有限的权力，而不是无限的权力。其次，特权的最终目的是为了恢复常态的法治秩序，而不是为了将国家带入无法无天的"自然状态"或行政权独大的专制状态。

如果说特权是一种法外政治行为，这是否意味着它不可能受到任何限制呢？洛克是否为特权提供了一个规范性框架？这个问题的核心在于，当特权被滥用时该怎么办。"谁来判断这个权力是否使用得当呢？"洛克的回答是，人民最终享有做出这个判断的权力。问题在于，人民能够承担如此艰巨的责任吗？当"9·11"事件发生后，当所有美国人都胆战心惊时，他们是否能够有足够的勇气与清醒的头脑去判断，又能用什么方法去判断：布什政府对美国公民的监视、秘密逮捕、刑讯逼供等法外行为是否超出了界限？人民在什么时候应当站起来反对政府的特权？人民如何才能判别政府是在维护人民的自由，还是已经在侵蚀人民的自由呢？人民如何才能防止自己做出错误的判断呢？对此，洛克并没有给出一个明确的答案，他也无法给出一个明确的答案。洛克赋予了政府以法外特权，也赋予了人民以制约这种特权的革命权。在洛克看来，法治社会可以有严格的制度设计与行为准则，但是法治并没有穷尽政治生活的全部，它无法一劳永逸地保障长治久安与自由幸福。人类的秩序不可能仅仅来自于成文的法律与政治学的知识，它还需要人类的实践智慧。

**延伸阅读材料：**

1.［美］哈维·C·曼斯菲尔德：《驯化君主》，冯克利译，222-243，南京，译林出版社，2005。

2. Douglas Casson, Emergency Judgment: Carl Schmitt, John Locke, and

the Paradox of Prerogative, *Politics & Policy*, Vol. 36, No. 6, pp. 944–971.

3. Sean Mattie, Prerogative and the Rule of Law in John Locke and the Lincoln Presidency, *The Review of Politics*, Vol. 67, No. 1 (Winter, 2005), pp. 77–111.

4. Pasquale Pasquino, Locke on King's Prerogative, *Political Theory*, Vol. 26, No. 2 (Apr., 1998), pp. 198–208.

5. Thomas S. Langston and Michael E. Lind, John Locke & the Limits of Presidential Prerogative, *Polity*, Vol. 24, No. 1 (Autumn, 1991), pp. 49–68.

英国国王威廉三世（King William Ⅲ, 1650—1702），即之前的奥兰治亲王威廉（William of Orange）。由戈弗雷·内勒（Godfrey Kneller）画于约1690年。洛克在《政府论两篇》的"前言"中写道：我这里所写的东西，"我希望能够确立我们伟大的政权恢复者、我们现在的国王威廉的王位。"

## § 159.

Where the legislative and executive power are in distinct hands, (as they are in all moderated monarchies and well-framed governments) there the good of the society requires, that several things should be left to the discretion of him that has the executive power: for the legislators not being able to foresee, and provide by laws, for all that may be useful to the community, the executor of the laws having the power in his hands, has by the common law of nature a right to make use of it for the good of the society, in many cases, where the municipal law has given no direction, till the legislative can conveniently be assembled to provide for it. Many things there are, which the law can by no means provide for; and those must necessarily be left to the discretion of him that has the executive power in his hands, to be ordered by him as the public good and advantage shall require: nay, it is fit that the laws themselves should in some cases give way to the executive power, or rather to this fundamental law of nature and government, viz. That, as much as may be, all the members of the society are to be preserved: for since many accidents may happen, wherein a strict and rigid observation of the laws may do harm; (as not to pull down an innocent man's house to stop the fire, when the next to it is burning) and a man may come sometimes within the reach of the law, which makes no distinction of persons, by an action that may deserve reward and pardon; it is fit the ruler should have a power, in many cases, to mitigate the severity of the law, and pardon some offenders: for the end of government being the preservation of all, as much as may be, even the guilty are to be spared, where it can prove no prejudice to the innocent.

## § 160.

This power to act according to discretion, for the public good, without the prescription of the law, and sometimes even against it, is that which is called prerogative: for since in some governments the law-making power is not always in being, and is usually too numerous, and so too slow for the dispatch requisite to execution; and because also it is impossible to foresee, and so by laws to provide for all accidents and necessities that may concern the public, or to make such laws as will do no harm, if they are executed with an inflexible rigour on all occasions, and upon all persons that may come in their way; therefore there is a latitude left to the executive power, to do many things of choice which the laws do not prescribe.

### § 161.

This power, whilst employed for the benefit of the community, and suitably to the trust and ends of the government, is undoubted prerogative, and never is questioned; for the people are very seldom or never scrupulous or nice in the point; they are far from examining prerogative, whilst it is in any tolerable degree employed for the use it was meant; that is, for the good of the people, and not manifestly against it: but if there comes to be a question between the executive power and the people, about a thing claimed as a prerogative, the tendency of the exercise of such prerogative to the good or hurt of the people will easily decide that question.

### § 162.

It is easy to conceive, that in the infancy of governments, when commonwealths differed little from families in number of people, they differed from them too but little in number of laws: and the governors being as the fathers of them, watching over them, for their good, the government was almost all prerogative. A few established laws served the turn, and the discretion and care of the ruler supplied the rest. But when mistake or flattery prevailed with weak princes to make use of this power for private ends of their own, and not for the public good, the people were fain by express laws to get prerogative determined in those points wherein they found disadvantage from it: and thus declared limitations of prerogative were by the people found necessary in cases which they and their ancestors had left, in the utmost latitude, to the wisdom of those princes who made no other but a right use of it; that is, for the good of their people.

## § 163.

And therefore they have a very wrong notion of government, who say, that the people have encroached upon the prerogative, when they have got any part of it to be defined by positive laws: for in so doing they have not pulled from the prince any thing that of right belonged to him, but only declare, that that power which they indefinitely left in his or his ancestors hands, to be exercised for their good, was not a thing which they intended him when he used it otherwise: for the end of government being the good of the community, whatsoever alterations are made in it, tending to that end, cannot be an encroachment upon any body, since nobody in government can have a right tending to any other end: and those only are encroachments which prejudice or hinder the public good. Those who say otherwise, speak as if the prince had a distinct and separate interest from the good of the community, and was not made for it; the root and source from which spring almost all those evils and disorders which happen in kingly governments. And indeed, if that be so, the people under his government are not a society of rational creatures, entered into a community for their mutual good; they are not such as have set rulers over themselves, to guard and promote that good; but are to be looked on as an herd of inferior creatures under the dominion of a master, who keeps them and works them for his own pleasure or profit. If men were so void of reason, and brutish, as to enter into society upon such terms, prerogative might indeed be, what some men would have it, an arbitrary power to do things hurtful to the people.

## § 164.

But since a rational creature cannot be supposed, when free, to put himself into subjection to another, for his own harm; (though, where he finds a good and wise ruler, he may not perhaps think it either necessary or useful to set precise bounds to his power in all things) prerogative can be nothing but the people's permitting their rulers to do several things, of their own free choice, where the law was silent, and sometimes too against the direct letter of the law, for the public good; and their acquiescing in it when so done: for as a good prince, who is mindful of the trust, put into his hands, and careful of the good of his people, cannot have too much prerogative, that is, power to do good; so a weak and ill prince, who would claim that power which his predecessors exercised without the direction of the law, as a prerogative belonging to him by right of his office, which he may exercise at his pleasure, to make or promote an interest distinct from that of the public; gives the people an occasion to claim their right, and limit that power, which, whilst it was exercised for their good, they were content should be tacitly allowed.

## § 165.

And therefore he that will look into the history of England, will find, that prerogative was always largest in the hands of our wisest and best princes; because the people, observing the whole tendency of their actions to be the public good, contested not what was done without law to that end: or, if any human frailty or mistake (for princes are but men, made as others) appeared in some small declinations from that end; yet it was visible, the main of their conduct tended to nothing but the care of the public. The people therefore, finding reason to be satisfied with these princes, whenever they acted without, or contrary to the letter of the law, acquiesced in what they did, and, without the least complaint, let them enlarge their prerogative as they pleased; judging rightly, that they did nothing herein to the prejudice of their laws, since they acted conformably to the foundation and end of all laws, the public good.

### § 166.

Such God-like princes indeed had some title to arbitrary power by that argument, that would prove absolute monarchy the best government, as that which God himself governs the universe by; because such kings partook of his wisdom and goodness. Upon this is founded that saying, That the reigns of good princes have been always most dangerous to the liberties of their people: for when their successors, managing the government with different thoughts, would draw the actions of those good rulers into precedent, and make them the standard of their prerogative, as if what had been done only for the good of the people was a right in them to do, for the harm of the people, if they so pleased; it has often occasioned contest, and sometimes public disorders, before the people could recover their original right, and get that to be declared not to be prerogative, which truly was never so: since it is impossible that any body in the society should ever have a right to do the people harm; though it be very possible, and reasonable, that the people should not go about to set any bounds to the prerogative of those kings, or rulers, who themselves transgressed not the bounds of the public good: for "prerogative is nothing but the power of doing public good without a rule."

### § 167.

The power of calling parliaments in England, as to precise time, place, and duration, is certainly a prerogative of the king, but still with this trust, that it shall be made use of for the good of the nation, as the exigencies of the times, and variety of occasions, shall require: for it being impossible to foresee which should always be the fittest place for them to assemble in, and what the best season, the choice of these was left with the executive power, as might be most subservient to the public good, and best suit the ends of parliaments.

## § 168.

The old question will be asked in this matter of prerogative, "But who shall be judge when this power is made a right use of?" I answer: between an executive power in being, with such a prerogative, and a legislative that depends upon his will for their convening, there can be no judge on earth; as there can be none between the legislative and the people, should either the executive or the legislative, when they have got the power in their hands, design, or go about to enslave or destroy them. The people have no other remedy in this, as in all other cases where they have no judge on earth, but to appeal to heaven: for the rulers, in such attempts, exercising a power the people never put into their hands, (who can never be supposed to consent that any body should rule over them for their harm) do that which they have not a right to do. And where the body of the people, or any single man[1], is deprived of their right, or under the exercise of a power without right, and have no appeal on earth, then they have a liberty to appeal to heaven, whenever they judge the cause of sufficient moment. And therefore, though the people cannot be judge, so as to have, by the constitution of that society, any superior power to determine and give effective sentence in the case; yet they have, by a law antecedent and paramount to all positive laws of men, reserved that ultimate determination to themselves which belongs to all mankind, where there lies no appeal on earth, viz. to judge, whether they have just cause to make their appeal to heaven.—And this judgment they cannot part with, it being out of a man's power so to submit himself to another, as to give him a liberty to destroy him; God and nature never allowing a man so to abandon

---

[1] 有些人认为这是洛克最为无政府主义的一个说法。

himself, as to neglect his own preservation: and since he cannot take away his own life, neither can he give another power to take it. Nor let any one think, this lays a perpetual foundation for disorder; for this operates not, till the inconveniency is so great, that the majority feel it, and are weary of it, and find a necessity to have it amended. But this the executive power, or wise princes, never need come in the danger of: and it is the thing, of all others, they have most need to avoid, as of all others the most perilous.

# Chapter XV
## Of Paternal, Political, and Despotical Power, Considered Together

### 导 读

这一章并没有进一步推进《政府论（下篇）》的论证，而仅仅是对本书此前结论的总结。洛克在第一章中就指出，我们必须要弄清楚不同"权力彼此之间的区别"。这些不同的权力最主要的就是父权、政治权力与专制权力。其中最为主要的问题就是政治权力的内涵是什么。到本章为止，洛克已经基本上完成了这个任务。

为什么洛克将区分不同性质的权力作为其主要任务呢？从物理层面上讲，人的权力的实质就是人的力量。人们之所以赋予不同性质的力量以不同的名称，是因为人类具有反思现象的能力。力量有不同的形态。它可以是一个人行使的，也可以是多个人行使的；它可以是通过暴力来行使的，也可以通过"软"方式来行使；它可以是为了光荣与梦想而被行使的，也可以是为了报复与打击而被行使的。这些是政治学关注的问题，但并不是政治学关注的首要问题。政治生活必然需要人的力量，政治共同体的存在必然需要公共力量并对其加以行使。问题在于，什么样的公共力量是正当的，是具有道德基础的。或者说，什么样的公共力量才能被恰当地称为"政治权力"。

人无法改变权力的物理性质，但是人可以通过反思不同的

权力来改变力量的道德性质。反思的方法就是对不同的权力分别做出定义与比较。政治学就是通过定义与比较来重新理解人的基本政治经验，从而在政治的物理性维度之上添一个道德性的维度。如果人们无法对不同的权力做出界定与辨析，那么他们就会生活在权力的物理性维度上。更为糟糕的是，这些遭受权力压迫与奴役的人在传统、习俗、意识形态的灌输下，可能会以为这些权力是正当的。洛克之所以认为区分不同的权力至关重要，是因为只有当我们明白了正当权力的目的、性质与界限时，我们才能够自我启蒙，追求自由与幸福。

洛克之前已经具体分析了父权与政治权力的内涵，在本章中他简明地重述了自己的论点。他着重强调了专制权力是一种对他人财产（包括人身与财物）的绝对的、专断的权力。专制权力就是政治权力的对立面。专制君主行使专制权力，因此他是"野兽或毒虫"，放弃了"理性所启示的和平道路"，与人民处于"战争状态"。

这一章是洛克在1689年加入到原稿中的，其目的就是要强调詹姆斯二世在光荣革命前的统治就是一种专制统治。詹姆斯二世在统治时期为了恢复一种天主教君主制，破坏英格兰既有的实定法，越权制定新的法律，并通过各种手段干涉人民的宗教信仰，侵害人民的生命与财产。依照洛克的学说，詹姆斯二世显然就是一位专制君主（despot），他恣意行使的权力就是一种专制权力（despotical power）。洛克通过自己的学说为人们评判政府权力的正当性提供了一个标准，使得他们对政府的来源、目的与性质有了更为清晰的认识。

英国国王詹姆斯二世（James Ⅱ，1633—1701）。洛克与沙夫茨伯里及其领导的辉格党人曾试图阻止詹姆斯二世上台，随后又试图控制詹姆斯二世的王权。沙夫茨伯里遭到詹姆斯二世的迫害，而客死他乡，而洛克最终见证了光荣革命的胜利与詹姆斯二世的下台。《政府论（下篇）》中有多处对詹姆斯二世暴政的控诉。

## § 169.

Though I have had occasion to speak of these separately before, yet the great mistakes of late about government having, as I surpose, arisen from confounding these distinct powers one with another, it may not, perhaps, be amiss to consider them here together.

## § 170.

First, then, paternal or parental power is nothing but that which parents have over their children, to govern them for the children's good, till they come to the use of reason, or a state of knowledge, wherein they may be supposed capable to understand that rule, whether it be the law of nature, or the municipal law of their country, they are to govern themselves by: capable, I say, to know it, as well as several others, who live as freemen under that law. The affection and tenderness which God hath planted in the breast of parents towards their children, makes it evident that this is not intended to be a severe arbitrary government, but only for the help, instruction, and preservation of their offspring. But happen it as it will, there is, as I have proved, no reason why it should be thought to extend to life and death, at any time, over their children, more than over any body else; neither can there be any pretence why this parental power should keep the child, when grown to a man, in subjection to the will of his parents, any farther than having received life and education from his parents, obliges him to respect, honour, gratitude, assistance and support, all his life, to both father and mother. And thus, it is true, the paternal is a natural government, but not at all extending itself to the ends and jurisdictions of that which is political. The power of the father doth not reach at all to the property of the child, which is only in his own disposing.

## § 171.

Secondly, political power is that power, which every man

having in the state of nature, has given up into the hands of the society, and therein to the governors, whom the society hath set over itself, with this express or tacit trust, that it shall be employed for their good, and the preservation of their property: now this power, which every man has in the state of nature, and which he parts with to the society in all such cases where the society can secure him, is to use such means for the preserving of his own property, as he thinks good, and nature allows him; and to punish the breach of the law of nature in others, so as (according to the best of his reason) may most conduce to the preservation of himself, and the rest of mankind. So that the end and measure of this power, when in every man's hands in the state of nature, being the preservation of all of his society, that is, all mankind in general; it can have no other end or measure, when in the hands of the magistrate, but to preserve the members of that society in their lives, liberties, and possessions; and so cannot be an absolute arbitrary power, over their lives and fortunes, which are as much as possible to be preserved; but a power to make laws, and annex such penalties to them, as may tend to the preservation of the whole, by cutting off those parts, and those only, which are so corrupt, that they threaten the sound and healthy, without which no severity is lawful. And this power has its original only from compact and agreement, and the mutual consent of those who make up the community.

### § 172.

Thirdly, despotical power is an absolute, arbitrary power one man has over another, to take away his life, whenever he pleases. This is a power, which neither nature gives, for it has made no such distinction between one man and another; nor compact can convey: for man not having such an arbitrary power over his own life, cannot give another man such a power over it; but it is the effect only of forfeiture which the aggressor makes of his own life, when he puts himself into the state of war with another; for having quitted reason, which God hath given to be the rule betwixt man and man, and the common bond whereby human kind is united into one fellowship and society; and having renounced the way of peace which that teaches, and made use of the force of war, to compass his unjust ends upon another, where he has no right; and so revolting from his own kind to that of beasts, by making force, which is their's, to be his rule of right; he renders himself liable to be destroyed by the injured person, and the rest of mankind, that will join with him in the execution of justice, as any other wild beast, or noxious brute, with whom mankind can have neither society nor security[1]. And thus captives, taken in a just and lawful war, and such only, are subject to a despotical power; which, as it arises not from compact, so neither is it capable of any, but is the state of war continued: for what compact can be made with a man that is not master of his own life? what condition can he perform? and if he be once allowed to be master of his own life, the despotical arbitrary power of his master ceases. He that is master of himself, and his own life, has a right too to the means of preserving it; so that, as soon as compact enters, slavery ceases, and he so far quits his absolute power, and puts an end to the state of war, who enters into conditions with his captive.

## § 173.

Nature gives the first of these, viz. paternal power, to parents for the benefit of their children during their minority, to supply their want of ability and understanding how to manage their property. (By property I must be understood here, as in other places, to mean that property which men have in their persons as well as

---

[1] 在第三版中，洛克重写与扩展了从 for having 到这里的内容。这很显然是对詹姆斯二世的影射，因此很有可能是 1689 年时加入到原稿中去的。

goods.) Voluntary agreement gives the second, viz. political power to governors for the benefit of their subjects, to secure them in the possession and use of their properties. And forfeiture gives the third despotical power to lords, for their own benefit, over those who are stripped of all property.

## § 174.

He, that shall consider the distinct rise and extent, and the different ends of these several powers, will plainly see, that paternal power comes as far short of that of the magistrate, as despotical exceeds it; and that absolute dominion, however placed, is so far from being one kind of civil society, that it is as inconsistent with it, as slavery is with property. Paternal power is only where minority makes the child incapable to manage his property; political, where men have property in their own disposal; and despotical, over such as have no property at all.

# Chapter XVI
## Of Conquest

### 导　读

　　从古到今，人类所栖居的这片土地上就不断地燃烧着战火。除了小规模的地区冲突外，还有不少国家之间的大规模战争。在洛克生活的年代以及他所了解的古代，为了争夺王位、领土与财富，家族之间的战争、王公之间的战争、国家之间为了征服对方而发动的战争此起彼伏，数不胜数。征服的正当性基础在哪儿？征服对征服者与被征服者意味着什么？征服与国家的建立之间是什么关系？这些问题显然具有重大的现实意义。洛克在这一章中将对这些问题提出自己的看法。

　　在英国的政治话语中，征服问题一直以来都是受到高度关注且备受争议的一个问题，因为英国的世袭君主制始于一位征服者：威廉一世。罗马人离开后，5世纪中叶，三个日耳曼人部落入侵不列颠。在之后五百多年间，这座岛屿内外战争不断，时而分裂，时而被侵占，时而统一。1066年，英国国王忏悔者爱德华病逝。法国的诺曼底公爵威廉与爱德华血缘关系较近，要求继承英格兰王位。当时英国的中央机构贤人会议因其是私生子而加以拒绝，并推荐戈德温家族的哈德罗为国王。威廉于当年向英格兰宣战，并大胜哈德罗的军队。当年圣诞节，威廉在威斯敏斯特加冕，称威廉一世，史称"征服者威廉"。威廉结束了英国的盎格鲁－撒克逊时代，成为英格兰的第一位诺曼人

国王。威廉的这次征服被简称为"诺曼征服"。由于英格兰后来一直按照世袭君主制的方式延续着威廉的王权,因此"诺曼征服"被人们看做是英格兰这个国家的起点。当人们讨论英格兰的国家性质、国王与人民的关系等重大问题时,都无可避免地要涉及对"诺曼征服"的性质与影响的界定。一直到17世纪,如何理解"诺曼征服"还是国王与议会、托利党人与辉格党人争论不休的问题。其中的一个重要问题是,"诺曼征服"是否意味着威廉一世是不受人民约束的绝对君主,是否意味着英格兰从一开始就是一个绝对君主制国家。洛克在本章中就对这个问题做出了自己的解释。

对洛克同时代的英国人来说,征服问题还涉及另一个更具有紧迫性的问题,即光荣革命的性质问题。1688年6月30日,七名主教联名致信詹姆斯二世的女婿、时任荷兰执政官的奥兰治的威廉,邀请他率军来英格兰保护英国人民的"宗教、自由与财产"。同年11月5日,威廉率大军登陆英格兰。詹姆斯二世于12月11日出逃,并将国玺投入泰晤士河,后被抓回。威廉感到把他留在英国不免会生出别的麻烦,就故意放他逃走。詹姆斯二世先逃到爱尔兰,后又逃往法国。11月21日,威廉召集了查理二世时期最后三届的议员、伦敦市参议员与市政委员会开会。12月26日,大会召开。会议授权威廉以临时元首的名义向全国发出通知,召集举行一场大会。这场大会于1689年1月22日召开,2月13日议会两院向威廉与玛丽呈上王冠与《权利法案》。

从事实上讲,威廉的入侵就是一场军事征服。按照洛克在本章中所提出的理论,即使是基于正义战争的征服也"不等于建立任何政府"。洛克认为,征服仅仅是拆除了旧的房屋,但是为了重建新屋,建立新的国家,必须要取得人民的同意。也就是说,征服发生后,新的国家必须要基于人民的自愿选择才具有正当性。按照洛克的讲法,威廉与玛丽作为征服者并不当然成为英格兰的统治者。就这一点而言,主导光荣革命的英国贵族们是赞同的,但是他们所采用的理论与实际做法其实是存在问题的。

从宪法层面上讲，当詹姆斯二世出逃后，英国的最高权力机构"王在巴列门中"就不存在了，因为其中的"王"不存在了，上下议院就不再具有最高权力。明白了这一点后，我们再来看光荣革命的具体情况。

按照英格兰的宪法原则，议会的召开必须要有国王的召集令，议会法案的通过必须要有国王的御准。但是，1月21日的会议是在威廉这位亲王（而非国王）的号召下召开的，从严格意义上讲，它并不是议会（Parliament），而仅仅是"协商会议"（Convention）。《权利宣言》（Declaration of Rights, 1689.2）与《权利法案》（Bill of Rights, 1689.10）也并没有国王的御准就成为了法律。那么，"协商会议"本身以及它所通过的《权利宣言》与《权利法案》的正当性基础在哪里呢？《权利宣言》与《权利法案》对这一非常做法给出的解释是：由于詹姆斯二世"放弃政府，使得王位虚空"，"协商会议"的所有成员决定"威廉与玛丽被宣为英格兰的国王与王后"。问题在于，如果将"协商会议"看做是某种议会，那么它就不再是传统意义上的议会，因为它享有宣布国王的任命与通过法律的单独权力。如此一来，议会就具有了至高主权，这无疑摧毁了英格兰原有的宪法原则。

光荣革命的官方解释是辉格党与托利党相互妥协的结果。英国的托利党人不愿意将光荣革命解释为：国王被人民废除，从而承认人民的革命权。因此，他们将其解释为国王的主动放弃，将王权的变动纳入原有的世袭君主制框架中。在洛克看来，这一解释存在严重的逻辑问题，并且无视此次事件的时代意义。洛克认为唯一合理且符合时代潮流的解释是：詹姆斯二世的出逃意味着政府的解体，光荣革命及其后续法律的正当性基础在于人民的"革命权"与"立宪权"。在第十九章中，我们将会看到洛克的这一学说的具体内容。

洛克对征服问题的分析不仅具有现实意义，而且具有思想史上的理论价值。由于征服问题关系重大，所以许多大思想家都对其做出了理论分析，例如格劳秀斯、霍布斯、普芬道夫。他们的观点与洛克不尽相同，甚至有截然对立的地方，我们可以将其进行比较。

**延伸阅读材料：**

1. 关于诺曼征服的历史参见：

——阎照祥：《英国政治制度史》，北京，人民出版社，1999，第二章。

——程汉大：《英国政治制度史》，北京，中国社会科学出版社，1995，第二章。

2. 关于光荣革命的历史参见：

——阎照祥：《英国政治制度史》，北京，人民出版社，1999，第192-203页。

——程汉大：《英国政治制度史》，北京，中国社会科学出版社，1995，第199-209页。

——［英］梅特兰：《英格兰宪政史》，李红海译，北京，中国政法大学出版社，2010，第181-183页。

3.《权利宣言》与《权利法案》的原文。

4. 霍布斯对征服的讨论：［英］霍布斯：《利维坦》，黎思复、黎廷弼译，杨昌裕校，北京，商务印书馆，1997，第二部分第二十章"论宗法的管辖权与专制的管辖权"。

5. 格劳秀斯对征服的讨论：Hugo Grotius, *The Rights of War and Peace*, edited and with an introduction by Richard Tuck, from the edition by Jean Barbeyrac. Indianapolis, Liberty Fund, 2005, Book iii, Chapter iv-xvi.

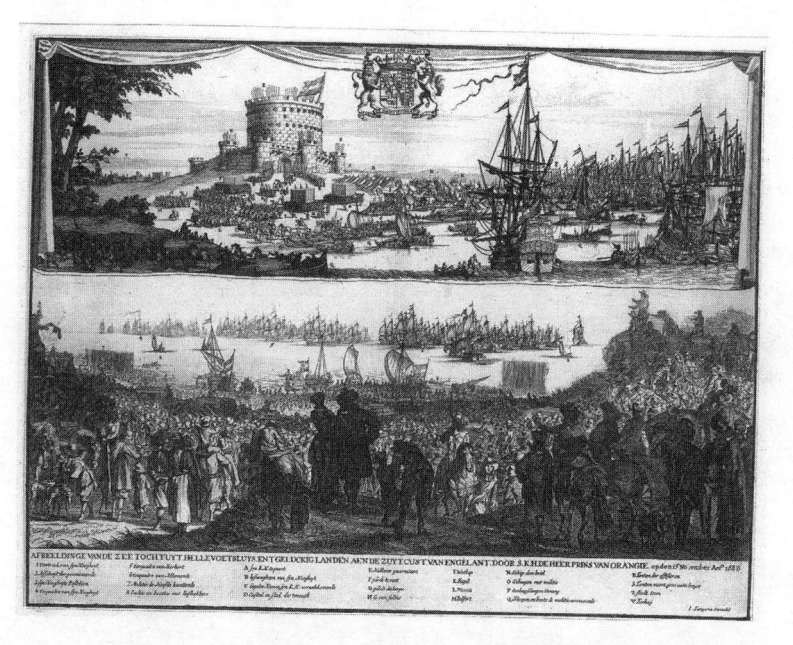

此图描绘了1688年在英国发生的光荣革命。此图上半部分是奥兰治亲王威廉（William of Orange, 1650—1702）于1688年11月13日率领舰队在荷兰的海勒武特斯莱斯（Hellevoetsluis）登船启程驶向英国。此图的下半部分是威廉的舰队于1688年11月5日在英国德文郡的托贝（Torbay, Devon）登陆英国。

## § 175.

Though governments can originally have no other rise than that before-mentioned, nor politics be founded on any thing but the consent of the people; yet such have been the disorders ambition has filled the world with, that in the noise of war, which makes so great a part of the history of mankind, this consent is little taken notice of: and therefore many have mistaken the force of arms for the consent of the people, and reckon conquest as one of the originals of government. But conquest is as far from setting up any government, as demolishing an house is from building a new one in the place. Indeed, it often makes way for a new frame of a commonwealth, by destroying the former; but, without the consent of the people, can never erect a new one.

## § 176.

That the aggressor, who puts himself into the state of war with another, and unjustly invades another man's right, can, by such an unjust war, never come to have a right over the conquered, will be easily agreed by all men, who will not think, that robbers and pirates have a right of empire over whomsoever they have force enough to master; or that men are bound by promises, which unlawful force extorts from them. Should a robber break into my house, and with a dagger at my throat, make me seal deeds to convey my estate to him, would this give him any title? Just such a title, by his sword, has an unjust conqueror, who forces me into submission. The injury and the crime are equal, whether committed by the wearer of the crown, or some petty villain. The title of the offender, and the number of his followers, make no difference in the offence, unless it be to aggravate it. The only difference is, great robbers punish little ones, to keep them in their obedience; but the great ones are rewarded with laurels and triumphs; because they are too big for the weak hands of justice in this world, and have the power in their own possession, which should punish offenders. What is my remedy against a robber, that so broke into my house? Appeal to the law for justice. But perhaps justice is denied, or I am crippled and cannot stir, robbed and have not the means to do it. If God has taken away all means of seeking remedy, there is nothing left but patience. But my son, when able, may seek the relief of the law, which I am denied: he or his son may renew his appeal, till he recover his right. But the conquered, or their children, have no court, no arbitrator on earth to appeal to. Then they may appeal, as Jephthah did, to heaven, and repeat their appeal till they have recovered the native right of their ancestors, which was, to have such a legislative over them, as the majority should approve, and freely acquiesce in. If it be objected, this would cause endless trouble; I answer, no more than justice does, where she lies open to all that appeal to her. He that troubles his neighbour without a cause, is punished for it by the justice of the court he appeals to: and he that appeals to heaven must be sure he has right on his side; and a right too that is worth the trouble and cost of the appeal, as he will answer at a tribunal that cannot be deceived, and will be sure to retribute to every one according to the mischiefs he hath created to his fellow-subjects; that is, any part of mankind: from whence it is plain, that he that "conquers in an unjust war, can thereby have no title to the subjection and obedience of the conquered."

### § 177.

But supposing victory favours the right side, let us consider a conqueror in a lawful war, and see what power he gets, and over whom.

First, it is plain, "he gets no power by his conquest over those that conquered with him." They that fought on his side cannot suffer by the conquest, but must at least be as much freemen as they were before. And most commonly they serve upon terms, and on conditions to share with their leader, and enjoy a part of the spoil, and other advantages that attended the conquering sword; or at least have a part of the subdued country bestowed upon them. And "the conquering people are not, I hope, to be slaves by conquest," and wear their laurels only to show they are sacrifices to their leader's triumph. They that found absolute monarchy upon the title of the sword, make their heroes, who are the founders of such monarchies, arrant Drawcansirs[1], and forget they had any officers and soldiers that fought on their side in the battles they won, or assisted them in the subduing, or shared in possessing, the countries they mastered. We are told by some, that the English monarchy is founded in the Norman conquest[2], and that our princes have thereby a title to absolute dominion: which if it were true, (as by the history it appears otherwise) and that William had a right to make war on this island; yet his dominion by conquest could reach no farther than to the Saxons and Britons, that were then inhabitants of this country. The Normans that came with him, and helped to conquer, and all descended from them, are freemen, and no subjects by conquest, let that give what dominion it will. And if I, or any body else, shall claim freedom, as derived from them, it will be very hard to prove the contrary: and it is plain, the law, that has made no distinction between the one and the other, intends not there should be any difference in their freedom or privileges.

## § 178.

But supposing, which seldom happens, that the conquerors and conquered never incorporate into one people, under the same laws and freedom; let us see next "what power a lawful conqueror has over the subdued:" and that I say is purely despotical. He has an absolute

---

[1] 德洛坎塞（Drawcansirs）是英国的白金汉二世公爵乔治·维勒（George Villiers, 2nd Duke of Buckingham）的笑剧《排练》（The Rehearsal）中的一个人物。这部剧于1663年至1664年间创作，于1671年首演。德洛坎塞在剧中是一个性情凶残的人，在战场上不分敌我，乱杀一气。

[2] 关于"诺曼征服"及下文中的"威廉王"参见本章的导读。

power over the lives of those who by an unjust war have forfeited them; but not over the lives or fortunes of those who engaged not in the war, nor over the possessions even of those who were actually engaged in it.

### § 179.

Secondly, I say then the conqueror gets no power but only over those who have actually assisted, concurred, or consented to that unjust force that is used against him: for the people having given to their governors no power to do an unjust thing, such as is to make an unjust war, (for they never had such a power in themselves) they ought not to be charged as guilty of the violence and injustice that is committed in an unjust war, any farther than they actually abet it; no more than they are to be thought guilty of any violence or oppression their governors should use upon the people themselves, or any part of their fellow-subjects, they having impowered them no more to the one than to the other. Conquerors, it is true, seldom trouble themselves to make the distinction, but they willingly permit the confusion of war to sweep all together: but yet this alters not the right; for the conqueror's power over the lives of the conquered being only because they have used force to do, or maintain an injustice, he can have that power only over those who have concurred in that force; all the rest are innocent; and he has no more title over the people of that country, who have done him no injury, and so have made no forfeiture of their lives, than he has over any other, who without any injuries or provocations, have lived upon fair terms with him.

### § 180.

Thirdly, the power a conqueror gets over those he overcomes in a just war, is perfectly despotical: he has an absolute power over the lives of those, who, by putting themselves in a state of war, have forfeited them; but he has not thereby a right and title to their possessions. This I doubt not but at first sight will seem a strange doctrine, it being so quite contrary to the practice of the world; there being nothing more familiar in speaking of the dominion of countries, than to say such an one conquered it; as if conquest, without any more ado, conveyed a right of possession. But when we consider, that the practice of the strong and powerful, how universal soever it may be, is seldom the rule of right, however it be one part of the subjection of the conquered, not to argue against the conditions cut out to them by the conquering sword.

### § 181.

Though in all war there be usually a complication of force and damage, and the aggressor seldom fails to harm the estate, when he uses force against the persons of those he makes war upon; yet it is the use of force only that puts a man into the state of war: for whether by force he begins the injury, or else, having quietly, and by fraud, done the injury, he refuses to make reparation, and by force maintains it, (which is the same thing, as at first to have done it by force) it is the unjust use of force that makes the war: for he that breaks open my house, and violently turns me out of doors; or, having peaceably got in, by force keeps me out; does in effect the same thing; supposing we are in such a state, that we have no common judge on earth, whom I may appeal to, and to whom we are both obliged to submit: for of such I am now speaking. It is the "unjust use of force then, that puts a man into the state of war" with another; and thereby he that is guilty of it makes a forfeiture of his life: for quitting reason, which is the rule given between man and man, and using force, the way of beasts, he becomes liable to be destroyed by him he uses force against, as any savage ravenous beast, that is dangerous to his being.

## § 182.

But because the miscarriages of the father are no faults of the children, and they may be rational and peaceable, not withstanding the brutishness and injustice of the father; the father, by his miscarriages and violence, can forfeit but his own life, but involves not his children in his guilt or destruction. His goods, which nature, that willeth the preservation of all mankind as much as is possible, hath made to belong to the children, to keep them from perishing, do still continue to belong to his children: for supposing them not to have joined in the war, either through infancy, absence, or choice, they have done nothing to forfeit them: nor has the conqueror any right to take them away, by the bare title of having subdued him that by force attempted his destruction; though perhaps he may have some right to them, to repair the damages he has sustained by the war; and the defence of his own right; which how far it reaches to the possessions of the conquered, we shall see by and by. So that he that by conquest has a right over a man's person to destroy him if he pleases, has not thereby a right over his estate to possess and enjoy it: for it is the brutal force the aggressor has used, that gives his adversary a right to take away his life, and destroy him if he pleases as a noxious creature; but it is damage sustained that alone gives him title to another man's goods: for, though I may kill a thief that sets on me in the highway, yet I may not (which seems less) take away his money and let him go: this would be robbery on my side. His force, and the state of war he put himself in, made him forfeit his life, but gave me no title to his goods. The right then of conquest extends only to the lives of those who joined in the war, not to their estates, but only in order to make reparation for the damages received, and the charges of the war; and that too with the reservation of the right of the innocent wife and children.

### § 183.

Let the conqueror have as much justice on his side as could be supposed, he has no right to seize more than the vanquished could forfeit: his life is at the victor's mercy; and his service and goods he may appropriate, to make himself reparation; but he cannot take the goods of his wife and children: they too had a title to the goods he enjoyed, and their shares in the estate he possessed: for example, I in the state of nature (and all commonwealths are in the state of nature one with another) have injured another man, and refusing to give satisfaction it comes to a state of war, wherein my defending by force what I had gotten unjustly makes me the aggressor. I am conquered: my life, it is true, as forfeit, is at mercy, but not my wife's and children's. They made not the war, nor assisted in it. I could not forfeit their lives; they were not mine to forfeit. My wife had a share in my estate; that neither could I forfeit. And my children also, being born of me, had a right to be maintained out of my labour or substance. Here then is the case: the conqueror has a title to reparation for damages received, and the children have a title to their father's estate for their subsistence: for as to the wife's share, whether her own labour, or compact, gave her a title to it, it is plain, her husband could not forfeit what was hers. What must be done in the case? I answer; the fundamental law of nature being, that all, as much as may be, should be preserved, it follows, that if there be not enough fully to satisfy both, viz. for the conqueror's losses, and children's maintenance, he that hath, and to spare, must remit something of his full satisfaction, and give way to the pressing and preferable title of those who are in danger to perish without it.

### § 184.

But supposing the charge and damages of the war are to be made up to the conqueror, to the utmost farthing; and that the children of the vanquished, spoiled of all their father's goods, are to be left to starve and perish; yet the satisfying of what shall, on this score, be due to the conqueror, will scarce give him a title to any country he shall conquer: for the damages of war can scarce amount to the value of any considerable tract of land, in any part of the world, where all the land is possessed, and none lies waste. And if I have not taken away the conqueror's land, which, being vanquished, it is impossible I should; scarce any other spoil I have done him can amount to the value of mine, supposing it equally cultivated, and of an extent any way coming near what I had over-run of his. The destruction of a year's product or two (for it seldom reaches four or five) is the utmost spoil that usually can be done: for as to money, and such riches and treasure taken away, these are none of nature's goods, they have but a fantastical imaginary value: nature has put no such upon them: they are of no more account by her standard, than the wampompeke[1] of the Americans to an European prince, or the silver money of Europe would have been formerly to an American. And five years product is not worth the perpetual inheritance of land, where all is possessed, and none remains waste, to be taken up by him that is disseized: which will be easily granted, if one do but take away the imaginary value of money, the disproportion being more than between five and five hundred; though, at the same time, half a year's product is more worth than the inheritance, where there being more land than the inhabitants possess and make use of, any one has liberty to make use of the waste: but there conquerors take little care to possess themselves of the lands of the vanquished. No damage therefore, that men in the state of nature (as all princes and governments are in reference to one another) suffer from one another, can give a conqueror power to dispossess the posterity of the vanquished, and turn them out of that inheritance which ought to be the possession of them and their descendants to all generations.

---

[1] 阿尔贡金语（北美印第安语族）中有 Wampumpeag 这样一个词，意思是"贝壳串珠"，wampompeke 是 Wampumpeag 的口语表达。17 世纪北美洲的印第安人将贝壳串珠（而非金银）当作交换手段来使用。Wampumpeag 在英语中被简化为 wampum，既有"贝壳串珠"的意思，也有"金钱"的意思。

The conqueror indeed will be apt to think himself master: and it is the very condition of the subdued not to be able to dispute their right. But if that be all, it gives no other title than what bare force gives to the stronger over the weaker; and, by this reason, he that is strongest will have a right to whatever he pleases to seize on.

### § 185.

Over those then that joined with him in the war, and over those of the subdued country that opposed him not, and the posterity even of those that did, the conqueror, even in a just war, hath, by his conquest, no right of dominion: they are free from any subjection to him, and if their former government be dissolved, they are at liberty to begin and erect another to themselves.

### § 186.

The conqueror, it is true, usually, by the force he has over them, compels them, with a sword at their breasts, to stoop to his conditions, and submit to such a government as he pleases to afford them; but the inquiry is, what right he has to do so? If it be said, they submit by their own consent, then this allows their own consent to be necessary to give the conqueror a title to rule over them. It remains only to be considered, whether promises extorted by force, without right, can be thought consent, and how far they bind. To which I shall say, they bind not at all; because whatsoever another gets from me by force, I still retain the right of, and he is obliged presently to restore. He that forces my horse from me, ought presently to restore him, and I have still a right to retake him. By the same reason, he that forced a promise from me, ought presently to restore it, i. e. quit me of the obligation of it: or I may resume it myself, i. e. choose whether I will perform it: for the law of nature laying an obligation on me only by the rules she prescribes, cannot oblige me by the violation of her rules: such is the extorting any thing from me by force. Nor does it at all alter the case to say, "I gave my promise," no more than it excuses the force, and passes the right, when I put my hand in my pocket and deliver my purse myself to a thief, who demands it with a pistol at my breast.

### § 187.

From all which it follows, that the government of a conqueror, imposed by force, on the subdued, against whom he had no right of war, or who joined not in the war against him, where he had right, has no obligation upon them.

### § 188.

But let us suppose that all the men of that community, being all members of the same body politic, may be taken to have joined in that unjust war, wherein they are subdued, and so their lives are at the mercy of the conqueror.

### § 189.

I say this concerns not their children who are in their minority: for since a father hath not, in himself, a power over the life or liberty of his child, no act of his can possibly forfeit it. So that the children, whatever may have happened to the fathers, are freemen, and the absolute power of the conqueror reaches no farther than the persons of the men that were subdued by him, and dies with them: and should he govern them as slaves subjected to his absolute arbitrary power, he has no such right or dominion over their children. He can have no power over them but by their own consent, whatever he may drive them to say or do; and he has no lawful authority, whilst force, and not choice, compels them to submission.

### § 190.

Every man is born with a double right: first, a right of freedom to his person, which no other man has a power over, but the free disposal of it lies in himself. Secondly, a right, before any other man, to inherit with his brethren his father's goods.

### § 191.

By the first of these, a man is naturally free from subjection to any government, though he be born in a place under its jurisdiction; but if he disclaim the lawful government of the country he was born in, he must also quit the right that belonged to him by the laws of it, and the possessions there descending to him from his ancestors, if it were a government made by their consent.

### § 192.

By the second, the inhabitants of any country, who are descended, and derive a title to their estates from those who are subdued, and had a government forced upon them against their free consents, retain a right to the possession of their ancestors, though they consent not freely to the government, whose hard conditions were by force imposed on the possessors of that country: for, the first conqueror never having had a title to the land of that country, the people who are the descendants of, or claim under those who were forced to submit to the yoke of a government by constraint, have always a right to shake it off, and free themselves from the usurpation or tyranny which the sword hath brought in upon them, till their rulers put them under such a frame of government as they willingly and of choice consent to. Who doubts but the Grecian christians, descendants of the ancient possessors of that country, may justly cast off the Turkish yoke, which they have so long groaned under, whenever they have an opportunity to do it? For no government can have a right to obedience from a people who have not freely consented to it; which they can never be supposed to do, till either they are put in a full state of liberty to choose their government and governors, or at least till they have such standing laws, to which they have by themselves or their representatives given their free consent; and also till they are allowed their due property, which is, so to be proprietors of what they have, that nobody can take away any part of it without their own consent, without which, men under any government are not in the state of freemen, but are direct slaves under the force of war.

### § 193.

But granting that the conqueror in a just war has a right to the estates, as well as power over the persons of the conquered; which, it is plain, he hath not: nothing of absolute power will follow from hence, in the continuance of the government; because the descendants of these being all freemen, if he grants them estates and possessions to inhabit his country, (without which it would be worth nothing) whatsoever he grants them, they have, so far as it is granted, property in.—The nature whereof is, that "without a man's own consent, it cannot be taken from him."

### § 194.

Their persons are free by a native right, and their properties, be they more or less, are their own, and at their own dispose, and not at his; or else it is no property. Supposing the conqueror gives to one man a thousand acres, to him and his heirs for ever; to another he lets a thousand acres for his life, under the rent of 50*l*. or 500*l*. per annum, has not the one of these a right to his thousand acres for ever, and the other during his life, paying the said rent? and hath not the tenant for life a property in all that he gets over and above his rent, by his labour and industry during the said term, supposing it to be double the rent? Can any one say, the king, or conqueror, after his grant, may, by his power of conqueror, take away all, or part of the land from the heirs of one, or from the other during his life, he paying the rent? or can he take away from either the goods or money they have got upon the said land, at his pleasure? If he can, then all free and voluntary contracts cease, and are void in the world; there needs nothing to dissolve them at any time but power enough: and all the grants and promises of men in power are but mockery and collusion: for can there be any thing more ridiculous than to say, I give you and yours this for ever, and that in the surest and most solemn way of conveyance can be devised; and yet it is to be understood, that I have a right, if I please, to take it away from you again tomorrow?

### § 195.

I will not dispute now, whether princes are exempt from the laws of their country; but this I am sure, they owe subjection to the laws of God and nature. Nobody, no power, can exempt them from the obligations of that eternal law. Those are so great, and so strong, in the case of promises, that omnipotency itself can be tied by them. Grants, promises, and oaths, are bonds that hold the Almighty: whatever some flatterers say to princes of the world, who all together, with all their people joined to them, are in comparison of the great God, but as a drop of the bucket, or a dust on the balance, inconsiderable, nothing.

### § 196.

The short of the case in conquest is this: the conqueror, if he have a just cause, has a despotical right over the persons of all that actually aided, and concurred in the war against him, and a right to make up his damage and cost out of their labour and estates, so he injure not the right of any other. Over the rest of the people, if there were any that consented not to the war, and over the children of the captives themselves, or the possessions of either, he has no power; and so can have, by virtue of conquest, no lawful title himself to dominion over them, or derive it to his posterity; but is an aggressor, if he attempts upon their properties, and thereby puts himself in a state of war against them: and has no better a right of principality, he, nor any of his successors, than Hingar, or Hubba, the Danes, had here in England;[1] or Spartacus[2], had he conquered Italy, would have had; which is to have their yoke cast off, as soon as God shall give those under their subjection courage and opportunity to do it. Thus, notwithstanding whatever title the kings of Assyria had over Judah, by the sword, God assisted Hezekiah to throw off the dominion of that conquering empire. "And the Lord was with Hezekiah, and he prospered; wherefore he went forth, and he rebelled against the king of Assyria, and served him not," 2 Kings, xviii. 7. Whence it is plain, that shaking off a power, which force, and not right, hath set over any one, though it hath the name of rebellion, yet is no offence before God, but is that which he allows and countenances, though even promises and covenants, when obtained by force, have intervened: for it is very probable, to any one that reads the story of Ahaz and Hezekiah attentively, that the Assyrians subdued Ahaz, and deposed him, and made Hezekiah king in his father's life-time; and that Hezekiah by agreement had done him homage, and paid him tribute all this time.[3]

---

[1] 欣加尔（Hingar）与胡巴（Hubba）应该是《盎格鲁－撒克逊编年史》中所记载的860年左右入侵英格兰的两位丹麦领袖。

[2] 斯巴达克斯（Spartacus，约公元前120年—约公元前70年）是巴尔干半岛东北部的色雷斯人。罗马侵入北希腊时，他被俘虏，并被卖为角斗士奴隶，送到卡普亚城一所角斗士学校参训。他和他的同伴克雷斯和奥梅尼奥斯在角斗士学校发起暴动，逃到维苏威火山上发动起义。起义队伍由七十余名角斗士很快发展为十余万人，并多次战胜罗马军队。罗马军队四面围剿，终于在阿普里亚决战中将起义镇压下去，斯巴达克斯战死，余部在意大利许多地区坚持战斗达十年之久。

[3] 希西家（Hezekiah）是犹大国（Judah）末年的君主。希西家25岁时就登基作王，在位29年。在国家危急之秋，希西家行耶和华上帝眼中正确的事，因而得上帝的怜悯，得以成功脱离亚述（Assyria）大军的攻击和一场致死的大病。由于希西家积极倡导百姓重新敬拜上帝，并遵守上帝的命令，所以被犹太人认为是一位好君王。

# Chapter XVII
## Of Usurpation

### 导 读

　　人类的政治史在某种意义上就是争夺权力与运用权力的历史。翔实地描述打天下与治天下的生动历史是历史学家的任务。政治学家的任务是为我们判断这种政治行为正当与否提供标准。

　　权力的获得与运作可以通过正当的方式，也可以通过不正当的方式。洛克在第十六章分析了征服这种特殊的方式。在他看来，对于征服，我们需要区分不同的情况。征服并不一定是不正当的，而且征服还可以为征服者带来某种有限的权力，或者是创造一个获得统治权的机会（如果能够通过人民的同意）。在第十七章与十八章中，洛克将要分析一种完全不正当的权力获得方式与一种完全不正当的运用权力的方式，即篡夺与暴政。

　　英文单词"暴君"（tyrant）与"暴政"（tyranny）起于希腊单词 tyrannos 与 tyrannis。暴君与暴政在现代用法中具有明显的贬义，但是在古希腊历史中并不一定是贬义的。因此，研究古希腊的学者往往将 tyrannos 与 tyrannis 翻译为"僭主"与"僭政"。僭主主要是指通过不合法的方式成为王的政权篡夺者。"僭政"就是这种政权篡夺者的统治。早期古希腊诗人使用"僭主"一词往往与"王"一词交替使用，并不赋予其否定涵义。原因也许是有不少僭主是贤明的、受到人民拥戴的。当柏拉图与亚里士多德对政体问题进行理论反思的时候，他们往往将僭政归为一种不好的政体。这是因为，虽然僭主有时候是贤明的，但是这取决于僭主的个人特征。要为僭政奠定一个抽象的正当性基础是非常困难的。柏拉图与亚里士多德都指出，僭主非常容易被人民诛杀。

到了中世纪，人们依然会讨论古希腊人所讲的这种"僭主"，即非法夺取王权的人。中世纪的人基本上认为，这种僭主因为破坏了世袭君主制所以是不合法的。因此，用贬义的"暴君"来指代僭主就更为准确了。洛克在第十七章中所讲的"篡夺者"也就是这种暴君。洛克也同样认为篡夺者是不合法的，但是他的理由有所不同。他的理由是：表面上看，通过这种方式上台的统治者破坏了国家关于如何选择统治者的基本法（这种基本法规定的可能是世袭君主制，也可能是其他制度），但从根本上看，篡夺者不具有合法性是因为他并没有获得人民的同意。

在中世纪，人们还用 tyrant 与 tyranny 来指代另一种的暴君与暴政概念。这种统治者具有拥有王权的正当性，但是却败坏了。例如，国王个人品德上出现了缺陷（残忍、贪婪、对宗教不虔诚等），或者实施有损人民利益的行为（如横征暴敛、错误地发动战争、治国不善等），或者仅仅因为与教会对抗都可能被人民、思想家、教会定义为暴君。此外，中世纪还慢慢发展出了"反抗暴君"的学说。早期的教父思想家往往坚持绝对服从原理，因为在他们看来，暴君是上帝对人类的惩罚，人不可反抗上帝的安排。后来，一些基督教思想家慢慢提出了暴君应当受到制约的说法，但是对究竟应当由谁来制约（教会、贵族还是人民），究竟应当通过什么方式来制约（进谏、要求退位还是诛杀）这两个重要问题并没有一致的看法。即使最为激进的思想家也并没有直接明了地将推翻暴君的权力赋予人民。中世纪的"反抗暴君"思想之所以略显保守的一个主要原因是，中世纪的君权神授观念占据主导，而人民主权概念还没有发展出来。要赋予人民推翻暴政的权力，必须彻底转化中世纪的国家学说，重新解释个人与国家的关系。

洛克在第十八章中所讲的暴政与中世纪所讲的这种暴政相

同,但是洛克进一步发展了这种学说。理解洛克对暴政问题的分析需要把握两个要点。第一个要点,是洛克赋予了暴政以全新的定义。中世纪对暴君的定义是复杂多样的,并没有一个统一的基础。洛克的定义非常简明,"法律一停止,暴政就开始"。当然,洛克这里所讲的"法律"并不是任何的法律,它具有特定的内容与形式。对此,洛克之前都已经讲过。第二个要点,是洛克赋予了人民用暴力来反抗暴政的权力。中世纪对反抗权的阐述主要是基于一种神学立场,即使是基于"人民同意学说"的反抗理论也没有一个系统的理论基础。由于洛克阐述了一种自然权利学说与法治国家学说,因此他可以明确赋予人民反抗暴政的权力,而这个权力是具有坚实理论基础的。

国家的统治究竟在哪些情况下会蜕变为暴政?人民应当是什么时候通过革命的方式来反抗暴政?人民的革命权的行使需要哪些条件呢?它会带来怎样的后果呢?革命与重新建国之间是怎样的关系呢?洛克在最后一章将对这些问题做出回答。

**延伸阅读材料:**

1. 古希腊的僭政问题:

——[古希腊]柏拉图:《理想国》,郭斌和、张竹明译,北京,商务印书馆,1986。

——[古希腊]亚里士多德:《政治学》,吴寿彭译,北京,商务印书馆,2007。

——[美]施特劳斯、科耶夫:《论僭政:色诺芬〈希耶罗〉义疏》,古热维奇、罗兹编,何地译,观溟校,北京,华夏出版社,2006。

——[英]A.安德鲁斯:《希腊僭主》,钟嵩译,北京,商务印书馆,1997。

——任东梅:《浅析古希腊早期僭主政治》,东北师范大学硕士论文,2008年。

2. 中世纪的暴政问题:

——[英]英萨尔兹伯利的约翰:《论政府原理》,北京,中国政法大学出版社,2003,特别是第18—20章。

——［英］奥卡姆的威廉：《僭主政体短论》，北京，中国政法大学出版社，2003。

——董玉洁：《中世纪英国有关暴君暴政的理论和暴君暴政的实际》，首都师范大学硕士论文，2009年。

——Wilfrid Parsons, The Medieval Theory of Tyrant, *The Review of Politics*, Vol. 4, No. 2 (Apr., 1942), pp.129–143.

洛克生前的最后一幅肖像，
由戈弗雷·内勒（Godfrey Kneller）画于1704年。

## § 197.

As conquest may be called a foreign usurpation, so usurpation is a kind of domestic conquest; with this difference, that an usurper can never have right on his side, it being no usurpation but where one is got into the possession of what another has right to. This, so far as it is usurpation, is a change only of persons, but not of the forms and rules of the government; for if the usurper extend his power beyond what of right belonged to the lawful princes, or governors of the commonwealth, it is tyranny added to usurpation.

## § 198.

In all lawful governments, the designation of the persons, who are to bear rule, is as natural and necessary a part, as the form of the government itself; and is that which had its establishment originally from the people; the anarchy being much alike to have no form of government at all, or to agree, that it shall be monarchical, but to appoint no way to design the person that shall have the power, and be the monarch. Hence all commonwealths, with the form of government established, have rules also of appointing those who are to have any share in the public authority, and settled methods of conveying the right to them: for the anarchy is much alike to have no form of government at all, or to agree that it shall be monarchical, but to appoint no way to know or design the person that shall have the power and be the monarch. Whoever gets into the exercise of any part of the power, by other ways than what the laws of the community have prescribed, hath no right to be obeyed, though the form of the commonwealth be still preserved; since he is not the person the laws have appointed, and consequently not the person the people have consented to. Nor can such an usurper, or any deriving from him, ever have a title, till the people are both at liberty to consent, and have actually consented to allow, and confirm in him the power he hath till then usurped.

# Chapter XVIII

# Of Tyranny[1]

### § 199.

As usurpation is the exercise of power, which another hath a right to, so tyranny is the exercise of power beyond right, which nobody can have a right to. And this is making use of the power any one has in his hands, not for the good of those who are under it, but for his own private separate advantage. When the governor, however intitled, makes not the law, but his will, the rule; and his commands and actions are not directed to the preservation of the properties of his people, but the satisfaction of his own ambition, revenge, covetousness, or any other irregular passion.

### § 200.

If one can doubt this to be truth, or reason, because it comes from the obscure hand of a subject, I hope the authority of a king

---

[1] 这一章从开头到第202段显然从属于从第16章开始的一系列主题，即几种非常的统治方式。这一章应该是写于1681年或1682年，其中一个重要的例子是第200段对英格兰国王"詹姆斯一世"的引用。但是从第202段开始，暴政这一主题被搁置，洛克转而讨论反抗问题。第202段往后的部分是后来加入的，但不太可能是1689年加入的，因为这里的内容读起来像是在描述一种设想中的反抗情形，而非已经发生的反抗活动（即光荣革命）。此外，这里对君主的描述更符合查理二世而非詹姆斯二世。因此，这一部分的大部分内容应该是洛克1683年离开英格兰去荷兰之前写成的。

will make it pass with him. King James[1] the first, in his speech to the parliament, 1603, tells them thus: "I will ever prefer the weal of the public, and of the whole commonwealth, in making of good laws and constitutions, to any particular and private ends of mine; thinking ever the wealth and weal of the commonwealth to be my greatest weal and worldly felicity; a point wherein a lawful king doth directly differ from a tyrant: for I do acknowledge, that the special and greatest point of difference that is between a rightful king and an usurping tyrant, is this, that whereas the proud and ambitious tyrant doth think his kingdom and people are only ordained for satisfaction of his desires and unreasonable appetites, the righteous and just king doth by the contrary acknowledge himself to be ordained for the procuring of the wealth and property of his people." And again, in his speech to the parliament, 1609, he hath these words: "The king binds himself by a double oath to the observation of the fundamental laws of his kingdom; tacitly, as by being a king, and so bound to protect as well the people, as the laws of his kingdom; and expressly, by his oath at his coronation; so as every just king, in a settled kingdom, is bound to observe that paction made to his people by his laws, in framing his government agreeable thereunto, according to that paction which God made with Noah after the deluge: Hereafter, seed-time and harvest, and cold and heat, and summer and winter, and day and night, shall not cease while the earth remaineth. And therefore a king governing in a settled kingdom, leaves to be a king, and degenerates into a tyrant, as soon as he leaves off to rule according to his laws." And a little after, "Therefore all kings that are not tyrants, or perjured, will be glad to bound themselves within the limits of their laws; and they that persuade them the contrary, are vipers, and pests, both against them and the commonwealth." Thus that learned king, who well understood the notions of things,

---

[1] 这里的"詹姆斯国王"(King James)是指詹姆斯一世(James I, 1566年6月19日—1625年3月27日), 1603年3月24日到1625年3月27日在位。

makes the difference betwixt a king and a tyrant to consist only in this, that one makes the laws the bounds of his power, and the good of the public the end of his government; the other makes all give way to his own will and appetite.

## § 201.

It is a mistake to think this fault is proper only to monarchies; other forms of government are liable to it, as well as that: for wherever the power, that is put in any hands for the government of the people, and the preservation of their properties, is applied to other ends, and made use of to impoverish, harass, or subdue them to the arbitrary and irregular commands of those that have it; there it presently becomes tyranny, whether those that thus use it are one or many. Thus we read of the thirty tyrants at Athens[1], as well as one at Syracuse[2]; and the intolerable dominion of the decemviri at Rome[3] was nothing better.

---

[1] 公元前404年，斯巴达人击败了雅典人，结束了长达27年的伯罗奔尼撒战争。斯巴达国王吕西斯特拉图（Lysistratus）在雅典建立了一个寡头政治的傀儡政府，处于斯巴达的保护下，称作三十人僭主（Thirty Tyrants）。三十人僭主集团由克里蒂亚斯（Critias）和年轻得多的查米德斯（Charmides）领导。这个集团在执政期间，处死了大量雅典公民，使得许多人流离逃亡。8个月后，三十人僭主集团垮台，民主制恢复，克里蒂亚斯和查米德斯被处死。

[2] 叙拉古（Syracuse）是古代希腊城邦，位于西西里岛东部，约公元前734年由科林斯的移民所建。公元前405年，狄奥尼修一世（Dionysius I）利用与迦太基人作战的紧张局势，在叙拉古重建僭主统治。之后，狄奥尼修一世的儿子狄奥尼修二世（Dionysius II）当政，继续维持僭主政体。柏拉图曾去叙拉古与狄奥尼修一世交谈，后又两次应邀去做狄奥尼修二世的导师。

[3] 十人委员会。Decemviri（单数为decemvir）是一个拉丁文的名词，表示"十人"。公元前452年，古罗马的平民与贵族同意组成一个十人委员会来进行立法。在十人委员会任职期间，所有其他的长官职务被暂时停止，而他们的决定将不被诉请民意公决。第一个十人委员会在公元前451年成立，完全由贵族组成。十人委员会中的每一人轮流管理政府一天，而且当天当政的委员就会有刀斧手持着刀斧、棍捆与仪仗来开道。十人委员会制度的成功促成公元前450年第二个十人委员会的任命。随后，这个十人委员会的统治变得越来越暴虐。当任期届满之时，十人委员会拒绝离开职位，也不允许继承人去接管职位。人们发起了反对十人委员会的暴动。公元前449年，十人委员会放弃了他们的职位，正规长官再次执政。

## § 202.

Wherever law ends, tyranny begins, if the law be transgressed to another's harm; and whosoever in authority exceeds the power given him by the law, and makes use of the force he has under his command, to compass that upon the subject, which the law allows not, ceases in that to be a magistrate; and, acting without authority, may be opposed as any other man, who by force invades the right of another. This is acknowledged in subordinate magistrates. He that hath authority to seize my person in the street, may be opposed as a thief and a robber if he endeavours to break into my house to execute a writ, notwithstanding that I know he has such a warrant, and such a legal authority, as will impower him to arrest me abroad. And why this should not hold in the highest, as well as in the most inferiour magistrate, I would gladly be informed. Is it reasonable that the eldest brother, because he has the greatest part of his father's estate, should thereby have a right to take away any of his younger brother's portions? or, that a rich man, who possessed a whole country, should from thence have a right to seize, when he pleased, the cottage and garden of his poor neighbour? The being rightfully possessed of great power and riches, exceedingly beyond the greatest part of the sons of Adam, is so far from being an excuse, much less a reason for rapine and oppression, which the endamaging another without authority is, that it is a great aggravation of it: for the exceeding the bounds of authority is no more a right in a great, than in a petty officer; no more justifiable in a king than a constable; but is so much the worse in him, in that he has more trust put in him, has already a much greater share than the rest of his brethren, and is supposed, from the advantages of his education, employment, and counsellors, to be more knowing in the measures of right and wrong.

## § 203.

"May the commands then of a prince be opposed? may he be

resisted as often as any one shall find himself aggrieved, and but imagine he has not right done him? This will unhinge and overturn all polities, and, instead of government and order, leave nothing but anarchy and confusion."

## § 204.

To this I answer, that force is to be opposed to nothing but to unjust and unlawful force; whoever makes any opposition in any other case, draws on himself a just condemnation both from God and man; and so no such danger or confusion will follow, as is often suggested: for,

## § 205.

First, as, in some countries[1], the person of the prince by the law is sacred; and so, whatever he commands or does, his person is still free from all question or violence, not liable to force, or any judicial censure or condemnation. But yet opposition may be made to the illegal acts of any inferiour officer, or other commissioned by him; unless he will, by actually putting himself into a state of war with his people, dissolve the government, and leave them to that defence which belongs to every one in the state of nature: for of such things who can tell what the end will be? and a neighbour kingdom has showed the world an odd example[2]. In all other cases the sacredness of the person exempts him from all inconveniencies, whereby he is secure, whilst the government stands, from all violence and harm whatsoever; than which there cannot be a wiser constitution; for the harm he can do in his own person not being likely to happen often, nor to extend itself far; nor being able by his single strength to subvert the laws, nor oppress the body of the people; should

---

[1] 这里的"有些国家"(some countries)是指英格兰。
[2] 从上文的 unless 到 example 的这部分内容应该是洛克在1689年加入到原稿中的。这段话直指詹姆斯二世将自己置于与人们的战争状态中,从而解散了政府。这里的 neighbour kingdom 也是指英格兰。

any prince have so much weakness and ill-nature as to be willing to do it, the inconveniency of some particular mischiefs that may happen sometimes, when a heady prince comes to the throne, are well recompensed by the peace of the public, and security of the government, in the person of the chief magistrate, thus set out of the reach of danger: it being safer for the body that some few private men should be sometimes in danger to suffer, than that the head of the republic should be easily, and upon slight occasions, exposed.

## § 206.

Secondly, but this privilege belonging only to the king's person, hinders not, but they may be questioned, opposed, and resisted, who use unjust force, though they pretend a commission from him, which the law authorizes not; as is plain in the case of him that has the king's writ to arrest a man, which is a full commission from the king; and yet he that has it cannot break open a man's house to do it, nor execute this command of the king upon certain days, nor in certain places, though this commission have no such exception in it; but they are the limitations of the law, which if any one transgress, the king's commission excuses him not: for the king's authority being given him only by the law, he cannot impower any one to act against the law, or justify him, by his commission, in so doing; the commission or command of any magistrate, where he has no authority, being as void and insignificant, as that of any private man; the difference between the one and the other being that the magistrate has some authority so far, and to such ends, and the private man has none at all: for it is not the commission, but the authority, that gives the right of acting; and against the laws there can be no authority. But notwithstanding such resistance, the king's person and authority are still both secured, and so no danger to governor or government.

## § 207.

Thirdly, supposing a government wherein the person of the chief magistrate is not thus sacred; yet this doctrine of the lawfulness of resisting all unlawful exercises of his power, will not upon every slight occasion endanger him, or embroil the government: for where the injured party may be relieved, and his damages repaired by appeal to the law, there can be no pretence for force, which is only to be used where a man is intercepted from appealing to the law: for nothing is to be accounted hostile force, but where it leaves not the remedy of such an appeal: and it is such force alone, that puts him that uses it into a state of war, and makes it lawful to resist him. A man with a sword in his hand, demands my purse in the highway, when perhaps I have not twelve-pence in my pocket: this man I may lawfully kill. To another I deliver £100 to hold only whilst I alight, which he refuses to restore me, when I am got up again, but draws his sword to defend the possession of it by force, if I endeavour to retake it. The mischief this man does me is an hundred, or possibly a thousand times more than the other perhaps intended me (whom I killed before he really did me any;) and yet I might lawfully kill the one, and connot so much as hurt the other lawfully. The reason whereof is plain; because the one using force, which threatened my life, I could not have time to appeal to the law to secure it: and when it was gone, it was too late to appeal. The law could not restore life to my dead carcase, the loss was irreparable: which to prevent, the law of nature gave me a right to destroy him, who had put himself into a state of war with me, and threatened my destruction. But in the other case, my life not being in danger, I may have the benefit of appealing to the law, and have reparation for my £100 that way.

## § 208.

Fourthly, but if the unlawful acts done by the magistrate be maintained (by the power he has got) and the remedy which is due by law, be by the same power obstructed: yet the right of resisting, even in such manifest acts of tyranny, will not suddenly, or on slight occasions, disturb the government: for if it reach no farther than some private men's cases, though they have a right to defend themselves, and to recover by force what by unlawful force is taken from them: yet the right to do so will not easily engage them in a contest, wherein they are sure to perish; it being as impossible for one, or a few oppressed men to disturb the government, where the body of the people do not think themselves concerned in it, as for a raving madman, or heady malecontent, to overturn a well-settled state, the people being as little apt to follow the one, as the other.

### § 209.

But if either these illegal acts have extended to the majority of the people; or if the mischief and oppression has lighted only on some few, but in such cases, as the precedent and consequences seem to threaten all; and they are persuaded in their consciences, that their laws, and with them their estates, liberties, and lives are in danger, and perhaps their religion too: how they will be hindered from resisting illegal force, used against them, I cannot tell. This is an inconvenience, I confess, that attends all governments whatsoever, when the governors have brought it to this pass, to be generally suspected of their people; the most dangerous state which they can possibly put themselves in; wherein they are less to be pitied, because it is so easy to be avoided; it being as impossible for a governor, if he really means the good of his people, and the preservation of them, and their laws together, not to make them see and feel it, as it is for the father of a family, not to let his children see he loves and takes care of them.

### § 210.

But if all the world shall observe pretences of one kind, and actions of another; arts used to elude the law, and the trust of prerogative, (which is an arbitrary power in some things left in the prince's hand to do good, not harm, to the people) employed contrary to the end for which it was given: if the people shall find the ministers and subordinate magistrates chosen suitable to such ends, and favoured, or laid by, proportionably as they promote or oppose them: if they see several experiments made of arbitrary power, and that religion underhand favoured (though publicly proclaimed against) which is readiest to introduce it; and the operators in it supported, as much as may be; and when that cannot be done, yet approved still, and liked the better: if a long train of actions show the councils all tending that way; how can a man any more hinder himself from being persuaded in his own mind, which way things are going; or from casting about how to save himself, than he could from believing the captain of the ship he was in, was carrying him, and the rest of the company, to Algiers, when he found him always steering that course, though cross winds, leaks in his ship, and want of men and provisions did often force him to turn his course another way for some time, which he steadily returned to again, as soon as the wind, weather, and other circumstances would let him?

法国国王路易十四（Louis XIV, 1638—1715），自号太阳王。路易十四是洛克所极力批判的绝对君主的典范。

# Chapter XIX

# Of the Dissolution of Government

## 导 读

本章不仅是《政府论（下篇）》中最长的一章，也是《政府论（下篇）》中最为重要、影响最为深远的一章。可以说，《政府论（下篇）》之前的内容都是为这一章做准备的。

我们可以将本章的主要内容归纳为人民革命学说。如果我们了解了《政府论（下篇）》之前的内容，那么我们是不难理解为何洛克认为人民享有革命权。简单来说，由于政府是受人民的委托来保护所有人的权利，因此当政府违背委托、滥用权力时，人民当然有权将其推翻。在阅读此章的时候，我们需要不断地回忆《政府论（下篇）》之前对人的权利、社会契约、委托、政府权力的论述。

"革命"这一字眼无疑会使我们想起英国的光荣革命。在当时，对于光荣革命有两种不同的理解。第一种理解是，王位是詹姆斯二世的，由于詹姆斯二世自愿放弃了王位，王位被空出了。此时，王位应当根据原有的君权神授的世袭继承法来加以确定。第二种理解是，詹姆斯二世的不端行为使得他被迫退位，因此国王与人民之间的原初契约或委托就被打破了。王位彻底虚空，由协商议会（Convention Parliament）来全权加以决定。英国人最终采纳了后一种理解。这种理解其实包含着非常激进的理念。

其一，人民拥有废除国王的权利，或者说人民拥有革命的权利。其二，人民可以重新设定国王及相关宪制制度，或者说人民拥有建国的权利。《政府论（下篇）》充分展示了这些激进的理念，赋予相应的政治举措以合法性，并将它们整合在一个完整的政府学说中。尽管如此，这种激进的思路完全超出了当时英格兰知识界与政治界大部分人的观念。因为，这相当于彻底摧毁英国的宪制传统（包括"王在巴列门中"与君权神授的世袭继承制度），在理论上将"人民"作为宪制的基础。其实，洛克在谈论光荣革命的具体问题时，也弱化了《政府论（下篇）》中的激进立场。他并没有直接主张一种无君的共和制，没有将"人民"等同于所有成年英国人。他还在信件中表示，"恢复"英国的传统宪制是光荣革命后的一个主要任务。洛克是一位思想家也是一位政治家，他的学说无疑指出了现代政治的方向，但是他也懂得政治言说与政治变革需要审慎的精神。

让我们回到洛克的人民革命学说本身中。即使人们勉强接受洛克的这一解释，许多人还是会反对将革命权赋予人民。一个重要理由是：革命导致国家陷入无政府状态。无政府状态对于一个国家来说是最大的灾难，因为它可能会带来无法无天的暴民统治，可能会带来导致国家四分五裂的内战，还可能导致外敌入侵。即使对于现代人来说，革命在许多人脑中都是一个不好的事情。对于还没有目睹过美国革命与法国大革命的英国人（特别是英国贵族）来说，"政府的解体"无疑是一个令人感到恐慌且不可思议的论断。为了应对将革命与无政府状态相等同的想法，洛克区分了"政府的解体"与"社会的解体"。他想告诉人们，"政府的解体"并不等于"社会的解体"。在政府解体后，社会仍然能够做出一致行动，重建政府。

这个问题并不像看上去那么简单，不然的话洛克也不会花那么大的篇幅来谈这个问题。对政治现实具有敏锐观察力的人一般都会认为，当一个政府彻底败坏的时候，几乎每个政府机构与大部分政府官员也已经都败坏了。也就是说，这个国家政治制度已经彻底"病入膏肓来不及救治"。此时，如果人民能够起来反抗的话，国家肯定是像一个被蛀空的大树完全丧失生命

力，一推就连根拔起了。此时，政府机构的任何一部分都无法继续运行，"人民变成了没有秩序或联系的杂乱群众"。洛克并不像一般人所认为的那样乐观甚至天真，他完全明白这一点。以上引号里的话就是洛克的原话。

洛克认为这种"政府的解体"是对人类政治自由的"愚弄"，因为人类让自己沦落到"奴隶"的境地。因此，洛克所讲的"政府的解体"还有另一种情况。在这种情况下，人类有能力也有责任去防止悲剧的发生。在这种情况下，严格地讲，政府并还没有违背人民的委托，而是"试图"、"企图"违背委托。此时，也许只是某个立法机构或某个执行机构试图滥用权力，并且已经出现明显的征兆。此时，人民也可以并需要加以反抗或革命。此时，旧制的某些部分仍然保持着一定的健康状态，人民（包括部分原有的政治人物）仍有很大一部分没有陷入奴役或堕落状态。洛克认为，此时社会是不会解体的。人民完全有能力去"建立一个新的政府，或在旧的政府形式下把立法权交给他们认为适当的新人"。

如果洛克认为人民明智而及时的反抗是防止自由政体沦为暴政、防止国家彻底解体的必要措施，那么是否只有当大部分国民都具有了对自由之宝贵的透彻了解与真正热爱，具有了对保卫国家的基本知识与行动力后，社会才可能成功地完成革命与随后的重建呢？换句话说，人民的革命是一种必然还是一种选择呢？如果革命是人民的一种选择，它就取决于人民的政治知识与政治能力。那么，人民是否会做出错误的选择，或者根本就不做出选择呢？

从古代到近代，许多思想家都对人民的政治行动抱有极大的怀疑。在他们看来，民众通常是无知的、懦弱的，他们非常容易被洗脑、被操纵，让人民担任政治的主角无疑是危险的。洛克充分认识到了这一点，他所讲的人民必须具备特定的品质。只有当一个国家在平时能够成功培养出这种人民时，这些公民才能够在危机时刻承担其民族重任。这种品质包括哪些？如何来加以培养？要了解这些问题，我们就必须去阅读洛克的另一部著作：《教育片论》。

**延伸阅读材料：**

1. 关于洛克及其学说与光荣革命的关系参见：

——［英］彼得·拉斯莱特：《洛克〈政府论〉导论》，冯克利译，北京，生活·读书·新知三联书店，2007，第三章《政府论两篇》与1689年革命"。

——James Farr and Clayton Roberts, John Locke on the Glorious Revolution: A Rediscovered Document, *The Historical Journal*, Vol. 28, No. 2 (Jun., 1985), pp. 385–398.

——Lois G. Schwoerer, Locke, Lockean Ideas, and the Glorious Revolution, *Journal of the History of Ideas*, Vol. 51, No. 4 (Oct. - Dec., 1990), pp. 531–548.

——Richard Ashcraft and M. M. Goldsmith, Locke, Revolution Principles, and the Formation of Whig Ideology, *The Historical Journal*, Vol. 26, No. 4 (Dec., 1983), pp. 773–800.

——Richard Ashcraft, Revolutionary Politics and Locke's Two Treatises of Government: Radicalism and Lockean Political Theory, *Political Theory*, Vol. 8, No. 4 (Nov., 1980), pp. 429–486.

——Richard Ashcraft, *Revolutionary Politics and Locke's "Two Treatises of Government"*, Princeton University Press (1 Aug. 1986).

2. 关于洛克人民革命学说的内在逻辑参见：

——李猛：《革命政治：洛克的政治哲学与现代自然法的危机》，载吴飞主编：《洛克与自由社会》，2012年。

——Nathan Tarcov, Locke's "Second Treatise" and "The Best Fence Against Rebellion", *The Review of Politics*, Vol. 43, No. 2 (Apr., 1981).

——M. Susan Power, John Locke: Revolution, Resistance, or Opposition?, *Interpretation*, Vol. 9/2 & 3 (Sep., 1981).

——Ruth W. Grant, *John Locke' Liberalism*, The University of Chicago Press, 1987, pp. 136–178.

——Robert C. Grady, II., Obligation, Consent, and Locke's Right to Revolution: "Who Is to Judge?", *Canadian Journal of Political Science*, Vol. 9, No. 2 (Jun., 1976).

——Martin Seliger, Locke's Theory of Revolutionary Action, *The Western Political Quarterly*, Vol. 16, No. 3 (Sep., 1963), pp. 548–568.

3. 洛克对公民品格的论述：［英］洛克：《教育片论》，熊春文译，上海，上海人民出版社，2006。

此图描绘了英国议会于1689年2月13日向威廉与玛丽呈上王冠与《权利法案》。

## § 211.

He that will with any clearness speak of the dissolution of government, ought in the first place to distinguish between the dissolution of the society and the dissolution of the government. That which makes the community, and brings men out of the loose state of nature into one politic society, is the agreement which every one has with the rest to incorporate, and act as one body, and so be one distinct commonwealth. The usual, and almost only way whereby this union is dissolved, is the inroad of foreign force making a conquest upon them; for in that case, (not being able to maintain and support themselves, as one entire and independent body) the union belonging to that body which consisted therein, must necessarily cease, and so every one return to the state he was in before, with a liberty to shift for himself, and provide for his own safety, as he thinks fit, in some other society. Whenever the society is dissolved, it is certain the government of that society cannot remain. Thus conquerors swords often cut up governments by the roots, and mangle societies to pieces, separating the subdued or scattered multitude from the protection of, and dependance on, that society which ought to have preserved them from violence. The world is too well instructed in, and too forward to allow of, this way of dissolving of governments, to need any more to be said of it; and there wants not much argument to prove, that where the society is dissolved, the government cannot remain; that being as impossible, as for the frame of a house to subsist when the materials of it are scattered and dissipated by a whirlwind, or jumbled into a confused heap by an earthquake.

## § 212.

Besides this overturning from without, governments are dissolved from within,

First, when the legislative is altered. Civil society being a state of peace, amongst those who are of it, from whom the state of war is excluded by the umpirage, which they have provided in their legislative, for the ending all differences that may arise amongst any of them; it is in their legislative, that the members of a commonwealth are united, and combined together into one coherent living body. This is the soul that gives form, life, and unity to the commonwealth: from hence the several members have their mutual influence, sympathy, and connexion; and therefore, when the legislative is broken, or dissolved, dissolution and death follows: for, the essence and union of the society consisting in having one will, the legislative, when once established by the majority, has the declaring, and as it were keeping of that will. The constitution of the legislative is the first and fundamental act of society, whereby provision is made for the continuation of their union, under the direction of persons, and bonds of laws, made by persons authorized thereunto, by the consent and appointment of the people; without which no one man, or number of men, amongst them, can have authority of making laws that shall be binding to the rest. When any one, or more, shall take upon them to make laws, whom the people have not appointed so to do, they make laws without authority, which the people are not therefore bound to obey; by which means they come again to be out of subjection, and may constitute to themselves a new legislative, as they think best, being in full liberty to resist the force of those, who without authority would impose any thing upon them. Every one is at the disposure of his own will, when those who had, by the delegation of the society, the declaring of the public will, are excluded from it, and others usurp the place, who have no such authority or delegation.

## § 213.

This being usually brought about by such in the commonwealth who misuse the power they have, it is hard to consider it aright, and know at whose door to lay it, without knowing the form of government in which it happens. Let us suppose then the legislative placed in the concurrence of three distinct persons.

1. A single hereditary person, having the constant, supreme, executive power, and with it the power of convoking and dissolving the other two, within certain periods of time.

2. An assembly of hereditary nobility.

3. An assembly of representatives chosen pro tempore, by the people. Such a form of government supposed, it is evident,

## § 214.

First, that when such a single person, or prince, sets up his own arbitrary will in place of the laws, which are the will of the society, declared by the legislative, then the legislative is changed: for that being in effect the legislative, whose rules and laws are put in execution, and required to be obeyed; when other laws are set up, and other rules pretended, and enforced, than what the legislative, constituted by the society, have enacted, it is plain that the legislative is changed. Whoever introduces new laws, not being thereunto authorized, by the fundamental appointment of the society, or subverts the old; disowns and overturns the power by which they were made, and so sets up a new legislative.

## § 215.

Secondly, when the prince hinders the legislative from assembling in its due time, or from acting freely, pursuant to those ends for which it was constituted, the legislative is altered: for it is not a certain number of men, no, nor their meeting, unless they have also freedom of debating, and leisure of perfecting, what is for the good of the society, wherein the legislative consists: when these are taken away or altered, so as to deprive the society of the due exercise of their power, the legislative is truly altered: for it is not names that constitute governments, but the use and exercise of those powers that were intended to accompany them; so that he, who takes away the freedom, or hinders the acting of the legislative in its due seasons, in effect takes away the legislative, and puts an end to the government.

### § 216.

Thirdly, when, by the arbitrary power of the prince, the electors, or ways of election, are altered, without the consent, and contrary to the common interest of the people, there also the legislative is altered: for, if others than those whom the society hath authorized thereunto, do choose, or in another way than what the society hath prescribed, those chosen are not the legislative appointed by the people.

### § 217.

Fourthly, the delivery also of the people into the subjection of a foreign power, either by the prince, or by the legislative, is certainly a change of the legislative, and so a dissolution of the government: for the end why people entered into society being to be preserved one intire, free, independent society, to be governed by its own laws; this is lost, whenever they are given up into the power of another.

### § 218.

Why, in such a constitution as this, the dissolution of the government in these cases is to be imputed to the prince, is evident; because he, having the force, treasure, and offices of the state to employ, and often persuading himself, or being flattered by others, that as supreme magistrate, he is uncapable of control; he alone is in a condition to make great advances toward such changes, under pretence of lawful authority, and has it in his hands to terrify or suppress opposers, as factious, seditious, and enemies to the government: whereas no other part of the legislative, or people, is capable by themselves to attempt any alteration of the legislative, without open and visible rebellion, apt enough to be taken notice of; which, when, it prevails, produces effects very little different from foreign conquest. Besides, the prince in such a form of government having the power of dissolving the other parts of the legislative, and thereby rendering them private persons, they can never in opposition to him, or without his concurrence, alter the legislative by a law, his consent being necessary to give any of their decrees that sanction. But yet, so far as the other parts of the legislative any way contribute to any attempt upon the government, and do either promote, or not (what lies in them) hinder such designs; they are guilty, and partake in this, which is certainly the greatest crime men can be guilty of one towards another.

### § 219.

There is one way more whereby such a government may be dissolved, and that is, when he who has the supreme executive power neglects and abandons that charge, so that the laws already made can no longer be put in execution. This is demonstratively to reduce all to anarchy, and so effectually to dissolve the government: for laws not being made for themselves, but to be, by their execution, the bonds of the society, to keep every part of the body politic in its due place and function; when that totally ceases, the government visibly ceases, and the people become a confused multitude, without order or connexion. Where there is no longer the administration of justice, for the securing of men's rights, nor any remaining power within the community to direct the force, or provide for the necessities of the public; there certainly is no government left. Where the laws cannot be executed, it is all one as if there were no laws; and a government without laws is, I suppose, a mystery in politics, inconceivable to human capacity, and inconsistent with human society.

## § 220.

In these and the like cases, when the government is dissolved, the people are at liberty to provide for themselves, by erecting a new legislative, differing from the other, by the change of persons, or form, or both, as they shall find it most for their safety and good: for the society can never, by the fault of another, lose the native and original right it has to preserve itself; which can only be done by a settled legislative, and a fair and impartial execution of the laws made by it. But the state of mankind is not so miserable that they are not capable of using this remedy, till it be too late to look for any. To tell people they may provide for themselves, by erecting a new legislative, when by oppression, artifice, or being delivered over to a foreign power, their old one is gone, is only to tell them, they may expect relief when it is too late, and the evil is past cure. This is in effect no more than to bid them first be slaves, and then to take care of their liberty; and when their chains are on, tell them, they may act like freemen. This, if barely so, is rather mockery than relief; and men can never be secure from tyranny, if there be no means to escape it till they are perfectly under it: and therefore it is, that they have not only a right to get out of it, but to prevent it.

## § 221.

There is, therefore, secondly, another way whereby governments are dissolved, and that is, when the legislative, or the prince, either of them, act contrary to their trust.

First, The legislative acts against the trust reposed in them, when they endeavour to invade the property of the subject, and to make themselves, or any part of the community, masters, or arbitrary disposers of the lives, liberties, or fortunes of the people.

## § 222.

The reason why men enter into society, is the preservation of their property; and the end why they choose and authorize a legislative, is, that there may be laws made, and rules set, as guards and fences to the properties of all the members of the society: to limit the power, and moderate the dominion, of every part and member of the society: for since it can never be supposed to be the will of the society, that the legislative should have a power to destroy that which every one designs to secure by entering into society, and for which the people submitted themselves to legislators of their own making; whenever the legislators endeavour to take away and destroy the property of the people, or to reduce them to slavery under arbitrary power, they put themselves into a state of war with the people, who are thereupon absolved from any farther obedience, and are left to the common refuge, which God hath provided for all men, against force and violence. Whensoever therefore the legislative shall transgress this fundamental rule of society; and either by ambition, fear, folly or corruption, endeavour to grasp themselves, or put into the hands of any other, an absolute power over the lives, liberties, and estates of the people; by this breach of trust they forfeit the power the people had put into their hands for quite contrary ends, and it devolves to the people, who have a right to resume their original liberty, and, by the establishment of a new legislative, (such as they shall think fit) provide for their own safety and security, which is the end for which they are in society. What I have said here, concerning the legislative in general, holds true also concerning the supreme executor, who having a double trust put in him, both to have a part in the legislative, and the supreme execution of the law, acts against both, when he goes about to set up his own arbitrary will as the law of the society. He acts also contrary to his trust, when he either employs the force, treasure, and offices of the society to corrupt the representatives, and gain them to his purposes; or openly pre-engages the electors, and prescribes to their choice, such, whom he has, by solicitations, threats, promises, or otherwise, won to his designs: and employs them to bring in such, who have promised beforehand what to vote, and what to enact. Thus to regulate candidates and electors, and new-model the ways of election, what is it but to cut up the government by the roots, and poison the very fountain of public security? for the people having reserved to themselves the choice of their representatives, as the fence to their properties, could do it for no other end, but that they might always be freely chosen, and so chosen, freely act, and advise, as the necessity of the commonwealth, and the public good should, upon examination and mature debate, be judged to require. This, those who give their votes before they hear the debate, and have weighed the reasons on all sides, are not capable of doing. To prepare such an assembly as this, and endeavour to set up the declared abettors of his own will, for the true representatives of the people, and the law-makers of the society, is certainly as great a breach of trust, and as perfect a declaration of a design to subvert the government, as is possible to be met with. To which if one shall add rewards and punishments visibly employed to the same end, and all the arts of perverted law made use of, to take off and destroy all that stand in the way of such a design, and will not comply and consent to betray the liberties of their country, it will be past doubt what is doing. What power they ought to have in the society, who thus employ it contrary to the trust that went along with it in its first institution, is easy to determine; and one cannot but see, that he, who has once attempted any such thing as this, cannot any longer be trusted.

§ 223.

To this perhaps it will be said, that the people being ignorant, and always discontented, to lay the foundation of government in the unsteady opinion and uncertain humour of the people, is to expose it to certain ruin; and no government will be able long to subsist, if the people may set up a new legislative, whenever they take offence at the old one. To this I answer, quite the contrary. People are not so easily got out of their old forms as some are apt to suggest. They are hardly to be prevailed with to amend the acknowledged faults in the frame they have been accustomed to. And if there be any original defects, or adventitious ones introduced by time, or corruption: it is not an easy thing to get them changed, even when all the world sees there is an opportunity for it. This slowness and aversion in the people to quit their old constitutions, has in the many revolutions which have been seen in this kingdom, in this and former ages, still kept us to, or, after some interval of fruitless attempts, still brought us back again to, our old legislative of king, lords, and commons: and whatever provocations have made the crown be taken from some of our princes heads, they never carried the people so far as to place it in another line.

### § 224.

But it will be said, this hypothesis lays a ferment for frequent rebellion. To which I answer,

First, no more than any other hypothesis: for when the people are made miserable, and find themselves exposed to the ill-usage of arbitrary power, cry up their governors as much as you will, for sons of Jupiter; let them be sacred or divine, descended, or authorized from heaven; give them out for whom or what you please, the same will happen. The people generally ill-treated, and contrary to right, will be ready upon any occasion to ease themselves of a burden that sits heavy upon them. They will wish, and seek for the opportunity, which in the change, weakness, and accidents of human affairs, seldom delays long to offer itself. He must have lived but a little while in the world, who has not seen examples of this in his time;

and he must have read very little, who cannot produce examples of it in all sorts of governments in the world.

## § 225.

Secondly, I answer, such revolutions happen not upon every little mismanagement in public affairs. Great mistakes in the ruling part, many wrong and inconvenient laws, and all the slips of human frailty, will be borne by the people without mutiny or murmur. But if a long train of abuses, prevarications and artifices, all tending the same way, make the design visible to the people, and they cannot but feel what they lie under, and see whither they are going; it is not to be wondered, that they should then rouse themselves, and endeavour to put the rule into such hands which may secure to them the ends for which government was at first erected; and without which, ancient names, and specious forms, are so far from being better, that they are much worse, than the state of nature, or pure anarchy; the inconveniencies being all as great and as near, but the remedy farther off and more difficult.

## § 226.

Thirdly, I answer, that this doctrine of a power in the people of providing for their safety anew, by a new legislative, when their legislators have acted contrary to their trust, by invading their property, is the best fence against rebellion, and the probablest means to hinder it: for rebellion being an opposition, not to persons, but authority, which is founded only in the constitutions and laws of the government; those, whoever they be, who by force break through, and by force justify their violation of them, are truly and properly rebels: for when men, by entering into society and civil government, have excluded force, and introduced laws for the preservation of property, peace, and unity amongst themselves; those who set up force again in opposition to the laws, do *rebellare*, that is, bring back again the state of war, and are properly rebels; which they who are in power, (by the pretence they have to authority, the temptation of force they have in their hands, and the flattery of those about them) being likeliest to do; the properest way to prevent the evil, is to show them the danger and injustice of it, who are under the greatest temptation to run into it.

### § 227.

In both the forementioned cases, when either the legislative is changed, or the legislators act contrary to the end for which they were constituted, those who are guilty are guilty of rebellion; for if any one by force takes away the established legislative of any society, and the laws by them made pursuant to their trust, he thereby takes away the umpirage, which every one had consented to, far a peaceable decision of all their controversies, and a bar to the state of war amongst them. They who remove, or change the legislative, take away this decisive power, which nobody can have but by the appointment and consent of the people; and so destroying the authority which the people did, and nobody else can set up, and introducing a power which the people hath not authorized, they actually introduce a state of war, which is that of force without authority; and thus by removing the legislative established by the society, (in whose decisions the people acquiesced and united, as to that of their own will) they untie the knot, and expose the people anew to the state of war. And if those, who by force take away the legislative, are rebels, the legislators themselves, as has been shown, can be no less esteemed so; when they, who were set up for the protection and preservation of the people, their liberties and properties, shall by force invade and endeavour to take them away; and so they putting themselves into a state of war with those who made them the protectors and guardians of their peace, are properly, and with the greatest aggravation, *rebellantes*, rebels.

## § 228.

But if they, who say, "it lays a foundation for rebellion," mean that it may occasion civil wars, or intestine broils, to tell the people they are absolved from obedience when illegal attempts are made upon their liberties or properties, and may oppose the unlawful violence of those who were their magistrates, when they invade their properties contrary to the trust put in them; and that therefore this doctrine is not to be allowed, being so destructive to the peace of the world: they may as well say, upon the same ground, that honest men may not oppose robbers or pirates, because this may occasion disorder or bloodshed. If any mischief come in such cases, it is not to be charged upon him who defends his own right, but on him that invades his neighbour's. If the innocent honest man must quietly quit all he has, for peace sake, to him who will lay violent hands upon it, I desire it may be considered, what a kind of peace there will be in the world, which consists only in violence and rapine; and which is to be maintained only for the benefit of robbers and oppressors. Who would not think it an admirable peace betwixt the mighty and the mean, when the lamb, without resistance, yielded his throat to be torn by the imperious wolf? Polyphemus's den gives us a perfect pattern of such a peace, and such a government, wherein Ulysses and his companions had nothing to do, but quietly to suffer themselves to be devoured. And no doubt Ulysses, who was a prudent man, preached up passive obedience, and exhorted them to a quiet submission, by representing to them of what concernment peace was to mankind; and by showing the inconveniencies might happen, if they should offer to resist Polyphemus, who had now the power over them.[1]

---

[1] 洛克这里引用的是古希腊诗人荷马（Homer）的史诗《奥德赛》（Odyssey）中主人公奥德修斯（Ulysses）的故事。奥德修斯于回家途中登陆西西里岛，落在独眼巨人波吕斐摩斯（Polyphemus）手中。波吕斐摩斯每天要吃掉奥德修斯的伙伴。奥德修斯忍住愤怒，谋划计策，最终带领伙伴成功逃脱。（《奥德赛》第九卷）

## § 229.

The end of government is the good of mankind: and which is best for mankind, that the people should be always exposed to the boundless will of tyranny; or that the rulers should be sometimes liable to be opposed, when they grow exorbitant in the use of their power, and employ it for the destruction, and not the preservation of the properties of their people?

## § 230.

Nor let any one say, that mischief can arise from hence, as often as it shall please a busy head, or turbulent spirit, to desire the alteration of the government. It is true, such men may stir, whenever they please; but it will be only to their own just ruin and perdition: for till the mischief be grown general, and the ill designs of the rulers become visible, or their attempts sensible to the greater part, the people, who are more disposed to suffer than right themselves by resistance, are not apt to stir. The examples of particular injustice or oppression, of here and there an unfortunate man, moves them not. But if they universally have a persuasion, grounded upon manifest evidence, that designs are carrying on against their liberties, and the general course and tendency of things cannot but give them strong suspicions of the evil intention of their governors, who is to be blamed for it? Who can help it, if they, who might avoid it, bring themselves into this suspicion? Are the people to be blamed, if they have the sense of rational creatures, and can think of things no otherwise than as they find and feel them? And is it not rather their fault, who put things into such a posture, that they would not have them thought to be as they are? I grant, that the pride, ambition, and turbulency of private men, have sometimes caused great disorders in commonwealths, and factions have been fatal to states and kingdoms. But whether the mischief hath oftener begun in the people's wantonness, and a desire to cast off the lawful authority of their rulers, or in the rulers insolence, and endeavours to get and exercise an arbitrary power over their people; whether oppression, or disobedience, gave the first rise to the disorder; I leave it to impartial history to determine. This I am sure, whoever, either ruler or subject, by force goes about to invade the rights of either prince or people, and lays the foundation for overturning the constitution and frame of any just government; is highly guilty of the greatest crime, I think, a man is capable of; being to answer for all those mischiefs of blood, rapine, and desolation, which the breaking to pieces of governments bring on a country. And he who does it, is justly to be esteemed the common enemy and pest of mankind, and is to be treated accordingly.

### § 231.

That subjects or foreigners, attempting by force on the properties of any people, may be resisted with force, is agreed on all hands. But that magistrates, doing the same thing, may be resisted, hath of late been denied: as if those who had the greatest privileges and advantages by the law, had thereby a power to break those laws, by which alone they were set in a better place than their brethren: whereas their offence is thereby the greater, both as being ungrateful for the greater share they have by the law, and breaking also that trust which is put into their hands by their brethren.

### § 232.

Whosoever uses force without right, as every one does in society, who does it without law, puts himself into a state of war with those against whom he so uses it; and in that state all former ties are cancelled, all other rights cease, and every one has a right to defend himself, and to resist the aggressor. This is so evident, that Barclay himself, that great assertor of the power and sacredness of kings, is forced to confess, that it is lawful for the people, in some cases, to resist their king; and that too in a chapter, wherein he pretends to show, that the divine law shuts up the people from all manner of rebellion. Whereby it is evident, even by his own doctrine, that, since they may in some cases resist, all resisting of princes is not rebellion. His words are these. "Quod siquis dicat, Ergone populus tyrannicæ crudelitati & furori jugulum semper præbebit? Ergone multitudo civitates suas fame, ferro, & flammâ vastari, seque, conjuges, & liberos fortunæ ludibrio & tyranni libidini exponi, inque omnia vitæ pericula omnesque miserias & molestias à rege de luci patientur? Num illis quod omni animantium generi est à naturâ tributum, denegari debet, ut sc. vim vi repellant, seseq; ab injuria tueantur? Huic brevitur responsum sit, Populo universo negari defensionem, quæ juris naturalis est, neque ultionem quæ præter naturam est adversus regem concedi debere. Quapropter si rex non in singulares tantum personas aliquot privatum odium exerceat, sed corpus etiam reipublicæ, cujus ipse caput est, i. e. totum populum, vel insignem aliquam ejus partem immani & intolerandâ sævitia seu tyrannide divexet; populo quidem hoc casu resistendi ac tuendi se ab injuriâ potestas competit; sed tuendi se tantum, non enim in principem invadendi: & restituendæ injuriæ illatæ, non recedendi à debitâ reverentiâ propter acceptam injuriam. Præsentem denique impetum propulsandi non vim præteritam ulciscendi jus habet. Horum enim alterum à naturâ est, ut vitam scilicet corpusque tueamur. Alterum vero contra naturam, ut inferior de superiori supplicium sumat. Quod itaque populus malum, antequam factum sit, impedire potest, ne fiat; id postquam factum est, in regem authorem sceleris vindicare non potest: populus igitur hoc ampliùs quam privatus quispiam habet: quod huic, vel ipsis adversariis judicibus, excepto Buchanano, nullum nisi in patientia remedium superest. Cùm ille si intolerabilis tyrannus est (modicum enim ferre omnino debet) resistere cum reverentia possit." Barclay[1] contra Monarchom. l. iii. c. 8."

In English Thus:

### § 233.

"But if any one should ask, Must the people then always lay themselves open to the cruelty and rage of tyranny? Must they see their cities pillaged and laid in ashes, their wives and children exposed to the tyrant's lust and fury, and themselves and families reduced by their king to ruin, and all the miseries of want and oppression; and yet sit still? Must men alone be debarred the common privilege of opposing force with force, which nature allows so freely to all other creatures for their preservation from injury? I answer: Self-defence is a part of the law of nature; nor can it be denied the community, even against the king himself: but to revenge themselves upon him, must by no means be allowed them; it being not agreeable to that law. Wherefore if the king should show an hatred, not only to some particular persons, but sets himself against the body of the commonwealth, whereof he is the head, and shall, with intolerable ill-usage, cruelly tyrannize over the whole, or a considerable part of the people, in this case the people have a right to resist and defend themselves from injury: but it must be with

---

[1] 巴尔克莱（William Barclay, 1546—1608），苏格兰法学家。巴尔克莱出生于苏格兰的阿伯丁郡（Aberdeenshire），求学于阿伯丁大学（University of Aberdeen）。1573 年，巴尔克莱来到法国，在波纪斯大学（University of Bourges）学习法律并获得了博士学位。查理三世洛林公爵（Charles Ⅲ, Duke of Lorraine）任命他为刚成立的穆松大学（University of Pont-à-Mousson）的民法教授及国事大臣。1603 年，因与耶稣会交恶，巴尔克莱离开法国，来到英格兰。詹姆斯六世意欲封给巴尔克莱以显赫职位，只要他愿意成为英国国教的成员。巴尔克莱拒绝了这份邀请，于 1604 年回到法国。他被任命为昂热大学（University of Angers）的民法教授。巴尔克莱最主要的著作是 De Regno et Regali Potestate (1600) 与 De Potestate Papae (1609)。这两本书是对绝对君权的有力辩护。洛克拥有巴尔克莱这两本书的一个合集（1612 年版）。洛克在《政府论（上篇）》的第 4 段与第 67 段曾提到过巴尔克莱，但没有做出评论。

this caution, that they only defend themselves, but do not attack their prince: they may repair the damages received, but must not for any provocation exceed the bounds of due reverence and respect. They may repulse the present attempt, but must not revenge past violences: for it is natural for us to defend life and limb, but that an inferiour should punish a superiour, is against nature. The mischief which is designed them the people may prevent before it be done; but when it is done, they must not revenge it on the king, though author of the villainy. This therefore is the privilege of the people in general, above what any private person hath; that particular men are allowed by our adversaries themselves (Buchanan[1] only excepted) to have no other remedy but patience; but the body of the people may with reverence resist intolerable tyranny; for, when it is but moderate, they ought to endure it."

### § 234.

Thus far that great advocate of monarchical power allows of resistance.

### § 235.

It is true, he has annexed two limitations to it, to no purpose.

First, he says, it must be with reverence.

Secondly, it must be without retribution, or punishment; and the reason he gives is, "Because an inferiour cannot punish a superiour."

First, how to resist force without striking again, or how to strike with reverence, will need some skill to make intelligible. He that shall oppose an assault only with a shield to receive the blows, or in any more respectful posture, without a sword in his hand, to abate the confidence and force of the assailant, will quickly be at an end

---

[1] 布坎南（George Buchanan，1506—1582）是文艺复兴时期的苏格兰历史学家与人文主义学者。布坎南主张，国王是通过人民同意依法进行统治的人，而当国王为了私欲而随意统治时就变成了暴君，人民有权利进行反抗。

of his resistance, and will find such a defence serve only to draw on himself the worse usage. This is as ridiculous a way of resisting, as Juvenal[1] thought it of fighting; "ubi tu pulsas, ego vapulo tantum."[2] And the success of the combat will be unavoidably the same he there describes it:

—*Libertas pauperis hæc est:*
*Pulsatus rogat, & pugnis concisus, adorat,*
*Ut liceat paucis cum dentibus inde reverti.*

This will always be the event of such an imaginary resistance, where men may not strike again. He therefore who may resist, must be allowed to strike. And then let our author, or any body else, join a knock on the head, or a cut on the face, with as much reverence and respect as he thinks fit. He that can reconcile blows and reverence, may, for aught I know, deserve for his pains a civil, respectful cudgelling, wherever he can meet with it.

Secondly, as to his second, "An inferiour cannot punish a superiour;" that is true, generally speaking, whilst he is his superiour. But to resist force with force, being the state of war that levels the parties, cancels all former relation of reverence, respect, and superiority: and then the odds that remains, is, that he, who opposes the unjust aggressor, has this superiority over him, that he has a right when he prevails, to punish the offender, both for the breach of the peace, and all the evils that followed upon it. Barclay therefore, in another place, more coherently to himself, denies it to be lawful to resist a king in any case. But he there assigns two cases, whereby a king may unking himself. His words are,

"Quid ergo, nulline casus incidere possunt quibus populo sese

---

[1] 尤维纳利斯（Juvenal），生活于公元1至2世纪的古罗马诗人，作品常讽刺罗马社会的腐化和人类的愚蠢。洛克以下引用的是尤维纳利斯的《讽刺诗集》（*Satires*）。

[2] 此句诗文翻译为英文是"I writhe with the blows you put upon me."出自《讽刺诗集》第三卷第289—290行。

erigere atque in regem impotentius dominantem arma capere & invadere jure suo suâque authoritate liceat? Nulli certe quamdiu rex manet. Semper enim ex divinis id obstat, Regem honorificato; & qui potestati resistit, Dei ordinationi resistit: non aliàs igitur in eum populo potestas est quam si id committat propter quod ipso jure rex esse desinat. Tunc enim se ipse principatu exuit atque in privatis constituit liber: hoc modo populus & superior efficitur, reverso ad eum sc. jure illo quod ante regem inauguratum in interregno habuit. At sunt paucorum generum commissa ejusmodi quæ hunc effectum pariunt. At ego cum plurima animo perlustrem, duo tantam invenio, duos, inquam, casus quibus rex ipso facto ex rege non regem se facit & omni honore & dignitate regali atque in subditos potestate destituit; quorum etiam meminit Winzerus. Horum unus est, Si regnum disperdat, quemadmodum de Nerone fertur, quod is nempe senatum populumque Romanum, atque adeo urbem ipsam ferro flammaque vastare, ac novas sibi sedes quærere, decrevisset. Et de Caligula, quod palam denunciarit se neque civem neque principem senatui amplius fore, inque animo habuerit interempto utriusque ordinis electissimo quoque Alexandriam commigrare, ac ut populum uno ictu interimeret, unam ei cervicem optavit. Talia cum rex aliquis meditatur & molitur serio, omnem regnandi curam & animum ilico abjicit, ac proinde imperium in subditos amittit, ut dominus servi pro derelicto habiti dominium."

*§ 236.*

"Alter casus est, Si rex in alicujus clientelam se contulit, ac regnum quod liberum à majoribus & populo traditum accepit, alienæ ditioni mancipavit. Nam tunc quamvis forte non eâ mente id agit populo plane ut incommodet: tamen quia quod præcipuum est regiæ dignitatis amisit, ut summus scilicet in regno secundum Deum sit, & solo Deo inferior, atque populum etiam totum ignorantem vel invitum, cujus libertatem sartam & tectam conservare debuit in alterius gentis ditionem & potestatem dedidit, hâc velut quadam regni ab alienatione efficit, ut nec quod ipse in regno imperium habuit retineat, nec in eum cui collatum voluit, juris quicquam transferat; atque ita eo facto liberum jam & suæ potestatis populum relinquit, cujus rei exemplum unum annales Scotici suppeditant. "Barclay contra Monarchom. l. iii. c. 16."

Which in English runs thus:

## § 237.

"What then, can there no case happen wherein the people may of right, and by their own authority, help themselves, take arms, and set upon their king imperiously domineering over them? None at all, whilst he remains a king. Honour the king, and he that resists the power, resists the ordinance of God; are divine oracles that will never permit it. The people therefore can never come by a power over him, unless he does something that makes him cease to be a king: for then he divests himself of his crown and dignity, and returns to the state of a private man, and the people become free and superiour, the power which they had in the interregnum, before they crowned him king, devolving to them again. But there are but few miscarriages which bring the matter to this state. After considering it well on all sides, I can find but two. Two cases there are, I say, whereby a king, ipso facto, becomes no king, and loses all power and regal authority over his people; which are also taken notice of by Winzerus."

"The first is, if he endeavour to overturn the government, that is, if he have a purpose and design to ruin the kingdom and commonwealth; as it is recorded of Nero[1], that he resolved to cut off the senate and people of Rome, lay the city waste with fire and

---

[1] 尼禄（Nero Claudius Drusus Germanicus，37年12月15日—68年6月9日），古罗马帝国的皇帝，54年—68年在位。后世关于他的史料与创作相当多，但普遍对他的形象描述不佳。世人称之为"嗜血的尼禄"。他是古罗马帝国朱里亚·克劳狄王朝的最后一任皇帝，是古罗马乃至欧洲历史上有名的残酷暴君。

sword, and then remove to some other place.—And of Caligula[1], that he openly declared, that he would be no longer a head to the people or senate, and that he had it in his thoughts to cut off the worthiest men of both ranks, and then retire to Alexandria: and he wished that the people had but one neck, that he might dispatch them all at a blow. Such designs as these, when any king harbours in his thoughts, and seriously promotes, he immediately gives up all care and thought of the commonwealth; and consequently forfeits the power of governing his subjects, as a master does the dominion over his slaves whom he hath abandoned."

### § 238.

"The other case is, When a king makes himself the dependent of another, and subjects his kingdom which his ancestors left him, and the people put free into his hands, to the dominion of another: for however perhaps it may not be his intention to prejudice the people, yet because he has hereby lost the principal part of regal dignity, viz. to be next and immediately under God supreme in his kingdom; and also because he betrayed or forced his people, whose liberty he ought to have carefully preserved, into the power and dominion of a foreign nation. By this, as it were, alienation of his kingdom, he himself loses the power he had in it before, without transferring any the least right to those on whom he would have bestowed it; and so by this act sets the people free, and leaves them at their own disposal. One example of this is to be found in the Scottish Annals."

### § 239.

In these cases Barclay, the great champion of absolute monarchy, is forced to allow, that a king may be resisted, and ceases to be a

---

[1] 卡里古拉（Caligula）是罗马帝国朱利亚·克劳狄王朝的第三位皇帝盖约·恺撒（Gaius Julius Caesar Augustus Germanicus，12年8月31日—41年1月24日，37年—41年在位）的别名，意思是"小军靴"。卡里古拉作为留名史册的暴君典范，继位没几年就被禁卫军杀死。

king. That is, in short, not to multiply cases, in whatsoever he has no authority, there he is no king, and may be resisted: for wheresoever the authority ceases, the king ceases too, and becomes like other men who have no authority. And these two cases the instances differ little from those above-mentioned, to be destructive to governments, only that he has omitted the principle from which his doctrine flows; and that is, the breach of trust, in not preserving the form of government agreed on, and in not intending the end of government itself, which is the public good and preservation of property. When a king has dethroned himself, and put himself in a state of war with his people, what shall hinder them from prosecuting him who is no king, as they would any other man, who has put himself into a state of war with them; Barclay and those of his opinion would do well to tell us. This farther I desire may be taken notice of out of Barclay, that he says, "The mischief that is designed them, the people may prevent before it be done: whereby he allows resistance when tyranny is but in design. Such designs as these (says he) when any king harbours in his thoughts and seriously promotes, he immediately gives up all care and thought of the commonwealth;" so that, according to him, the neglect of the public good is to be taken as an evidence of such design, or at least for a sufficient cause of resistance. And the reason of all, he gives in these words, "Because he betrayed or forced his people, whose liberty he ought carefully to have preserved." What he adds, "into the power and dominion of a foreign nation," signifies nothing, the fault and forfeiture lying in the loss of their liberty, which he ought to have preserved, and not in any distinction of the persons to whose dominion they were subjected. The people's right is equally invaded, and their liberty lost, whether they are made slaves to any of their own, or a foreign nation; and in this lies the injury, and against this only have they the right of defence. And there are instances to be found in all countries, which show, that it is not the change of nations in the persons of their governors, but the change of government, that gives the offence. Bilson[1], a bishop of our church, and a great stickler for the power and prerogative of princes, does, if I mistake not, in his treatise of christian subjection, acknowledge, that princes may forfeit their power, and their title to the obedience of their subjects; and if there needed authority in a case where reason is so plain, I could send my reader to Bractan[2], Fortescue[3], and the author of the Mirror[4], and others, writers that cannot be suspected to be ignorant of our government, or enemies to it. But I thought Hooker alone might be enough to satisfy those men, who relying on him for their ecclesiastical polity, are by a strange fate carried to deny those principles upon which he builds it. Whether they are herein made the tools of cunninger workmen, to pull down their own fabric, they were best look. This I am sure, their civil policy is so new, so dangerous, and so destructive to both rulers and people, that as former ages never could bear the broaching of it; so it may be hoped, those to come, redeemed from the impositions

---

[1] 比尔逊（Thomas Bilson，1547 年—1616 年 6 月 18 日），英格兰温彻斯特（Winchester）主教与伍斯特（Worcester）主教，温彻斯特学院（Winchester College）的校长。洛克这里提到的是他的《基督教徒的服从与非基督教徒的谋反之间真正的区别》(*The True Difference Between Christian Subjection and Unchristian Rebellion*，1585) 一书。比尔逊经常被绝对主义的反对者所引用，因为虽然他是一位绝对王权的支持者，但是他认为臣民在一些紧要关头可以反抗君主。

[2] 应为 Bracton。布拉克顿（Henry de Bracton，约 1210 年—1268 年），英格兰法学家。他最重要的作品是大约于 1235 年前所写的《论英格兰的法律与习惯》(*De Legibus et Consuetudinibus Angliae*，英译为：*The Laws and Customs of England*)。

[3] 亨利·福蒂斯丘爵士（Sir Henry Fortescue，约 1395 年—约 1477 年），英格兰王座法院首席法官。他最重要的作品是《英格兰法律礼赞》(*In Praise of the Laws of England*) 与《论英格兰的政制》(*The Governance of England*)。中译本参见：[英] 福蒂斯丘：《论英格兰的法律与政制》，袁瑜琤译，北京大学出版社 2008 年版。

[4] 这里指的可能是安德鲁·霍恩（Andrew Home）。霍恩据传是 14 世纪早期出现的《司法之镜》(*The Mirror of Justices*) 一书的作者。这本集语言、幽默故事与政治法律思想于一身的奇书体现了一种古老的宪政思想。17 世纪 40 年代，这本书被翻译出版，成为议会党人抨击专制王权、维护臣民权利的重要思想武器。相关介绍参见：陈敬刚：《〈司法之镜〉中体现的宪政思想》，载《普通法的中世纪渊源》，知识产权出版社 2011 年版。

of these Egyptian under task-masters, will abhor the memory of such servile flatterers, who, whilst it seemed to serve their turn, resolved all government into absolute tyranny, and would have all men born to, what their mean souls fitted them for, slavery.

### § 240.

Here, it is like, the common question will be made, "Who shall be judge, whether the prince or legislative act contrary to their trust?" This, perhaps, ill-affected and factious men may spread amongst the people, when the prince only makes use of his due prerogative. To this I reply, "The people shall be judge;" for who shall be judge whether his trustee or deputy acts well, and according to the trust reposed in him, but he who deputes him, and must by having deputed him, have still a power to discard him, when he fails in his trust? If this be reasonable in particular cases of private men, why should it be otherwise in that of the greatest moment, where the welfare of millions is concerned, and also where the evil, if not prevented, is greater, and the redress very difficult, dear, and dangerous?

### § 241.

But farther, this question, ("Who shall be judge?") cannot mean that there is no judge at all: for where there is no judicature on earth, to decide controversies amongst men, God in heaven is judge. He alone, it is true, is judge of the right. But every man is judge for himself, as in all other cases, so in this, whether another hath put himself into a state of war with him, and whether he should appeal to the supreme judge, as Jephthah did.

### § 242.

If a controversy arise betwixt a prince and some of the people, in a matter where the law is silent, or doubtful, and the thing be of great consequence, I should think the proper umpire, in such a case, should be the body of the people: for in cases where the prince hath a trust reposed in him, and is dispensed from the common ordinary rules of the law; there, if any men find themselves aggrieved, and think the prince acts contrary to, or beyond that trust, who so proper to judge as the body of the people, (who, at first, lodged that trust in him) how far they meant it should extend? But if the prince, or whoever they be in the administration, decline that way of determination, the appeal then lies no where but to heaven; force between either persons, who have no known superior on earth, or which permits no appeal to a judge on earth, being properly a state of war, wherein the appeal lies only to heaven; and in that state the injured party must judge for himself, when he will think fit to make use of that appeal, and put himself upon it.

### § 243.

To conclude, The power that every individual gave the society, when he entered into it, can never revert to the individuals again, as long as the society lasts, but will always remain in the community; because without this there can be no community, no commonwealth, which is contrary to the original agreement: so also when the society hath placed the legislative in any assembly of men, to continue in them and their successors, with direction and authority for providing such successors, the legislative can never revert to the people whilst that government lasts; because, having provided a legislative with power to continue for ever, they have given up their political power to the legislative, and cannot resume it. But if they have set limits to the duration of their legislative, and made this supreme power in any person, or assembly, only temporary; or else, when by the miscarriages of those in authority, it is forfeited; upon the forfeiture, or at the determination of the time set, it reverts to the society, and the people have a right to act as supreme, and continue the legislative in themselves; or erect a new form, or under the old form place it in new hands, as they think good.

图书在版编目（CIP）数据

政府论.下篇：英文/（英）洛克著；王涛导读.—北京：中国人民大学出版社，2013.4
（世界大师原典文库：中文导读插图版/杨慧林，金莉总主编）
ISBN 978-7-300-17228-6

Ⅰ.政… Ⅱ.①洛… ②王… Ⅲ.①英语–语言读物 ②政治制度–研究
Ⅳ.① H319.4：D

中国版本图书馆 CIP 数据核字（2013）第 059440 号

世界大师原典文库（中文导读插图版）
总主编　杨慧林　金莉

**政府论（下篇）**

［英］约翰·洛克（John Locke）　著
王　涛　导读

Zhengfu Lun (Xiapian)

| | | | |
|---|---|---|---|
| 出版发行 | 中国人民大学出版社 | | |
| 社　　址 | 北京中关村大街 31 号 | 邮政编码 | 100080 |
| 电　　话 | 010-62511242（总编室） | 010-62511398（质管部） | |
| | 010-82501766（邮购部） | 010-62514148（门市部） | |
| | 010-62515195（发行公司） | 010-62515275（盗版举报） | |
| 网　　址 | http:// www.crup.com.cn | | |
| | http:// www.ttrnet.com（人大教研网） | | |
| 经　　销 | 新华书店 | | |
| 印　　刷 | 北京宏伟双华印刷有限公司 | | |
| 规　　格 | 148 mm×210 mm　32 开本 | 版　次 | 2013 年 4 月第 1 版 |
| 印　　张 | 9.25　插页 1 | 印　次 | 2013 年 4 月第 1 次印刷 |
| 字　　数 | 248 000 | 定　价 | 25.00 元 |

版权所有　　侵权必究　　印装差错　　负责调换

# 中国人民大学出版社外语出版分社读者信息反馈表

尊敬的读者：

感谢您购买和使用中国人民大学出版社外语出版分社的 _____ 一书，我们希望通过这张小小的反馈卡来获得您更多的建议和意见，以改进我们的工作，加强我们双方的沟通和联系。我们期待着能为更多的读者提供更多的好书。

请您填妥下表后，寄回或传真回复我们，对您的支持我们不胜感激！

1. 您是从何种途径得知本书的：
   □书店　　　　□网上　　　　□报纸杂志　　　　□朋友推荐
2. 您为什么决定购买本书：
   □工作需要　　□学习参考　　□对本书主题感兴趣　　□随便翻翻
3. 您对本书内容的评价是：
   □很好　　　　□好　　　　□一般　　　　□差　　　　□很差
4. 您在阅读本书的过程中有没有发现明显的专业及编校错误，如果有，它们是：
   _____
   _____
   _____

5. 您对哪些专业的图书信息比较感兴趣：
   _____
   _____
   _____

6. 如果方便，请提供您的个人信息，以便于我们和您联系（您的个人资料我们将严格保密）：
   您供职的单位：_____
   您教授的课程（教师填写）：_____
   您的通信地址：_____
   您的电子邮箱：_____

请联系我们：黄婷　程子殊　于真妮　商希建　鞠方安

电话：010-62512737，62513265，62515037，62514974，62515576

传真：010-62514961

E-mail：huangt@crup.com.cn　　chengzsh@crup.com.cn　　yuzn@crup.com.cn
　　　　shandysxj@163.com　　jufa@crup.com.cn

通信地址：北京市海淀区中关村大街甲59号文化大厦15层　　邮编：100872

中国人民大学出版社外语出版分社